A HUNDRED MERRY TALES

PAUL M. ZALL is a native of Massachusetts and holds degrees from Swarthmore College (B.A., 1948) and Harvard University (M.A., 1950; Ph.D., 1951). Now Associate Professor of English at Los Angeles State College, he formerly was Assistant to the Curator of the Wordsworth Collection at Cornell University, a member of the English faculty at the University of Oregon, and Technical Research Editor for Boeing Airplane Company. He is still a consultant at Boeing, and since 1956 has worked on such projects as the 707-type plane and on major weapon-systems such as Dyna-Soar, Minuteman, and Saturn. His studies on Elizabethan, late eighteenth century, and Romantic subjects have appeared in such publications as *PMLA*, *Bulletin of the New York Public Library*, *Modern Language Notes*, *ELH*, and the *Times Literary Supplement*. He is the author of *Elements of Technical Report Writing* (1962).

A Hundred Merry Tales

*and Other English Jestbooks of the
Fifteenth and Sixteenth Centuries*

Edited by

P. M. ZALL

University of Nebraska Press · Lincoln · 1963

Publishers on the Plains

UNP

MANUFACTURED IN THE UNITED STATES OF AMERICA

The illustrations in this book are reproduced by permission of the
Huntington Library, San Marino, California.

For L.

For L.

Table of Contents

The Natural History of Jestbooks:
An Introduction

THIS EDITION is intended to show milestones in the development of English jestbooks printed between 1484 and 1584, from the time of William Caxton to the time of William Shakespeare. These collections of short "merry" prose tales or witty remarks provided subsoil for the lush growth of Elizabethan prose fiction and comedy, yet they are generally unknown to modern readers —partly because they are considered beneath the notice of your practicing scholar, partly because they are scattered all over the English-speaking world in the major research libraries, and partly because they are not very nice to modern ears or the family reading circle. Our aim here is to provide basic texts in modern format and let the jestbooks speak for themselves.

The jestbooks are not "literary." Though often treating the same subject matter, they differ from the tales of Chaucer or Boccaccio and the witty sayings of the *Greek Anthology,* for those are works of art, with preconceived design and concern for artistic integrity of style and content. The jestbooks are more concerned with what is said than with how it is said, and generally make their point simply, succinctly and with as much zest as the jests will bear.

Because jests are meant to be said as well as read, their style is conversationally dramatic, vernacular vs. literary, and sometimes seemingly taken down from actual speech. This is to the advantage of the modern reader. For if he is familiar with the King James version of the Bible, he will feel right at home with the vernacular style of the jestbooks. The King James version closely follows the original translation begun in 1523 by William Tyndale, whose style is very similar to that in the early English jestbooks.

With the remarkable exception of *A C. Mery Talys,* or *A Hundred Merry Tales,* the earliest English jestbooks were translations from French, Flemish, and Latin. *A Hundred Merry Tales* seems to have been compiled from jests circulating by word-of-mouth. Taken altogether, Caxton's "fables"—from Alphonsus and Poggio, *Howleglas, A Hundred Merry Tales,* and *Tales and Quick Answers*—represent five distinct though crossbred strains deriving from classical, Oriental, Teutonic, Renaissance Italian, and domestic roots. A broad outline of the natural history of jestbooks is thus in order.

It may well be, as Coleridge somewhere says, that the first jests were told by Noah as the ark bounced across the flood, and that all jests thereafter derived from his originals. Whatever the origins, we find jests at a high stage of development in Homer's *Odyssey* and *Iliad.* In fact, the *Odyssey* features two distinctive types of jests—one about things done and the other about things said.

An example of the first is the jest about Hephaistos told by the blind minstrel: The famed craftsman of the gods enmeshes his wife and her lover in bed by means of a finely woven steel net, then hobbles out to call all the gods to witness the lovers caught in their perfidious act. As the gods look upon the hapless pair, "a roar of involuntary laughter rose from the blessed throats to see the skill of the master craftsman." And, of course, Odysseus's tale about escaping from the Cyclops is an extended jest about punning on the name "Nemo": When the Cyclops asks his name, Odysseus says it's "No Man," and then when the giant is asked who blinded him, he replies, "No Man," and his friends think he is mad.

The Greeks of Athens developed jests about things said into apothegms: short, pithy anecdotes about historical or living people bearing some kind of moral point. By Cicero's time, in the glory that was Rome, the apothegm was one of the commonest tools in the orator's bag of tricks. Then the first-century rhetorician Quintilian devoted an entire chapter in his major work to the art of telling them, for they were valuable in moving the hearts of listeners, disarming opponents in debate, or (quite frankly) keeping an audience awake. Many of Quintilian's examples, however, have lost the moral sentiment of apothegms and are unadulterated jests: Cato, struck by a ladder carried on the shoulder of a workman in a busy Roman street, replies to the workman's "Take heed, sir," with "Why? Do you carry anything else?" In his chapter, Quintilian formalizes the distinction between jests about things done and jests about things said. Since he was interested in the power of words to move men's hearts and minds, there is little question where his preference lies.

This classical preference for the witty word, the pun, the understatement, or the ambiguous remark leading to misunderstanding is obvious in the first collection of jests for their own sakes that appeared sometime in the fifth century. Previously, jests had been used incidentally, in isolation as examples or imbedded in extended narrative. Then, attached to the manuscript by Hierocles of Alexandria, "The Golden Words of Pythagoras," appeared a collection of twenty-one jests connected to Hierocles or Pythagoras only in the sense that they are about pedants and about words. Because seven other jests are also found attached to his works, Hierocles enjoys the reputation of archetypal jestbook-maker. Whether his or not, the jests are remarkable for focusing on one kind of wordplay: taking a word at face value to an absurd extreme without regard to reality or common sense.

The jests of Hierocles are not, however, new. Nor are they purely classical. Rather they are derivative of a timeless tradition that attributes to some cultural or ethnic class the facility for blundering by taking everything literally and by being completely impractical about matters of fact. Typical are these jests, based on the translation for the Rowfant Club's edition of Hierocles by Charles Clinch Bubb (1920):

> A pedant, desiring to see how he looked when asleep, stood in front of a mirror with his eyes closed.

> A pedant, seeing a deep well in his field, asked his hired man if the water was good to drink. "Oh, yes," was the reply. "Your ancestors drank from that well." The pedant said: "What long necks they must have had to drink from such depths!"

The jests of Hierocles are all about things said, but are more concerned with behavior. For example, one of the longer jests is about a pedant, a barber, and a bald-headed man who camp out in the wilds and agree to take turns at guard duty. The barber has first watch and, bored, shaves the head of the pedant before waking him. As the pedant awakens, he tries to run his hand through his hair, finds himself bald, and complains peevishly that the barber has awakened the wrong man: "He's wakened the bald-headed man instead of me!"

The pedant of Hierocles is representative of the ancient class of "wittols." Equally ancient, however, is the antithesis of the wittol or the innately wise common man who can outwit kings as wise as Solomon on any subject—learned or otherwise. Perhaps best known of this class is Marcolphus, of apparently Eastern origins, who debates the wise Solomon on biblical and philosophical matters and wins every time. Traditionally, Marcolphus uses mother wit to overcome Solomon's abstract, sententious aphorisms. But for some obscure reason, about the twelfth century Marcolphus is transformed from a brilliant wit to a dull, cloddish bumpkin who can do little but parody the sententious Solomon. He becomes, in effect, a Teutonic peasant, gradually acquires a trick or two, and eventually by the end of the fifteenth century develops into Til Eulenspiegel, whom we will see again as the English Howleglas.

A clearer melding of the classical and Eastern, or Oriental, strains in the development of jestbooks is the *Disciplina Cleri-*

calis of Petrus Alphonsus, dating from the twelfth century. Alphonsus, born Moses Sephardi in 1062, prepared a collection of Jewish and Arabic tales as a gift to his new church upon his conversion. Its sole purpose was to enable preachers to keep their congregations awake by providing entertaining *exempla,* or illustrations, to suit at least thirty texts (also provided as connecting links between the jests). At least two of the *exempla* are drawn patently from classical apothegms, and several from *Aesop's Fables,* in addition to those derivative of Jewish and Arabic lore.

Alphonsus' jests became household words in the medieval world and spread from Spain to Iceland or wherever missionaries wandered. They are chiefly short tales rather than jests about things said, and as "fabliaux," were readily absorbed into medieval literature. At the same time, however, preachers in the thirteenth and fourteenth centuries used them as bases for their private collections, exchanging new versions, adapting or adopting new jests in tavern, marketplace, or cloister. Often a private collection is found to contain three or four versions of the same jest because it may have been picked up in three or four different places or from as many people. Names, places, incidents, may change, but the basic jests are familiar.

Perhaps the finest private collection of jests built upon the *Disciplina Clericalis* is that of Johannes de Bromyard, an English Dominican monk, who took the trouble to arrange his material in encyclopedic fashion, after the pattern of the medieval *Alphabetum Narrationum,* and thus provided a handy dictionary of ninety-five jests appropriate to as many theological topics. But by the time Bromyard's work became generally available at the end of the fifteenth century, another strain of jestbook had sprouted full flower in Renaissance Florence.

This was the *Facetiae* of Poggio Bracciolini, Florentine, secretary to eight successive popes, discoverer of some of the finest classical manuscripts (hidden by previous generations of monks) in Northern Italy—including a manuscript of Quintilian's work. Although Poggio's *Liber Facetiarum* was not printed until 1477, after his death, his facetiae were compiled about mid-century, chiefly from conversations with friends (he claims in his preface). He wrote them down for two reasons: to relax his mind and to develop a good Latin vernacular prose style.

Poggio's jests derive from classical, Oriental, and Alphonsian sources, but they add something new as well. Where apothegms and *exempla* had been cloaked with the respectability of moral application, Poggio's jests dispensed with moral tags or parodied them. As a good Humanist, he was more concerned with things of this earth, the good life to be lived here and now, the curiosities about him—such as Latin-speaking sea monsters and two-headed calves. More important, he brings up eyewitnesses and cites the sources of his jests ("Razello of Bologna," "Cencio Romano," and others of his friends or, possibly, foes). His jests feature actual persons, places, and things as opposed to historical figures or "a pedant" or Marcolphus, even when the latter may have played the starring role in the original version.

The medieval in Alphonsus and the renaissance in Poggio were united with the ancient world of Aesop as soon as Poggio's jests were printed. In 1477, Heinrich Steinhowel, German physician, author of a treatise on plague, translator of Boccaccio into German, and of Apollonius of Tyre, compiled a Latin and a German collection of Aesop, complete with "biography" and appended jests (or "fables") from both Poggio and Alphonsus. Six years later, in 1483, his Latin version was literally translated into French by Jules de Machault, a monk of Lyons. And in the following year, Caxton faithfully translated Machault into English, thus providing the first jestbook in English.

Neither in Germany nor in England were Alphonsus or Poggio as popular as we might expect. In England, for example, early Humanists such as Sir Thomas More and Erasmus much preferred modeling their light writing after the apothegms of the classical world. In Germany, Heinrich Bebel and Sebastian Brandt (the former poet laureate of Emperor Maximilian and the latter author of *Ship of Fools*) followed Poggio's lead, but they had stiff competition from *Marcolphus* for popular favor. *Solomon and Marcolphus* appeared in English in 1492 and again in 1493, printed in Antwerp by Gerard Leeu—who, incidentally, was reprinting many of Caxton's works at that time, suggesting that perhaps Caxton had earlier printed an edition now lost to us.

An interesting sidelight is that the same woodcut prefacing *Solomon and Marcolphus* appears as frontispiece to *Howleglas* in 1528. *Howleglas'* earliest appearance in English dates from at least 1510 when it was printed in Antwerp, a faithful translation of *Eulenspiegel,* Marcolphus' best developed descendant. Marcolphus had other English descendants besides Howleglas: Scogin and the Parson of Kalenborowe are closer to the prototype. But since the former appears now only in a seventeenth-century text and the latter only in fragment, they are not included here. *Solomon and Marcolphus* is excluded as being an extended (and dull) dialogue rather than a jestbook.

Howleglas displays few of Marcolphus' bones, chiefly in some of the wittol-like jests and, conversely, in some of his "quick answers." Howleglas, as the central figure, thus displays both ends of the Marcolphus tradition. The result is what critics of the novel might call a "rounded" figure, consistently inconsistent yet readily lifelike because of it. From baptism to burial and re-burial, he is involved in a connected (geographically, at least, and chronologically) series of incidents that carry him across the spectrum of common life. He is, by turn, apprentice robber, cook's helper, clerk, butcher, baker, candlestickmaker, cobbler, pardoner, physician, and monk. A few of his exploits are cloacal, representative of the true "dirty joke" tradition in being concerned with such matters rather than with the more modern "sex." For the most part, Howleglas is an ur-Thurber hero as much sinned against as sinning.

With respect to both characterization and coherence, *Howleglas* is more modern than the distinctively haphazard compilation of jests attributed to Skelton that appeared in 1565–1566. Skelton is closer, in fact, to what we have of the *Parson of Kalenborowe,* a random in-gathering of jests associated with a name. Yet Skelton employs actual biographical data, much in the manner of

Poggio. In fact, until the nineteenth century, the jestbook was taken as gospel biography because of its realism. We can see the degree of realism by comparison of two jests on the same incident—Skelton's visit to the Bishop of Norwich—one in *Skelton* and the other in the earlier *A Hundred Merry Tales.*

A Hundred Merry Tales was printed in 1526 by John Rastell, Sir Thomas More's brother-in-law. Although Rastell was deeply concerned with the problem of providing translations to the "unlearned" (i.e., those having neither Latin nor Greek), *A Hundred Merry Tales* is the closest thing we have to a distinctively native English jestbook. It is relatively untouched by alien influences and seems to be attempting for a colloquial English style what Poggio had attempted for a colloquial Latin style. Also in the spirit of Poggio is its Humanist bias: Many of its jests are patently intended to familiarize the "unlearned" with such mysteries as the Pater Noster, the Creed, the Ave Maria, and the Seven Deadly Sins. Others are just as patently directed at teaching the newly "civilized" Welsh the rudiments of urban gentility. And, fundamentally, the majority of the jests illuminate the superiority of common sense over wittol-like logic-chopping or scholastic dogmatizing.

The realism of some of the jests, particularly those about things done by confidence men or hypocrites, is enhanced by detailed description of settings and by the language that often seems phonetically transcribed. Nevertheless, *A Hundred Merry Tales* pretends to be no more than it is—a random collection of jests compiled to the magic number one hundred.

Ten years after its appearance, however, *Tales and Quick Answers* (1536) discarded both the limits and the pattern of *A Hundred Merry Tales.* Both jestbooks retained the moral tag lines discarded by Poggio and *Howleglas,* but those in *A Hundred Merry Tales* are mere vestigial appendages, while those in *Tales and Quick Answers* are derived from the ancient apothegms via Erasmus. In effect, *Tales and Quick Answers* is a translation: Its "quick answers" are chiefly from Erasmus and its tales from Poggio or Sebastian Brandt. Its popularity redirected whatever development jestbooks might have shown had they followed *A Hundred Merry Tales* along a more native path.

But, as we have noted, the contemporary realism of *A Hundred Merry Tales* was also a part of *Howleglas* and of *Skelton*. This realism plus the characterization seen in *Howleglas* are combined in a jestbook-that-is-not-really-a-jestbook, Thomas Deloney's translation of Des Periers' *Mirrour of Mirth* of 1583.

Mirrour of Mirth represents a point where jestbook and prose fiction meet, for while it employs techniques of dramatic realism and characterization seen in the jestbooks, its concern for artistic form distinguishes it as a collection of humorous short stories. Plot, setting, characters, are focused on achieving the humorous effect, where in the "pure" jest little is important other than the incident or the punch line, and there is no time for development. With the pattern of *Mirrour of Mirth*, then, the jestbook-maker had the choice of moving into the heady realm of prose fiction or dramatic comedy, or following the eclectic *Tales and Quick Answers*, blazing the trail to the *Jests of Joe Miller* and Bennet Cerf's numerous jestbooks. There our story ends, and the jestbooks now speak for themselves.

It would have been self-defeating to let them speak in all the chaos of their original spelling, punctuation, and typography. Still, I have had to tamper only infrequently with the language itself—and then only to straighten out ambiguities resulting from the ubiquitous "which" or un-antecedented pronouns. I have chosen to gloss idioms and "hard" words that do not appear in a standard desk dictionary or are not clear from the context. Usually, reading aloud will clear up an apparent obscurity of diction.

Those interested in textual and historical matters will find valuable the standard study by Ernst Schulz, "Die Englischen Schwankbuecher," *Palaestra,* CXVII (1912), summarized and brought up to date by F. P. Wilson in *Huntington Library Quarterly,* II (1939), 121–158. A fifteenth-century Middle-English version of Alphonsus has been edited by W. H. Hulme, *Western*

Reserve Bulletin, XXII, 3, Cleveland, 1919. Poggio is available only in limited editions, so far as I know; e.g., by Isidore Liseux, Paris, 1879. *Solomon and Marcolphus* has been edited by E. Gordon Duff, London, 1892.

A brief note before each jestbook summarizes pertinent bibliography and the source of the present text, whether photostatic copy or original edition in the Henry E. Huntington Library. The staff of the library has been helpful and wise, particularly Miss Janet Hawkins. Professors George Mayhew and Irwin Swerdlow have been encouraging and patient. I am also grateful for the assistance received from the staffs of the British Museum and from the Library of Trinity College, from whose collections many of the selections in this book are garnered. And I have also to thank a gracious critic and part-time typist whose three small boys provided many modern analogues to the jests that follow.

P.M.Z.

William Caxton:
The Fables of Alfonce
and Poge (1484)

The "fables" of Alfonce and Poge were translated faithfully and printed at the end of William Caxton's Aesop, *1484, from the French of Jules de Machault's* Livre de Subtilles Histoires et Fables de Esope, *1483. Machault, in turn, translated from the Latin of Heinrich Steinhowel (who also printed a German version), about 1477. Steinhowel is credited with attaching the jests to Aesop, and also with collecting the variety of Aesopian tales flourishing in the Middle Ages. Machault omitted two of the fifteen jests from Alphonso, and so did Caxton. Caxton, however, added three at the end of Poggio—apparently originals.*

Caxton's Aesop *is one of his finest books and features his first use of wood-cut initial letters as well as illustrations in greater number than in any other of his books. Only three copies remain: in the Bodleian Library, the British Museum, and (the only perfect copy) the Royal Library at Windsor.*

The book was reprinted three times in the sixteenth century and three times in the seventeenth century. Its only modern appearance is in the limited edition by Joseph Jacobs, 2 vols. (London: David Nutt, 1889). The basis for the present text is the British Museum copy, Number 175 in the current (1962) Short Title Catalogue of Books Printed in England *. . . 1475–1640 (London, 1926).*

¶ The fyrst fable maketh mencion of theexhortacion of sapyence or wysedome and of loue

A Rabe of Lucanye sayd to his sone in this maner / My
sone beware & loke that the formye be not more prudent
or wyser / than thy self / the whiche gadreth & assembleth
to gyder in the somer all that to her nedeth to haue in the wynter / and beware that thou slepe no lenger / than the Cocke doth
the whiche watcheth and waketh atte matyns tyme / and that
he be not wyser and more sage than thy self / the whiche rulileth and goverueth wel in hennes / but hit suffyseth wel / that
thou ruble and gouerne one wel / And also that the dogge
be not more noble than thy self / whiche forgeteth neuer the gos
od / whiche is done to hym / but euer he remembryth it / ¶ Jam
my sone / suppose it not a lytyll thynge / to haue a good frend
but doubte not to haue a thousand frendes / ¶ And whanne
Arabe wold deye / he demaunded of his sone / My sone hath ma
ny good frendes hast thou / And his sone answerd to hym /
My fader I haue as I suppose an honderd frendes / And the

THE FABLES OF ALFONCE

The first fable maketh mention of the exhortation of sapience or wisdom and of love

A rabbi of Lucanye said to his son in this manner: "My son, beware and look that the formyce [1] be not more prudent or wiser than thyself, the which [2] gathereth and assembleth together in the summer all that to her needeth to have in the winter. And beware that thou sleep no longer than the cock doth, the which watcheth and waketh at matins time, and that he be not wiser and more sage than thyself, the which ruleth and governeth well nine hens. But it sufficeth well that thou rule and govern one well. And also that the dog be not more noble than thyself, which forgeteth never the good which is done to him, but ever he remembereth it."

Item: "My son, suppose it not a little thing to have a good friend, but doubt not to have a thousand friends."

And when a rabbi would die, he demanded [3] of his son: "My son, how many good friends hast thou?" And his son answered to him: "My father, I have as I suppose an hundred friends." And the father answered to him: "Beware and look well that thou suppose none to be thy friend without that thou hast as-

[1] *formyce:* ant
[2] *the which:* who (throughout these jestbooks "which" and "the which" = who)
[3] *demanded:* asked

sayed and proved him. For I have lived longer than thyself hast and unnethe [4] I have got half a friend, wherefore I marvel much how thou hast gotten so many friends."

And then the son, seeing the admiration or wonder of his father, demanded of him: "My father, I pray you that ye will give to me counsel how I shall mowe [5] prove and assay my friends." And his father said to him: "Go thou and kill a calf, and put it in a sack all bloody, and bear it to thy first friend and say to him that it is a man which thou hast slain, and that for the love of which he loveth thee that he will keep thy misdeed secretly and bury it to the end that he may save thee."

The which counsel his son did, to whom his friend said: "Return again to thy house, for if thou hast done evil, I will not bear the pain for thee, for within my house thou shalt not enter."

And thus one after other, he assayed all his friends and every of them made to him such an answer as the first did, whereof greatly he was abashed. And then he returned again to his father and told him how he had done. And his father answered to him: "Many one been friends of words only; but fewe been in fait or deed. But I shall tell to thee what thou shalt do. Go thou to my half-friend and bear to him thy calf, and thou shalt hear and see what he shall say to thee."

And when the son came to the half-friend of his father, he said to him as he did to the others. And when the half-friend understood his fait or deed, he anon took him secretly into his house, and led him into a sure and obscure place where he did bury his dead calf. Whereof the son knew the truth of the half-friend's love.

Then the son of a rabbi turned again toward his father and told to him all that his half-friend had done to him. And then the father said to his son that the philosopher sayeth that the very and true friend is found in the extreme need. Then asked the son of his father: "Sawest thou never man which in his

---

[4] *unnethe:* hardly (another frequent expression)
[5] *mowe:* may, may be able to

life got a whole friend?" And his father said to him: "I saw never none, but well have I heard it said." And the son answered: "My father, I pray thee that thou wilt rehearse it to me to the end that by adventure [6] I may get such a one."

And the father said to him: "My son, sometime have I heard of two merchants which never had seen each other. The one was of Egypt and the other was of Baldak, but they had knowledge each of the other by their letters which they sent and wrote friendly one to the other. It befell then that the merchant of Baldak came into Egypt for to chepe [7] and buy some ware or merchandise, whereof his friend was much glad and went to meet him and brought him benignly into his house.

"And after that he had cheered and feasted him by the space of nine days, the same merchant of Baldak waxed [8] and became sick, whereof his friend was sorrowful and full heavy, and incontinent [9] sent for physicians or leeches through all Egypt for to recover his health. And when the medecines [10] had seen and visited him and his urine also, they said that he had no bodily sickness, but that he was ravished of love. And when his friend heard these words, he came to him and said: 'My friend, I pray thee that thou wilt show and tell to me thy sickness.'

"And his friend said to him: 'I pray thee that thou wilt make to come hither all the women and maidens which been in thy house, for to see if she which my heart desireth is among them.' And anon his friend made to come before him both his own daughters and servants, among the which was a young maid which he had nourished [11] for his pleasure. And when the patient or sick man saw her, he said to his friend: 'The same is she which may be cause of my life or of my death.' The which his friend gave to him for to be his wife with all such goods [12]

[6] *by adventure:* by chance
[7] *chepe:* bargain
[8] *waxed:* paled
[9] *incontinent:* immediately (a very frequent expression)
[10] *medecines:* physicians
[11] *nourished:* reared
[12] *goods:* property (another very frequent expression)

as he had of her—the which he wedded and returned with her into Baldak with great joy.

"But within a while after, it happed and fortuned so that this merchant of Egypt fell in poverty, and for to have some consolation and comfort he took his way toward Baldak and supposed to go and see his friend. And about one evening he arrived to the city; and for as much that he was not well arrayed nor clothed, he had shame by daylight to go into the house of his friend, but went and lodged him within a temple nigh by his friend's house.

"It happed then that on that same night that he lay there, a man slew another man before the gate or entry of the said temple, wherefore the neighbors were sore troubled. And then all the people moved thereof came into the temple wherein they found nobody save only the Egyptian—the which they took and like a murderer interrogated him why he had slain that man which lay dead before the portal or gate of the temple.

"He then, seeing his infortune and poverty, confessed that he had killed him; for because of his evil fortune, he would rather die than live any more. Wherefore he was had before the judge and was condemned to be hanged. And when men led him toward the gallows, his friend saw and knew him and began to weep sore, remembering the benefits which he had done to him. Wherefore he went to the Justice and said: 'My lords, this man did not the homicide, for it was myself that did it, and therefore ye should do great sin if ye did put this innocent and guiltless to death.' And anon he was taken for to be had unto the gallows.

"And then the Egyptian said: 'My lords, he did it not, and therefore evil should ye do to put him to death.' And as the two friends would have been hanged each one for the other, he which had done the homicide came and knew and confessed there his sin, and addressed himself before the Justice and said: 'My lords, none of them both hath done the deed, and therefore punish not ye these innocents. For I alone ought to bear the pain.'

"Whereof all the Justice was greatly marvelled. And for the doubt which therein was great, the Justice took them all three and led them before the king. And when they had rehearsed to the king all the manner after inquest thereupon made, and that he knew the very truth of it, he granted his grace to the murderer and so all three were delivered. And the friend brought his friend into his house and received him joyously. And after, he gave to him both gold and silver, and the Egyptian turned again to his house."

And when the father had said and rehearsed all this to his son, his son said to him: "My father, I know now well that he which may get a good friend is well happy, and with great labor, as I suppose, I shall get such a one."

The second fable is of the commission of pecuny or money

A Spaniard arrived sometime into the land of Egypt, and because that he doubted to be robbed within the deserts of Arabia he purposed and bethought in himself that it were wisely done to take his money to some true man for to keep it unto his return again. And because that he heard some say that within the City was a true man, he anon went to him and took to him his silver for to keep it. And when he had done his voyage he came again to him and demanded of him his silver—which answered to him in this manner: "My friend, I ne wot [1] who thou art, for I saw thee never that I wote of, and if thou sayest or speakest any more words I shall make thee to be well beat."

Then was the Spaniard sorrowful and wroth, and thereof he would have made a plaint to his neighbors, as he did. And the neighbors said to him: "Certainly we be well abashed of that that ye tell to us, for he is among us all reputed and holden for a good man and true. And therefore return again to him and

[1] *ne wot:* know not

by sweet words tell him that. He will render to thee thy goods [2] again."

The which thing he did, and the old man answered to him more sharply and rigorously than he had done before—whereof the Spaniard was wonderly wroth. And as he departed out of the old man's house, he met with an old woman, the which demanded of him wherefore he was so troubled and heavy. And after that he had told to her the cause why, the old woman said to him: "Make good cheer, for if it be so as thou sayest, I shall counsel thee how thou shalt recover thy silver."

And then he demanded of her how it might be done, and she said to him: "Bring hither to me a man of thy country whom thou trustest, and do to be made [3] four fair chests, and fill them all with stones. And by thy fellows thou shalt make them to be borne into his house, and to him they shall say that the merchants of Spain send them to him for to be kept surely. And when the chests shall be within his house, thou shalt go and demand of him thy silver." Which thing he did.

And as the said chests were borne within his house, the Spaniard went with them that bare them. The which strangers said to the old man: "My lord, these four chests been all full of gold, of silver, and of precious stones which we bring to you as to the truest man and faithful that we know, for to keep them surely because that we fear and doubt the thieves which been within the desert."

After the which words said, came he which the old woman had counseled, and demanded of him his silver. And because that the old man doubted that the Spaniard would have dispraised him, he said thus to him: "Thou art welcome! I marveled how thou tarriest so long for to come." And incontinent [4] he restored to him his silver.

And thus by the counsel of the woman which he greatly thanked, he had his goods again and returned again into his country.

[2] *goods:* property
[3] *do to be made:* order to be made
[4] *incontinent:* immediately

The third fable speaketh of a subtle invention of a sentence given upon a dark and obscure cause

It befell sometime that a goodman laborer went from life to death, the which laborer left nothing to his son but only a house. The which son lived by the labor of his hands poorly. This young man had a neighbor which was much rich—which demanded of the said young man if he would sell his house, but he would not sell it because that it was come to him by inheritance and by patrimony. Wherefore the rich man his neighbor conversed and was full oft with him for to deceive him. But the young man fled his company as much as he might. And when the rich man perceived that the young man fled from him, he bethought himself of a great deception and falsehood, and demanded [1] of the poor young man that he would hire to him a part of his house for to delve and make a cellar, the which he should hold of him paying to him yearly rent. And the poor young man hired it to him.

And when the cellar was made, the rich man did do [2] bring therein ten tuns of oil, of the which five were full of oil and the other five were but half-full, and did do make a great pit in the earth and did do put the five tuns which were half-full in it and the other five above them. And then he shut the door of the cellar and delivered the key to the poor young man, and prayed him fraudulently to keep well his oil. But the poor young man knew not the malice and falsehood of his neighbor, wherefore he was content to keep the key.

And within a while after, as the oil became dear, the rich man came to the poor and asked of him his goods, and the young man took to him the key. This rich man then sold his oil to the merchants and warranted each tun all full. And when the merchants measured their oil, they found but five of the

[1] *demanded:* asked
[2] *did do:* ordered

ten tuns full. Whereof the rich man demanded of the poor young man restitution. And for to have his house, he made him to come before the judge.

And when the poor man was before the judge, he demanded term and space for to answer, for him thought and seemed that he had kept well his oil. And the judge gave and granted to him a day of advice. And then he went to a philosopher which was procurator of the poor people and prayed him, for charity, that he would give to him good counsel at his great need. And he rehearsed and told to him all his cause [3] and swore upon the holy evangels that he took none of the rich man's oil. And then the philosopher answered to him in this manner: "My son, have no fear, for the truth may not fail."

And the next morrow after, the philosopher went with the poor man into judgment, the which philosopher was constituted by the king for to give the just sentence of it. And after that the cause had been well defended and pleaded by both parties, the philosopher said: "The same rich man is of good renown and I suppose not that he demanded more than he should have. And also I believe not that this poor young man may be maculed [4] nor guilty of the blame which he putteth on him. But notwithstanding, for to know the truth of it, I ordain and give sentence that the pure and clean oil of the five tuns which are full be measured and also the lye [5] thereof; and, after, that the pure and clean oil of the five tuns which been but half-full be measured with the lye thereof; and that men look if the lye of the five tuns half-full is equal and like to the lye of the five tuns which been full. And if it be not so—that as much lye be found within the vessels which been but half-full as in the other—it shall then be sufficiently and right wisely proved that none oil hath been taken out of them. But if there not be found as much lye in the one as in the other, the poor shall be condemned." And with this sentence, the poor was content.

[3] *cause:* case
[4] *maculed:* guilty
[5] *lye:* dregs

And the truth was known, wherefore the poor man went quit [6] and the rich was condemned, for his great malice and falsehood was known and manifested. For there is no sin or misdeed done but that once it shall be known and manifested.

The fourth fable maketh mention of the sentence given upon the pecuny, or money, which was found

A rich man sometime went by a city, and as he walked from one side to the other, fell from him a great purse wherein were a thousand crowns, the which a poor man found and took them for to keep to his wife. Whereof she was full glad and said: "Thanked be God of all the goods which He sendeth to us. If He sendeth now this great sum, keep we it well."

And on the next morn after following, the rich man made to be cried through the city that whosomever had found a thousand crowns in a purse, he should restitute and bring them to him again, and that he should have for his reward an hundred of them. And after that the poor man had heard this cry, he ran incontinent to his wife and said to her: "My wife, that that we have found must be rendered or yielded again. For it is better to have a hundred crowns without sin than a thousand with sin and wrongfully."

And how be it the woman would have resisted, nevertheless in the end she was content. And thus the poor man restored the thousand crowns to the rich and demanded of him his hundred crowns. And the rich, full of fraud or falsehood, said to the poor man: "Thou renderest not to me all my gold which thou foundest, for of it I lack four hundred pieces of gold. And when thou shalt render and bring to me again the said four hundred pieces of gold, thou shalt have of me the hundred crowns which I promised to thee."

[6] *quit:* free, acquitted

And then the poor answered to him: "I have taken and brought to thee all that I have found." Wherefore they fell in great difference or strife insomuch that the cause came before the king to be decided and pleaded—of the which the king made to be called before him a great philosopher which was procurator of the poor. And when the cause was well disputed, the philosopher, moved with pity, called to him the poor man and to him said in this manner: "Come hither, my friend. By thy faith, hast thou restored all that goods which thou foundest in the purse?"

And the poor man answered to him: "Yes, sire, by my faith."

And then the philosopher said before the assistants: [1] "Since this rich man is true and faithful and that it is not to believe that he should demand more than he ought to do, he ought to be believed. And as to the other part, men must believe that this poor man is of good reknown and known for a true man. Wherefore," the philosopher said to the king, "Sire, I give by my sentence that thou take these thousand crowns, and that an hundred thou take of them, the which hundred thou shalt deliver to this poor man which found them. And after, when he that hath lost them shall come, thou restore them to him. And if it happeth that another person finds the thousand and four hundred crowns, they shall be rendered and taken again to the same good man which is here present which sayeth that he hath lost them."

The which sentence was much agreeable and pleasant to all the company. And when the rich man saw that he was deceived, he demanded misericorde [2] and grace of the king, saying in this manner: "Sire, this poor man that hath found my purse, truly he hath restored it to me all that I ought to have, but certainly I would have deceived him. Wherefore I pray thee that thou wilt have pity and misericorde on me." And then the king had misericorde on him. And the poor man was well contented and paid, and all the malice of the rich man was known and manifested.

[1] *assistants:* i.e., the court
[2] *misericorde:* mercy

The fifth fable is of the faith of three fellows

Oft if happeth that the evil which is procured to others cometh to him which procureth it, as it appeareth by the fellows—of the which twain were burgesses and the third a laborer [1]—the which assembled them together for to go to the holy sepulcher.

These three fellows made so great provision of flour for to make their pilgrimage in such wise that it was all chaffed and consumed except only for to make one loaf only. And when the burgesses saw the end of their flour, they said together: "If we find not the manner and cautele [2] for to beguile this villein— because that he is a right great gallant—we shall die for hunger. Wherefore we must find the manner and fashion that we may have the loaf which shall be made of all our flour."

And therefore they concluded together and said: "When the loaf shall be put within the oven, we shall go and lie us for to sleep, and he that shall dream best, the loaf shall be his. And because that we both been subtle and wise, he shall not mowe [3] dream as well as we shall, whereof the loaf shall be ours."

Whereof all they three were well content and all began to sleep. But when the laborer or villein knew and perceived all their fallacy [4] and saw that his two fellows were asleep, he went and drew the loaf out of the oven and ate it. And after, he feigned to be asleep.

And then one of the burgesses rose up and said to his fellows: "I have dreamed a wonder dream, for two angels have taken and borne me with great joy before the divine majesty."

And the other burgess, his fellow, awoke and said: "Thy dream

[1] *laborer:* rustic, villein
[2] *cautele:* trick
[3] *mowe:* be able to
[4] *fallacy:* deception

is marvelous and wonderful, but I suppose that the mine is fairer than thine is. For I have dreamed that two angels drew me on hard ground for to lead me into hell."

And after, they did awake the villein, which—as dread-full—said: "Who is there!"

And they answered: "We be thy fellows."

And he said to them: "How be ye so soon returned?"

And they answered to him: "How 'returned'? We departed not yet from hence."

And he said to them: "By my faith, I have dreamed that the angels had led one of you into paradise or heaven, and the other into hell. Wherefore, I supposed that ye should never have come again. And therefore I arose me from sleep and because I was hungry I went and drew out of the oven the loaf and ate it."

For oft it happeth that he which supposeth to beguile some other is himself beguiled.

The sixth fable is of the laborer and of the nightingale

Sometime there was a laborer which had a garden well pleasant and much delicious, into the which he oft went for to take his disport [1] and pleasure. And on a day at evening when he was weary and had travailed sore,[2] for to take his recreation he entered into his garden and set himself down under a tree, where he heard the song of a nightingale.

And for the great pleasure and joy which he took thereof, he sought and at the last found the means for to take the nightingale, to the end that yet greater joy and plaisance [3] he might have of it.

And when the nightingale was taken, he demanded of the

[1] *disport:* relaxation
[2] *travailed sore:* worked hard
[3] *plaisance:* pleasure

laborer: "Wherefore hast thou taken so great pains for to take me? For well thou knowest that of me thou mayst not have great profit."

And the villein answered thus to the nightingale: "For to hear the song of thee I have taken thee."

And the nightingale answered: "Certainly in vain thou hast pained and labored, for, for no good I will sing while that I am in prison."

And then the laborer or villein answered: "If thou singest not well I shall eat thee."

And then the nightingale said to him: "If thou put me within a pot for to be sodden,[4] little meat shalt thou then make of my body. And if thou settest me for to be roasted, less meat shall be then made of me. And therefore neither boiled nor roasted shall not be thy great belly filled of me. But if thou let me flee, it shall be to thee a great good and profit. For three doctrines I shall teach thee which thou shalt love better than three fat kine." And then the laborer let the nightingale flee.

And when he was out of his hands, and that he was upon a tree, he said to the villein in this manner: "My friend, I have promised to thee that I shall give to thee three doctrines, whereof the first is this—that thou believe no thing which is impossible. The second is that thou keep well what thine is. And the third is that thou take no sorrow of the thing lost which may not be recovered."

And soon after, the nightingale began to sing, and in his song said thus: "Blessed be God Which hath delivered me out of the hands of this villein or churl, which hath not known, seen, nor touched the precious diamond which I have within my belly. For if he had found it, he had been much rich and from his hands I had not escaped."

And then the villein which heard this song began to complain and to make great sorrow and after said: "I am well unhappy that have lost so fair a treasure which I had won. And now I have lost it."

[4] *sodden:* boiled

And the nightingale said then to the churl: "Now know I well that thou art a fool, for thou takest sorrow of that whereof thou shouldst have none, and soon thou hast forgotten my doctrine, because that thou weenest [5] that within my belly should be a precious stone of more weight than I am. And I told and taught to thee that thou shouldst never believe that thing which is impossible. And if that stone was thine, why hast thou lost it? And if thou hast lost it and mayst not recover it, why takest thou sorrow for it?"

And therefore it is folly to chastise or to teach a fool, which never believeth the learning and doctrine which is given to him.

The seventh fable is of a rhetorician and a crookback

A philosopher said once to his son that when he were fallen by fortune into some damage or peril, the sooner that he might, he should deliver him of it, to the end that afterwards he should no more be vexed nor grieved of it. As it appeareth by this fable of a rhetoric man, or fair speaker, which once demanded [1] of a king that of all them which should enter into the city having some fault of kind [2] on their bodies, as crooked or counterfeited, he might have and take of them at the entry of the gate a penny. The which demand the king granted to him and made his letters to be sealed and written under his signet.

And thus he kept himself still at the gate, and of every lame, scabbed, and of all such that had any counterfeiture on their bodies, he took a penny.

It happened then on a day that a crookbacked and counterfeited man would have entered within the city without giving of any penny, and bethought himself that he should take and put on him a fair mantle, and thus arrayed came to the gate.

[5] *weenest:* imagine
[1] *demanded:* petitioned
[2] *fault of kind:* natural fault

And then when the porter beheld him, he perceived that he was goggle-eyed, and said to him: "Pay me of my duty." And the goggle-eyed would pay nought, wherefore he took from him his mantle. And then he saw that he was crookbacked, and said to him: "Thou wouldest not 'tofore [3] pay a penny, but now thou shalt pay twain."

And while that they strived together, the hat and the bonnet fell from his head to the earth, and the porter which saw his scabbed head said to him: "Now shalt thou pay to me three pence." And then the porter yet again set his hands on him and felt that his body was all scabbed. And as they were thus wrestling together, the crookback fell to the ground and hurt himself sore on the leg. And the porter said then to him: "Now shalt thou pay five pence, for thy body is all counterfeited. Wherefore thou shalt leave here thy mantle, and if thou hadst paid a penny, thou hadst gone on thy way free and quit."

Wherefore he is wise that payeth that which he oweth of right to the end that thereof come not to him greater damage.

The eighth fable is of the disciple and the sheep

A disciple was sometime which took his pleasure to rehearse and tell many fables, the which prayed to his master that he would rehearse unto him a long fable. To whom the master answered: "Keep and beware well that it hap not to us as it happed to a king and to his fabulator." [1] And the disciple answered: "My master, I pray thee to tell to me how it befell." And then the master said to his disciple:

"Sometime was a king which had a fabulator the which rehearsed to him at every time that he would sleep, five fables for to rejoice the king and for to make him fall into a sleep.

"It befell then on a day that the king was much sorrowful

[3] *'tofore:* heretofore
[1] *fabulator:* storyteller

and so heavy that he could in no wise fall asleep. And after that the said fabulator had told and rehearsed his five fables, the king desired to hear more. And then the said fabulator recited unto him three fables well short, and the king then said to him: 'I would fain hear one well long and then shall I leave well thee sleep.'

"The fabulator then rehearsed unto him such a fable: Of a rich man which went to the market or fair for to buy sheep, the which man bought a thousand sheep. And as he was returning from the fair, he came unto a river. And because of the great waves of the water, he could not pass over the bridge. Nevertheless, he went so long to and fro on the rivage [2] of the said river that at the last he found a narrow way, upon the which might pass scant enough three sheep at once. And thus he passed and had them over one after another. And hitherto rehearsed of this fable, the fabulator fell on sleep.

"And anon after, the king awoke the fabulator and said to him in this manner: "I pray thee that thou wilt make an end of thy fable.'

"And the fabulator answered to him in this manner: 'Sire, this river is right great and the sheep is little, wherefore let the merchant do pass over his sheep. And after, I shall make an end of my fable.' And then was the king well appeased and pacified.

"And therefore be thou content of that I have rehearsed unto thee, for there is folk so superstitious or capax [3] that they may not be contented with few words."

[2] *rivage:* bank
[3] *capax:* impressionable

The ninth fable is of the wolf, of the laborer, of the fox, and of the cheese

Sometime was a laborer [1] which unnethe [2] might govern and lead his oxen because that they smote with their feet. Wherefore the laborer said to them: "I pray to God that the wolf may eat you." The which words the wolf heard, wherefore he hid himself nigh them until the night and then came for to eat them.

And when the night was come, the laborer unbound his oxen and let them go to his house. And then when the wolf saw them coming homeward, he said: "O thou laborer, many times on this day thou didst give to me thine oxen, and therefore hold thy promise to me."

And the laborer said to the wolf: "I promised to thee nought at all, in the presence of whom I am obliged or bound. I swore not neither to pay thee."

And the wolf answered: "I shall not leave thee go without that thou hold to me, that that thou promised and gavest to me." And as they had so great strife and dissension together, they remitted the cause to be discuted or pleaded before the judge. And as they were seeking a judge, they met with the fox, to whom they recounted or told all their difference and strife.

Then said the fox unto them: "I shall accord you both well and I shall give on your case or plea a good sentence. But I must speak with each one of you both apart or alone." And they were content.

And the fox went and told to the laborer: "Thou shalt give to me a good hen and another to my wife, and I shall it so make that thou with all thine oxen shalt freely go unto thy house." Whereof the laborer was well content.

And after, the fox went and said to the wolf: "I have well

[1] *laborer:* farmer
[2] *unnethe:* hardly

labored and wrought for thee, for the laborer shall give to thee therefore a great cheese, and let him go home with his oxen." And the wolf was well content.

And after, the fox said to the wolf: "Come thou with me and I shall lead thee whereas the cheese is." And then he led him to and fro, here and there, unto the time that the moon shined full brightly, and that they came to a well. Upon the which, the fox leaped and showed to the wolf the shadow of the moon which reluced [3] in the well, and said to him: "Look now, godsip,[4] how that cheese is fair great and broad. Hie thee, now, and go down and after take that fair cheese."

And the wolf said to the fox: "Thou must be the first of us both that shall go down, and if thou mayst not bring it with thee because of its greatness, I shall then go down for to help thee." And the fox was content because that two buckets were there, of which as the one came upward the other went downward, and the fox entered into one of the same buckets and went down into the well.

And when he was down, he said to the wolf: "Godsip, come hither and help me, for the cheese is so much and so great that I may not bear it up." And then the wolf was afraid that the fox should eat it and entered within the other bucket. And as fast as he went downward, the fox came upward. And when the wolf saw the fox coming upward, he said to him: "My godsip, ye go hence?"

"Thou sayest true," said the fox. "For thus it is of the world. For when one commeth down, the other goeth upward." And thus the fox went away and left the wolf within the well.

And thus the wolf lost both the oxen and the cheese. Wherefore, it is not good to leave that which is sure and certain for to take that which is uncertain. For many one been thereof deceived by the falsehood and deception of the advocate and of the judge.

[3] *reluced:* reflected
[4] *godsip:* "cousin"

The tenth fable is of the husband, and of the mother, and of his wife

Sometime was a merchant which married him to a young woman the which had yet her mother alive. It happed that this merchant would once have gone somewhere into a far country for to buy some ware or merchandise. And as he was going, he betook his wife to her mother for to keep and rule her honestly till he come again.

His wife then by the own consenting and will of her mother enamored herself of a right genteel, fair and young man which furnished to th' appointment.[1] And once as they three made good cheer, the husband came again from the fair and knocked at the door of the house, wherefore they were well abashed. Then said the old mother thus to them: "Have no fear, but do as I shall tell to you, and care you not."

And then she said to the young man: "Hold this sword and go thou to the gate and beware thyself that thou say not one word to him, but let me do."[2] And as the husband would have entered his house, and that he saw the young man holding a naked sword in his hands, he was greatly afraid. And then the old woman said to him: "My son, thou art right welcome. Be not afraid of this man, for three men ran right now after him for to have slain him, and by adventure he found the gate open —and this is the cause why he came here for to save his life."

And then the husband said to them: "Ye have done well, and I can you greatly thank." And thus the young amorous went his way surely[3] by the subtlety of the mother of his wife, to the which trust thyself not and thou shalt do as sage and wise.

[1] *furnished to th' appointment:* suited the purpose
[2] *let me do:* let me do the talking
[3] *surely:* securely, safely

The eleventh fable is of an old harlot or bawd

A nobleman was sometime which had a wife much chaste and was wonder fair. This nobleman would have gone on pilgrimage to Rome and left his wife at home because that he knew her for a chaste and a good woman. It happed on a day as she went into the town, a fair young man was esprised [1] of her love and took on him hardiness and required her of love and promised to her many great gifts. But she which was good had lever [2] die than to consent her thereto.

Wherefore the young man died almost for sorrow. To the which fellow came an old woman which demanded of him the cause of his sickness. And the young man manifested or discovered unto her all his courage [3] and heart, asking help and counsel of her. And the old woman wily and malicious said to him: "Be thou glad and joyous, and take good courage. For well I shall do and bring about thy fate insomuch that thou shalt have thy will fulfilled."

And after this, the old bawd went to her house and made a little cat which she had at home to fast three days one after another. And after, she took some bread with a great deal or quantity of mustard upon it and gave it to this young cat for to eat it. And when the cat smelled it, she began to weep and cry.

And the old woman or bawd went unto the house of the said young woman and bare her little cat with her. The which young and good woman received and welcomed her much honestly because that all the world held her for a holy woman. And as they were talking together the young woman had pity of the cat which wept and demanded of the old woman what the cat ailed. And the old woman said to her: "Ha a, my fair daughter and

[1] *esprised:* enflamed
[2] *lever:* rather
[3] *courage:* state of mind

my fair friend, renew not my sorrow." And saying these words
she began to weep and said: "My friend, for no good [4] will I tell
the cause why my cat weepeth."

And then the young woman said to her: "My good mother,
I pray you that ye will tell me the cause why and wherefore your
cat weepeth." And then the old woman said to her: "My friend,
I will well if thou wilt swear that thou shalt never rehearse it
to nobody." To the which promise the good and true young
woman accorded herself, supposing that it had been all good,
and said: "I will well."

And then the old woman said to her in this manner: "My
friend, this same cat which thou seest yonder was my daughter,
the which was wonder fair, gracious, and chaste, which a young
man loved much, and was so much esprised of her love that because that she refused him he died for her love. Wherefore the
gods, having pity on him, have turned my daughter into this
cat."

And the young woman, which supposed that the old woman
had said truth, said to her in this manner: "Alas, my fair mother,
I ne wote [5] what I shall do. For such a case might well hap to
me. For in this town is a young man which dieth almost for the
love of me. But for love of my husband, to whom I ought to keep
chastity, I have not granted his will. Nevertheless, I shall do that,
that thou shalt counsel to me."

And then the old woman said to her: "My friend, have thou
pity on him as soon as thou mayst, so that it befall not to thee
like as it did to my daughter."

The young woman then answered to her and said: "If he require me any more I shall accord me with him, and if he require me no more yet shall I proffer me to him. And to the end
that I offend not the gods, I shall do and accomplish it as soon
as I may."

The old woman then took leave of her and went forthwith
to the young man, and to him she rehearsed and told all these

---

[4] *for no good:* i.e., "not for all the money in the world"
[5] *ne wote:* know not

tidings. Whereof his heart was filled with joy, the which anon went toward the young woman and with her he fulfilled his will.

And thus ye may know the evils which been done by bawds and old harlots, that would to God that they were all burnt.

The twelfth fable is of a blind man and his wife

There was sometime a blind man which had a fair wife, of the which he was much jealous. He kept her so that she might go nowhere, for ever he had her by the hand. And after that she was enamoured of a genteel fellow, they could not find the manner nor no place for to fulfill their will. But notwithstanding, the woman, which was subtle and ingenious, counseled to her friend that he should come into her house and that he should enter into the garden and that there he should climb upon a pear tree. And he did as she told him.

And when they had made their enterprise, the woman came again into the house and said to her husband: "My friend, I pray you that ye will go into our garden for to disport us a little while there."

Of the which prayer the blind man was well content and said to his wife: "Well, my good friend, I will well. Let us go thither."

And as they were under the pear tree, she said to her husband: "My friend, I pray thee to let me go upon the pear tree, and I shall gather for us both some fair pears."

"Well, my friend," said the blind man, "I will well and grant thereto."

And when she was upon the tree, the young man began to shake the pear tree at one side and the young woman at the other side. And as the blind man heard thus hard shake the pear tree and the noise which they made, he said to them: "Ha a! evil woman, howbeit that I see it not, nevertheless I feel and understand it well. But I pray to the gods that they vouchsafe to send me my sight again." And as soon as he had made his prayer, Jupiter rendered to him his sight again.

And when he saw that pageant upon the pear tree, he said to his wife: "Ha, unhappy woman, I shall never have no joy with thee."

And because that the young woman was ready in speech and malicious, she answered forthwith to her husband: "My friend, thou art well beholden and bounden to me for because the gods have restored to thee thy sight, whereof I thank all the gods and goddesses which have enhanced and heard my prayer.

"For I, desiring much that thou might see me, ceased never day nor night to pray them that they would render to thee thy sight. Wherefore the goddess Venus visibly showed herself to me and said that if I would do some pleasure to the said young man, she should restore to thee thy sight. And thus I am cause of it."

And then the good man said to her: "My right dear wife and good friend, I remercy [1] you greatly, for right ye have done and I great wrong."

The thirteenth fable is of the tailor of a king and of his servants

A man ought not to do some other that which he would not that it were done to him, as it appeareth by this present fable of a king which had a tailor which was as good a workman of his craft as any was at that time in all the world. The which tailor had with him many good servants, whereof the one was called Medius which surmounted all the others in shaping or sewing. The king commanded to his steward that the said tailors should fare well and have of the best meats and of delicious drink.

It happed on a day that the master steward gave to them right

---

[1] *remercy:* thank

good and delicious meat in the which was some honey. And because that Medius was not at that feast, the steward said to the others that they should keep for him some of their meat. And then the master tailor answered: "He must none have, for if he were here he should not eat of it, for he eats never no honey."

And as they had done, Medius came and demanded of his fellows: "Why kept you not part of this meat for me?"

And the steward answered and said to him: "Because that thy master said to me that thou eat never no honey, no part of the meat was kept for thee."

And Medius answered then never one word but began to think how he might pay his master. And on a day as the steward was alone with Medius, he demanded of Medius if he knew no man that could work as well as his master. And Medius said nay and that it was great dommage [1] of a sickness that he had. And the steward demanded what sickness it was, and then Medius answered to him: "My lord, when he is entered into his phrenzy or wodeness [2] there cometh upon him a rage."

"And how shall I know it?" said the steward.

"Certainly, my lord," said Medius, "when ye shall see that he shall set at his work and that he shall look here and there and shall smite upon his board with his fist, then may ye know that his sickness commeth on him. And then, without ye take and bind him and also beat him well, he shall do great harm and damage."

And the steward said to him: "Care not thereof, my friend, for well I shall beware myself of him."

And on the morning next following, the steward came for to see the tailors. And then Medius, which knew well the cause of his coming, took away secretly his master's shears and hid them. And anon his master began for to look after them and saw and searched all about, here and there, and began to smite his fist upon the board. And then the master steward began to look on his manners and suddenly made him to be taken and

---

[1] *great dommage:* too bad
[2] *wodeness:* madness

held by his servants; and after, made him to be bound and well beaten.

Then was the master tailor all abashed and demanded of them: "My lords, wherefore do ye beat me so outrageously? What offense have I done wherefore I must be bound and thus be beat?"

And then the steward said to him in this manner: "Because that Medius told me that thou art frantic, and if thou be not well beat thou shouldest do great harm and damage."

And then the master came to his servant Medius and rigorously said to him: "Ha a! evil boy, filled with evil words! When sawest thou me mad?"

And his servant proudly answered to him: "My master, when diddest thou see that I eat no honey? And therefore I threw to thee one bowl for another." And the master steward and all his servants began then to laugh and said all that he had well done.

And therefore men ought not to do to any other that thing which they would not that men did to them.

Here enden the fables of Alfonce
And followen other fables of Poge the Florentyn

THE FABLES OF POGE

The first fable is of the subtlety of the woman for to deceive her husband

The cautele [1] or falsehood of woman is wonder marvelous, as it appeareth by this fable of a merchant which was wedded of new unto a fair and young woman—the which merchant went over the sea for to buy and sell and for to get somewhat for to live honestly.[2] And because that he dwelled too long, his wife supposed that he was dead. And therefore she enamored herself with another man which did to her mickle good,[3] as for to have do, make and build up his house anew, the which had great need of reparation. And also he gave to her all new utensils to keep a household.

And within a long time after the departing of the merchant, he came again into his house, which he saw new builded and saw dishes, pots, pans, and such other household goods. Wherefore he demanded of his wife how and in what manner she had found the fashion and the means for to have repaired so honestly his house. And she answered that it was by the grace of God. And he answered: "Blessed be God of it."

And when he was within the chamber, he saw the bed richly

[1] *cautele:* trick
[2] *honestly:* handsomely, prosperously
[3] *mickle good:* much good

covered and the walls well hanged, and demanded of his wife as he had done before. And she then answered to him in like manner as she did before. And therefore he thanked God as he had done 'tofore.

And as he would set him at his dinner, there was brought before him unto his wife a child of three years of age or thereabout. Wherefore he demanded of his wife: "My friend, to whom belongeth this fair child?" And she answered: "My friend, the Holy Ghost of His Grace hath sent it to me."

Then answered the merchant to his wife in this manner: "I render not graces nor thanks not to the Holy Ghost of this. For He hath taken too much pain and labor for to have made up mine own work, and I will that in no manner wise He meddle no more therewith. For such thing belongeth to me for to do it and not to the Holy Ghost."

The second fable is of the woman and of the hypocrite

The generation or birth of the hypocrite is much damnable and evil, as it appeareth by this fable, and as Poge rehearseth to us which saith that sometime he found himself in a good fellowship where he heard a fable which was there rehearsed, of the which the tenor followeth:

And sayeth the said Poge that of all the goods [1] of this world the hypocrites been possessors. For howbeit that an hypocrite have sometime will for to help some poor and indigent, nevertheless he hath a condition within himself—that is, to wit, that he should rather see a man at the point of death than for to save his life of an halfpenny. And this presumption is called hypocrisy, as ye shall hear hereafter by the fable following, the which sayeth (that one being in the fellowship of Poge rehearsed):

[1] *goods:* property

That sometime the custom of all the poor was that they went before the folks' doors without saying any word. It happed then on that time that a poor man, much fair and of good life, went to search his life from one door to another. And upon a day, among others he went and set himself upon a great stone before the gate of a widow, which widow was accustomed to give him ever somewhat.

And when the good woman knew that he was at her door, she did bring to him his portion as she was 'customed for to do. And as she gave to him the meat, she looked on him, and seeing him so fair and well made of body, she then filled of carnal concupiscence—and burning in the fire of love, required and instantly prayed him that he would return thither within three days, and promised to him that she should give to him a right good dinner. And the poor man said to her that he should do so.

And when he came again, he set himself as before at the door of the widow's house, which woman knew well when he should come, wherefore she came to the gate and said: "Come within, good man, for now we shall dine." To the which prayer the poor man assented and entered within the house.

The which widow gave to him good meat and good drink, and when they had well dined, the said widow pressed the good man strongly. And after, she kissed him, requiring him that she might have the copy of his love. And then the poor man, all ashamed and virginous, knowing her thought and her will, answered thus to her: "Certainly, my good lady, I dare not." But nevertheless, he would fain have done it.

And the widow, all embraced with love, beseeched and prayed him more and more. And then when the poor man saw that he might not excuse himself, he said to the widow in this manner: "My friend, sith that thou desirest it for to do so much and so great an evil, I take God to my witness that thou art causer of it. For I am not consenting to the fait or deed." But saying these words, he consented to her will.

*The third fable is of a young woman which accused her
husband of culp or blame*

Poge Florentine sayeth that sometime there was a man named
Nerus dePacis, the which of his age was among the Florentines
right sage and prudent and right rich. This Nerus had a fair
daughter the which he married with a right fair young man and
a rich and of good parentage or kindred. The which young man
the next day after the feast of his wedding did lead her into
his castle a little way without the city of Florence.

And within few days after, this young man brought his wife
again into Florence, into the house of her father Nerus—the
which made then a feast as it was 'customed to do at that time
in some places eight days after the wedding.

When this new married or wedded woman was come again
to her father's house, she made not over good cheer, but ever
she had her look downward to the earth, as full triste,[1] thoughtful, and melancholious. And when her mother perceived and
saw her daughter so sorrowful and of mourning countenance,
she called her within a wardropp [2] whereas nobody was but they
two, and asked of her the cause of her sorrow, saying: "How fare
ye, my daughter? What want you? Have you not all things coming to you after your desire and plaisance? [3] Wherefore take ye
so great thought and melancholy?"

And then the daughter, weeping full tenderly, said to the
mother in this manner: "Alas, my mother, ye have not married
me to a man. For of such a thing that a man ought to have,
he hath never a dele [4] save only a little part of that thing for
the which wedding is made."

And then the mother, right wroth and sorrowful of this evil
fortune, went toward her husband Nerus and told to him th'evil

---

[1] *triste:* sad
[2] *wardropp:* wardrobe, dressing room
[3] *plaisance:* pleasure
[4] *dele:* little bit

aventure [5] and hap of their daughter. Whereof he was greatly wroth and sore troubled. And soon after, this fortune was also divulged, manifested and known among all the lineage of Nerus. Whereof they were all sorrowful and greatly abashed how this fair young man to whom God had sent so many good virtues and that had so many gifts of grace—as is beauty, riches, and good renown—was indigent or faulty of that thing wherefore marriage is made.

Nevertheless, the tables were set and covered. And when the time of dinner came, the young man came into the house of Nerus with his friends and parents. And incontinent [6] they set them all at the table—some with heavy and sorrowful hearts, and the others with great joy and pleasure. And when the young man saw that all his friends made good cheer and that all the parents [7] of his wife were heavy and melancholious, he prayed and besought them that they would tell him the cause of their heaviness and sorrow. But none of them all answered.

Nevertheless, he prayed and besought them yet again. And then one of them—full of sorrow and more liberal than all the others—said thus to him: "Certainly, my fair son, thy wife hath told to us that thou art not man perfect."

For the which words the man began to laugh and said with a high [8] voice that all they that were there might understand what he said: "My lords and my friends, make good cheer. For the cause of your sorrow shall soon be 'peased." [9] And then he, being clothed with a short gown, untied his hose and took his member with his hand—which was great and much sufficient— upon the table so that all the fellowship might see it.

Whereof the said fellowship was full glad and joyful; whereof some of the men desired to have as much, and many of the women wished to their husbands such an instrument. And then some of the friends and parents of Nerus' daughter went toward

[5] *aventure:* occurrence
[6] *incontinent:* immediately
[7] *parents:* close relatives
[8] *high:* loud
[9] *'peased:* appeased

her and said to her that she had great wrong for to complain her of her husband, for he had well wherewith she might be contented, and blamed her greatly of her folly.

To whom the young daughter answered: "My friends, why blame ye me? I complain me not without cause, for our ass which is a brute beast hath well a member as great as mine arm and my husband which is a man, his member is unnethe [10] half so great." Wherefore the simple and young damsel weened that the man should have it as great and greater than asses.

Therefore it is said oft that much lacketh he of that, that a fool thinketh or weeneth.

The fourth fable is of the hunting and hawking

Poge Florentine rehearseth to us how once he was in a fellowship where men spake of the superfluous cure [1] of them which govern the dogs and hawks. Whereof a Milanese named Paulus began to laugh, and laughing required of Poge that he would rehearse some fable of the said hawks. And for love of all the fellowship, he said in this manner: Sometime was a medecine [2] which was a Milanese. This medecine healed all fools of all manner of folly, and how and in what manner he did heal them, I shall tell it to you.

This medecine or leech had within his house a great garden. And in the midst of it was a deep and a broad pit which was full of stinking and infected water. And within the same pit, the said medecine put the fools after the quantity of their foolishness—some unto the knees and the others unto the belly. And there he bound them fast at a post. But none he put deeper than unto the stomach, for doubt [3] of greater inconvenience.

[10] *unnethe:* hardly, scarcely
[1] *superfluous cure:* idle pastime
[2] *medecine:* physician
[3] *doubt:* fear

It happed then that among others was one brought to him which he put into the said water unto the thighs. And when he had been by the space of 15 days within the said water, he began to be peaceable and got his wit again. And for to have taken some disport [4] and consolation, he prayed to him which had the keeping of him that he would take him out of the water, and promised to him that he should not depart from the garden.

And then the keeper, that kept him, unbound him from the stake and had him out of the water. And when he had been many days out of the pit, he went well unto the gate of the garden but he durst not go out—lest that he should be put again within the said pit.

And on a time he went above upon the gate and as he looked all about, he saw a fair young man on horseback which bare a sparrow hawk on his fist and had with him two fair spaniels. Whereof the said fool was all abashed. And indeed as by case of novelty [5] he called the said young man and, after, he said to him benignly: "My friend, I pray thee that thou wilt tell me what is that whereupon thou art set?" And then the young son said to him that it was a horse which profited to him to the chase and bare him where he would.

And, after, the fool demanded [6] of him: "And what is that which thou bearest on thy fist, and whereto is it good?" And the young man answered to him: "It is a sparrow hawk, which is good for to take partridges and quails."

And, yet again, the fool demanded of him: "My friend, what are those that follow thee and whereto been they good?" And the young man answered to him: "They be dogs, which are good for to search and find partridges and quails. And when they have raised them, my sparrow hawk taketh them—whereof proceedeth to me great solace and pleasure."

And the fool demanded again: "To your advice,[7] the taking that ye do by them in a whole year—how much is it? Shall it

[4] *disport:* recreation
[5] *as . . . novelty:* out of curiosity
[6] *demanded:* asked
[7] *to your advice:* by your estimate

bear to thee great profit?" And the young man answered to him:
"Four or five crowns or thereabout, and no more."

Said the fool: "And to your advice, how much shall they dispend [8] in a year?" And the young man answered: "Forty or fifty
crowns." And when the fool heard these words, he said to the
said young man: "O, my friend, I pray thee that soon thou wilt
depart from hence. For if our physician come, he shall put thee
within the said pit because that thou art a fool. I was put in
it unto the thighs, but therein he should put thee unto the chin
—for thou dost the greatest folly that ever I heard speak of."

And therefore the study of the hunting and hawking is a slothful [9] cure, and none ought to do it without he be much rich
and a man of livelihood. And yet it ought not be done full oft,
but sometime for to take disport and solace, and to drive away
melancholy.

The fifth fable is of the recitation of some monsters

Poge of Florence reciteth how in his time one named Hugh,
Prince of the Medicis, saw a cat which had two heads and a calf
which also had two heads—and his legs both before and behind
were double, as they had been joined all together—as many folk
saw.

Item about the marches of Italy. Within a meadow was sometime a cow, the which made and delivered her of a serpent of
wonder and right marvelous greatness, right hideous and fearful. For, first, he had the head greater than the head of a calf.
Secondly, he had a neck of the length of an ass, and his body
made after the likeness of a dog, and his tail was wonder great,
thick, and long without comparison to any other.

And when the cow saw that she had made such a birth, and

[8] *how . . . dispend:* how much do you spend on them
[9] *slothful:* idle

that within her belly she had borne so right horrible a beast, she was all fearful and lifted herself up and supposed to have fled away. But the serpent with his wonder long tail enlaced her two hinder legs, and the serpent then began to suck the cow. And, indeed, so much and so long he sucked, till that he found some milk.

And when the cow might escape from him, she fled unto the other kine, and incontinent [1] her paps and her behinder legs and all that the serpent touched was all black a great space of time. And soon after, the said cow made a fair calf, the which marvel was announced or said to the said Pope, he being at Ferrare.

And yet again, soon after that, there was found within a great river a monster mariner of the sea, of the form or likeness which followeth: First, he had from the navel upward, the similitude or likeness of a man. And from the navel downward, he had the form or making of a fish—the which part was dual, that is, to wit, double. Secondly, he had a great beard, and he had two wonder great horns above his ears. Also he had great paps and a wonder great and horrible mouth. And his hands reached unto his entrails or bowels. And at the both his elbows, he had wings right broad and great, of fish's mails,[2] wherewith he swimmed and only he had but the head out of the water.

It happed then, as many women bouked [3] and washed at the port or haven of the said river, that this horrible and fearful beast was—for lack and default of meat—come swimming toward the said women. Of the which he took one by the hand and supposed to have drawn her into the water. But she was strong and well avised [4] and resisted against the said monster. And, as she defended herself, she began to cry with a high voice, "Help! Help!" To the which came running five women which, by hurling and drawing of stones, killed and slew the said

---

[1] *incontinent:* immediately
[2] *mails:* scales
[3] *bouked:* bathed
[4] *well avised:* determined

monster. For he was come too far within the sonde,[5] wherefore he might not return into the deep water.

And after, when he rendered his spirit, he made a right little cry, saying that he was so deformed and so much cruel—for he was of great corpulence more than any man's body. And yet, sayeth Poge in this matter, that he, being at Ferrare, saw the said monster and sayeth yet, that the young children were customed for to go bathe and wash them within the said river but they came not all again. Wherefore the women washed nor bouked no more their clothes at the said port. For the folk presumed and supposed that the monster killed the young children which were drowned.

Item. Also, within a little while after, it befell about the marches of Italy that a child of form human had two heads and two visages or faces beholding one upon the other, and the arms of each other embraced the body—the which body, from the navel upward, was joined save the two heads, and from the navel downward, the limbs were all separated one from other in such wise that the limbs of generation were showed manifestly. Of the which child, the tidings came unto the person of the Pope of Rome.

The sixth fable is of the parson, of his dog,
and of the bishop

Silver doth and causeth all things to be done, unto the hallowing again of a place which is profane or interdicted, as ye shall mowe[1] hear by this present fable of a priest dwelling in the country which sometime had a dog which he loved much. The which priest was much rich. The said dog, by process of time,

[5] *sonde:* channel
[1] *mowe:* be able to

died. And when he was dead, he entered and buried it in the church yard, for cause of the great love which he loved him.

It happed then on a day his bishop knew it by th'advertisement of some other. Wherefore he sent for the said priest and supposed to have of him a great sum of gold, or else he should make him to be straitly punished. And then he wrote a letter unto the said priest, of which the tenor contained only that he should come and speak with him.

And when the priest had read the letter, he understood well all the case, and presupposed or bethought in his courage [2] that he would have of him some silver. For he knew well enough the conditions [3] of his bishop. And forthwith, he took his breviary and an hundred crowns with him and went forth to speak to his prelate.

And when he came before him the prelate began to remember [4] and to show to him the enormity of his misdeed. And to him answered the priest, which was right wise, saying in this manner: "O, my right reverend father—if ye knew the sovereign prudence of which the said dog was filled, ye should not be marveled if he hath well deserved for to be buried honestly and worshipfully among the men. He was all filled with human wit as well in his life as in th'article of the death."

And then the bishop said: "How may that be? Rehearse to me then all his life."

"Certainly, right reverend father. Ye ought well to know that when he was at th'article and at the point of death, he would make his testament. And the dog, knowing your great need and indigence, he bequeathed to you an hundred crowns of gold—the which I bring now unto you."

And then the bishop for love of the money he absolved the priest and also granted the said sepulture. [5] And, therefore, silver causeth all things to be granted or done.

[2] *bethought in his courage:* knew in his heart
[3] *conditions:* habits
[4] *remember:* remind
[5] *sepulture:* burial

The seventh fable is of the fox, of the cock and of the dogs

All the salary or payment of them that mock others is for to be mocked at the last—as it appeareth by this present fable of a cock which sometime saw a fox coming toward him sore hungry and famished. Which cock supposed well that he came not toward him but for to eat some hens, for which cause the cock made all his hens to flee upon a tree. And when the fox began to approach to the said tree, he began to cry toward the cock: "Good tidings, good tidings!" And after, he saluted the cock right reverently and demanded [1] of him thus: "O, godsep,[2] what dost thou there so high, and thy hens with thee? Hast not thou heard the good tidings, worthy and profitable for us?"

And then the cock, full of malice, answered to him: "Nay, verily, godsep—but I pray thee tell and rehearse them unto us."

Then said the fox to the cock: "Certainly, godsep, they be the best that ever ye heard. For ye may go and come, talk and communicate, among all beasts without any harm or dommage.[3] And they shall do to you both pleasure and all service to them possible. For thus it is concluded and accorded and also confirmed by the great council of all beasts.

"And yet they have made commandment that none be so hardy to vex nor lett [4] in no wise any other, be it never so little a beast. For the which good tidings, I pray thee that thou wilt come down, to th'end that we may go and sing 'Te Deum Laudamus' for joy."

And the cock, which knew well the fallacies or falsehood of the fox, answered to him in this manner: "Certainly, my brother and my good friend, thou hast brought to me right good tidings, whereof more than hundred times I shall thank thee." And say-

[1] *demanded:* asked
[2] *godsep:* cousin
[3] *dommage:* sorrow, hurt
[4] *lett:* interfere with

ing these words, the cock lift up his neck and his feet and looked far from him.

And the fox said to him: "What, godsep, whereabout lookest thou?"

And the cock answered to him: "Certainly, my brother, I see two dogs strongly and lightly running hitherward with open mouths, which—as I suppose—come for to bring to us the tidings which thou hast told to us."

And then the fox, which shook for fear of the two dogs, said to the cock: "God be with you, my friend. It is time that I depart from hence ere these two dogs come nearer." And saying these words, he took his way and ran as fast as he might.

And then the cock demanded and cried after him: "Godsep, why runnest thou thus if the said pact is accorded? Thou oughtest not to doubt [5] nothing."

"Ha a, godsep," said the fox from afar, "I doubt that these two dogs have not heard the decree of the peace."

And, thus, when a beguiler is beguiled he receives the salary or payment which he ought to have. Wherefore let every man keep himself therefrom.

The eighth fable

Pogius rehearseth that there were two women in Rome which he knew, of diverse age and form, which came to a courtier because to have and win somewhat with their bodies—whom he received. And it happed that he knew the fairest of both twice, and that other once, and so departed.

And afterward, when they should depart, he gave to them a piece of linen cloth, not discerning how much each of them should have to her part and portion. And in the parting of the said cloth fell between the women a strife because one of them demanded two parts—after the exigency of her work—and that other, the half after their persons; each of them showing di-

[5] *doubt:* fear

versely their reasons: That one saying that she had suffered him twice to do his pleasure, and that other pretended that she was ready, and in her was no default.

And so from words they came to strokes and cratching with nails and drawing their hair, insomuch that their neighbors came to this battle for to depart them and also their own and proper husbands, not knowing the cause of their strife and debate, each of them defending his wife's cause. And, from the fighting of the women, it arose and came to their husbands— with buffets and casting of stones so long that men ran between them. And, after the custom of Rome, both the husbands were brought to prison, bearing enmity each to other, and knew nothing the cause wherefore.

The said cloth is set in the hands of the women secretly; yet [1] not departed, but is secretly argued among the women in what wise that this matter shall be decided. And I demand [2] of doctors [3] what the law is.

The ninth fable

He sayeth also that a merchant of Florence bought an horse of a man and made his covenant [1] with the seller for 25 ducats: for to pay forthwith in hand 15 ducats and, as for the rest, he should abide debtor and owe. And the seller was content and thereupon delivered the horse and received the 15 ducats.

After this a certain term, the seller demanded of the buyer the residue, and he denied the payment and bad him hold his covenant—for the buyer said: "We were accorded that I should be thy debtor. And if I should satisfy and pay thee, I should no more be thy debtor, et cetera." And so he abode debtor.

[1] *yet:* still
[2] *demand:* ask
[3] *doctors:* professors, scholars, wise men
[1] *covenant:* bargain

The tenth fable

He telleth also that there was a carrick [1] of Genoa hired into France for to make war against Englishmen, of the which carrick the patron bore in his shield painted an oxe head. Which a nobleman of France beheld and saw and said he would avenge him on him that bore those arms. Whereupon arose an altercation so much that the Frenchman provoked the Genoese to battle and fight therefore.

The Genoese accepted the provocation and came at the day assigned into the field, without any array or habilements of war. And that Frenchman came in much noble apparel into the field that was ordained. And then the patron of the carrick said: "Wherefore is it that we two should this day fight and make battle?"

"For I say," said that other, "that thine arms been mine and belonged to me 'tofore that thou haddest them."

"Then," the Genoese said, "it is no need to make any battle therefore. For the arms that I bear is not the head of an oxe, but it is the head of a cow." Which thing so spoken, the noble Frenchman was abashed and so departed half-mocked.

The eleventh fable

Also he sayeth that there was a physician dwelling in a city which was a great and a cunning man in that science. And he had a servant, a young man which made pills after a certain form that he showed to him. And when this young man had dwelled long with him and could perfectly make the pills, he departed from his master and went into strange country. Where,

[1] *carrick:* galley

as he was known, he let men there to understand that he was a cunning physician and could give medicine for all manner of maladies and sicknesses, and ministered always his pills to every man that came to him for any remedy.

And it was so that a poor man of that place where he was, came to him and complained how he had lost his ass, and prayed him to give to him a medicine for to find his ass again. And he gave to him the said pills and bad him to receive and take them, and he should find his ass.

And this poor man did so and, after, went into the fields and pastures to seek and look after his ass. And, so doing, the pills wrought so in his belly that he must needs go purge him, and went among the reeds and there eased him. And, anon! there he found his ass.

Whereof he, being much joyful, ran into the town and told and proclaimed that by the medicine that he had received of the physician he had found his ass. Which thing known, all the simple people reputed him for a much cunning man—which could nothing do but make pills.

And, thus, many fools are oft taken for wise and cunning. For he was reputed to heal all manner sicknesses and also to find asses.

The twelfth fable

There was in a certain town a widower wooed a widow for to have and wed her to his wife. And at the last, they were agreed and sured together. And when a young woman, being servant with the widow, heard thereof, she came to her mistress and said to her: "Alas, mistress, what have ye do?"

"Why?" said she.

"I have heard say," said the maid, "that ye be assured and shall wed such-a-man."

"And what then?" said the widow.

"Alas," said the maid. "I am sorry for you because I have heard say that he is a perilous man. For he lay so oft and knew so much his other wife that she died thereof. And I am sorry thereof that if ye should fall in like case."

To whom the widow answered and said: "Forsooth, I would be dead—for there is but sorrow and care in this world." This was a courteous excuse of a widow.

The thirteenth fable

Now, then, I will finish all these fables with this tale that followeth, which a worshipful priest and a parson told me late. He said that there were dwelling in Oxenford two priests, both masters of art—of whom that one was quick and could put himself forth, and that other was a good, simple priest.

And so it happed that the master that was pert and quick was anon promoted to a benefice or twain, and, after, to prebendies and to be a Dean of a great Prince's chapel—supposing and weening that his fellow, the simple priest, should never have been promoted but be always an annual [1] or at the most a parish priest.

So after a long time this worshipful man, this Dean, came riding into a good parish with ten or twelve horses like a prelate, and come into the church of the said parish, and found there this good, simple man sometime his fellow, which came and welcomed him lowly. And that other bad him, "good morrow, Master John," and took him slightly by the hand and asked him where he dwelled. And the good man said: "In this parish."

"How?" said he. "Are ye here a sole priest or a parish priest?"

"Nay, sir," said he. "For lack of a better, though I be not able nor worthy, I am parson and curate of this parish."

And then that other avaled [2] his bonnet and said: "Master

[1] *annual:* on yearly appointment
[2] *avaled:* doffed

parson, I pray you to be not displeased. I had supposed ye had not been beneficed. But, master," said he, "I pray you, what is this benefice worth to you a year?"

"Forsooth," said the good, simple man, "I wote [3] never, for I make never accounts thereof, how well [4] I have had it four or five years."

"And know ye not," said he, "what it is worth? It should seem a good benefice."

"No, forsooth," said he. "But I wote well what it shall be worth to me."

"Why," said he, "what shall it be worth?"

"Forsooth," said he, "if I do my true diligence in the cure of my parishioners, in preaching and teaching, and do my part belonging to my cure, I shall have heaven therefore. And if their souls been lost or any of them by my default, I shall be punished therefore. And hereof am I sure."

And with that word, the rich Dean was abashed and thought he should be the better and take more heed to his cures and benefices than he had done. This was a good answer of a good priest and an honest.

And herewith I finish this book translated and imprinted by me William Caxton at Westminster in th'Abbey and finished the xxvi day of March, the year of our lord MCCCClxxxiiii, and the first year of the reign of King Richard the third.

[3] *wote:* know, "I can't imagine"
[4] *how well:* although

A Hundred Merry Tales
(1526)

A C. Mery Talys, *dated 22 November 1526, was printed by John Rastell, brother-in-law of Sir Thomas More and a lawyer and playwright as well as a printer. His specialty was law books. In 1526, in addition to* A C. Mery Talys, *he published a very popular jestbook-in-verse modeled after Chaucer by a servant of More's named Smythe, entitled* The Merry Jests of the Widow Edith. A C. Mery Talys *remains anonymous.*

Three copies of the book are extant, and suggest two different editions—though both were printed by Rastell. The "copyright" to the book was assigned to John Walley in 1557/1558 and then to Samson Awdley and John Charlewood in 1582. We have no idea whether later editions by these printers ever appeared.

Of the three extant copies, that in the British Museum is fragmentary and was used for the edition by W. Carew Hazlitt in 1864—still the only generally available text. Another copy of this edition is in the Folger Library. The unique copy of the other edition is in the Royal Library at Göttingen and was edited by Dr. Herman Oesterly (London, 1866). In 1887, Hazlitt published a photo-copy of the original text in a limited edition, and this has been used as basis for the present edition. The original is Number 23664 in the Short Title Catalogue.

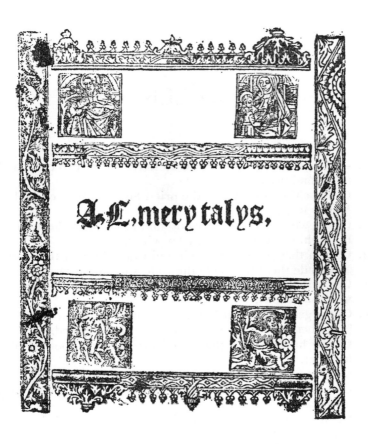

A C. mery talys,

THE KALENDER

1. Of the miller that said he heard never but of two command-ments and two doubts.
2. Of the citizen that called the priest Sir John & he called him Master Rafe.
3. Of the wife that made her husband to go sit in the arbor in the night while her 'prentice lay with her in bed.
4. Of him that played the devil and came through the warren and made them that stole the coneys to run away.
5. Of the sick man that bequeathed his third son a little ground with the gallows.
6. Of the gentleman that lost his ring in the gentlewoman's bed & another gentleman found it after in the same bed.
7. Of the husbandman that asked for Master Pispot the Phi-losopher.
8. Of the scholar that bore his shoes to clouting.
9. Of him that said that a woman's tongue was lightest meat of digestion.
10. Of the woman that followed her fourth husband's hearse & wept.
11. Of the woman that said her wooer came too late.
12. Of the miller with the golden thumb.
13. Of the horseman of Ireland that prayed O'Conner to hang up the friar.
14. Of the priest that said neither "corpus meus" nor "corpum meum."

15. Of the two friars, whereof the one loved not the eel head nor the other the tail.
16. Of the welchman that shrove him for breaking his fast on the Friday.
17. Of the merchant of London that put nobles in his mouth in his death bed.
18. Of the miller that stole the nuts & of the tailor that stole a sheep.
19. Of the four elements, where they should soon be found.
20. Of the woman that poured the pottage in the Judge's male.
21. Of the wedded men that came to heaven to claim their heritage.
22. Of the merchant that charged his son to find one to sing for his soul.
23. Of the maid washing clothes and answered the friar.
24. Of the three wise men of Gotham.
25. Of the gray friar that answered his penitent.
26. Of the gentleman that bare the siege board on his neck.
27. Of the merchant's wife that said she would take a nap at sermon.
28. Of the woman that said an' she lived another year, she would have a cuckold's hat of her own.
29. Of the gentleman that wished his tooth in the gentlewoman's tail.
30. Of the welchman that confessed him how he had slain a friar.
31. Of the welchman that could not get but a little male.
32. Of the gentlewoman that said to a gentleman "Ye have a beard above & none beneath."
33. Of the friar that said Our Lord fed five thousand people with two fishes.
34. Of the franklin that would have had the friar gone.
35. Of the good man that said to his wife he had ill fare.
36. Of the friar that bad his child make a-Latin.
37. Of the gentleman that asked the friar for his beaver.
38. Of the three men that chose the woman.
39. Of the gentleman that taught his cook the medicine for the toothache.

70. Of the friar that stole the pudding.
71. Of the franklin's son that came to take orders.
72. Of the husbandman that lodged the friar in his own bed.
73. Of the priest that would say two gospels for a groat.
74. Of the courtier that did cast the friar over the boat.
75. Of the friar that preached what men's souls were.
76. Of the husband that cried "ble" under the bed.
77. Of the shoemaker that asked the collier: "What tidings in hell?"
78. Of Saint Peter that cried: "Cause bob!"
79. Of him that adventured body and soul for his prince.
80. Of the parson that stole the miller's eels.
81. Of the welchman that saw one 40 shillings better than God.
82. Of the friar that said "dirige" for the hog's soul.
83. Of the parson that said mass of requiem for Christ's soul.
84. Of the herdman that said: "Ride apace—ye shall have rain."
85. Of him that said: "I shall have ne'er a penny."
86. Of the husband that said his wife and he agreed well.
87. Of the priest that said: "Comede, Episcope."
88. Of the woman that stole the pot.
89. Of Master Wittinton's dream.
90. Of the priest that killed his horse called "Modicum."
91. Of the maltman of Colbrook.
92. Of the welchman that stole the Englishman's cock.
93. Of him that brought a bottle to a priest.
94. Of the indictment of Jhesu of Nazareth.
95. Of him that preached against them that rode on the Sunday.
96. Of the one brother that found a purse.
97. Of the answer of the mistress to the maid.
98. Of a certain alderman's deeds of London.
99. Of the northern man that was all heart.
100. Of the burning of Old John.

Finis

A C. MERY TALYS

1.

A certain curate in the country there was that preached in the pulpit of the ten commandments, saying that there were ten commandments that every man ought to keep, and he that brake any of them committed grievous sin. Howbeit, he said that sometime it was deadly sin and sometime venial. But when it was deadly sin and when venial, there were many doubts therein. And a miller—a young man and a mad fellow that came seldom to church, and had been at very few sermons or none in all his life—answered him then shortly this wise: "I marvel, master parson, that ye say there been so many commandments and so many doubts. For I never heard tell but of two commandments—that is to say, 'command me to you,' and 'command[1] me from you.' Nor I never heard tell of mo' doubts but twain—that is to say, 'dout[2] the candle' and 'dout the fire.'" At which answer, all the people fell a-laughing.

By this tale a man may well perceive that they that be brought up without learning or good manners shall never be but rude and beastly, although they have good natural wits.

[1] *command:* the pun is on command = commend
[2] *dout:* the pun is on doubt = d'out (i.e., do out, or put out)

2.

On a time there was a jolly citizen walking in the country for sport, which met with a foolish priest, and in derision in communication called him Sir John. This priest understanding his mocking called him Master Rafe.

"Why," quod the citizen, "dost thou call me 'Master Rafe'?"

"Marry," quod the priest, "why callest me 'Sir John'?"

Then quod the citizen: "I call thee Sir John because every foolish priest most commonly is called Sir John."

"Marry," quod the priest, "and I call thee Master Rafe because every proud cuckold most commonly is called Master Rafe." At the which answer all that were by laughed apace because divers there supposed the same citizen to be a cuckold indeed.

By this tale ye may see that he that delighteth to deride and laugh others to scorn is sometime himself more derided.

3.

A wife there was which had appointed her 'prentice to come to her bed in the night—which servant had long wooed her to have his pleasure—which according to the appointment came to her bedside in the night, her husband lying by her. And when she perceived him there, she caught him by the hand and held him fast, and incontinent [1] wakened her husband and said: "Sir, it is so ye have a false and an untrue servant to you which is William your 'prentice, and hath long wooed me to have his pleasure, and because I could not avoid his importunate request, I have appointed him this night to meet me in the garden

---

[1] *incontinent:* immediately

in the arbor. And if ye will array yourself in mine array and go thither, ye shall see the proof thereof, and then ye may rebuke him as ye think best by your discretion."

This husband thus advertised by his wife put upon him his wife's raiment and went to the arbor. And when he was gone thither, the 'prentice came into bed to his mistress where for a season they were both content and pleased each other by the space of an hour or two. But when she thought time convenient, she said to the 'prentice: "Now go thy way into the arbor and meet him, and take a good waster [2] in thy hand, and say thou didst it but to prove whether I would be a good woman or no, and reward him as thou thinkest best."

This 'prentice, doing after his mistress' counsel, went to the arbor where he found his master in his mistress' apparel and said: "A, thou harlot! Art thou come hither? Now I see well— if I would be false to my master, thou wouldst be a strong whore. But I had lever [3] thou were hanged than I would do him so traitorous a deed. Therefore I shall give thee some punishment as thou, like an whore, hast deserved." And therewith he lapped him well about the shoulders and back and gave him a dozen or two good stripes.

The master, feeling himself somewhat to smart, said: "Peace, William, mine own true good servant—for God's sake, hold thy hands, for I am thy master and not thy mistress!"

"Nay, whore," quod he, "thou liest—thou art but an harlot, and I did but to prove thee—" and smote him again.

"Alas, man," quod the master, "I beseech thee—no more—for I am not she—for I am thy master—feel, for I have a beard!" And therewith he spared his hand and felt his beard.

"Alas, master," quod the 'prentice, "I cry you mercy." And then the master went unto his wife and she asked him how he had sped and he answered: "I wis,[4] wife, I have been shrewdly beaten. Howbeit, I have cause to be glad, for I thank God I

[2] *waster:* i.e., a big club
[3] *I had lever:* I had rather
[4] *I wis:* I know

have as true a wife and as true a servant as any man hath in England."

By this tale ye may see that it is not wisdom for a man to be ruled always after his wife's counsel.

4.

It fortuned that in a market town in the county of Suffolk there was a stage play, in the which play one called John Adroyns (which dwelled in another village two miles from thence) played the devil. And when the play was done, this John Adroyns in the evening departed from the said market town to go home to his own house. And because he had there no change of clothing, he went forth in his devil's apparel.

In the way coming homeward, he came through a warren of conies [1] belonging to a gentleman of the village where himself dwelt. At which time, it fortuned a priest—a vicar of a church thereby—with two or three other unthrifty [2] fellows had brought with them a horse, a hey,[3] and a ferret, to the intent there to get conies. And when the ferret was in the earth, and the hey set over the pathway wherein this John Adroyns should come, this priest and these other fellows saw him come in the devil's raiment—and considering that they were in the devil's service (and stealing of conies) and supposing it had been the devil indeed, for fear ran away.

This John Adroyns in the devil's raiment, because it was somewhat dark, saw not the hey but went forth in haste and stumbled thereat and fell down and with the fall, he had almost broke. But when he was a little revived, he looked up and spied it was a hey to catch conies; and looked further and saw that they ran away

[1] *conies:* rabbits
[2] *unthrifty:* loose living
[3] *hey:* snare

for fear of him; and saw a horse tied to a bush, laden with conies which they had taken.

And he took the horse and the hey and leaped upon the horse and rode to the gentleman's place that was lord of the warren—to the intent to have thanks [4] for taking such a prey—and when he came, knocked at the gates. To whom anon one of the gentleman's servants asked who was there, and suddenly opened the gate—and as soon as he perceived him in the devil's raiment, was suddenly abashed and sparred [5] the door again, and went in to his master and said and sware to his master that the devil was at the gate and would come in.

The gentleman, hearing him say so, called another of his servants and bad him go to the gate to know who was there. This second servant came to the gate, durst not open it but asked with loud voice who was there. This John Adroyns in the devil's apparel answered with a high voice and said: "Tell thy master I must needs speak with him ere I go."

This second servant, hearing that answer, supposing also it had been the devil, went in again to his master and said thus: "Master, it is the devil indeed that is at the gate and saith he must needs speak with you ere he go hence."

The gentleman then began a little to bash [6] and called the steward of his house—which was the wisest servant that he had—and bad him to go to the gate and to bring him sure word who was there. This steward, because he thought he would see surely [7] who was there, came to the gate and looked through the chinks of the gate in divers places, and saw well that it was the devil and sat upon an horse, and hanging about the saddle on every side saw the conie heads hanging down. Then he came to his master, afraid, in great haste and said: "By God's body, it is the devil indeed that is at the gate, sitting upon an horse laden all with souls—and by likelihood he is come for your soul purposely

---

[4] *thanks:* reward
[5] *sparred:* barred
[6] *to bash:* to become abashed
[7] *surely:* securely, safely

—and lacketh but your soul—and if he had your soul I ween he should be gone."

This gentleman then marvelously abashed called up his chaplain and made the holy candle to be lighted and gat holy water and went to the gate with as many of his servants as durst go with him—where the chaplain with holy words of conjuration said: "In the name of the Father, Son and Holy Ghost—I conjure thee and charge thee in the Holy Name of God to tell me why and wherefore thou commest hither."

This John Adroyns in the devil's apparel, hearing them begin to conjure after such manner, said: "Nay, nay, be not afeard of me, for I am a good devil. I am John Adroyns, your neighbor, dwelling in this town, and he that played the devil today in the play. I have brought my master a dozen or two of his own conies that were stolen in his warren—and their horse and their hey—and made them for fear to run away."

And when they heard him thus speak, by his voice they knew him well enough and opened the gate and let him come in. And so all the foresaid fear and dread was turned to mirth and disport.

By this tale ye may see that men fear many times more than they need—which hath caused men to believe that spirits and devils have been seen in divers places when it hath been nothing so.

5.

There was a rich man which lay sore sick in his bed like to die, wherefore his eldest son came to him and beseeched him to give him his blessing. To whom the father said: "Son, thou shalt have God's blessing and mine. And for that, that thou hast been ever good of conditions,[1] I give and bequeath thee all my land."

---

[1] *conditions:* behavior, habits

To whom he answered and said: "Nay, father, I trust you shall live and occupy them yourself full well by God's grace."

Soon after, came his second son to him likewise, and desired his blessing. To whom the father said: "Because thou hast been ever kind and gentle, I give thee God's blessing and mine and also I bequeath thee all my movable goods." [2] To whom he answered and said: "Nay, father, I trust ye shall live and do well and spend and use your goods yourself by God's grace."

Anon after, the third son came to him and desired his blessing. To whom the father answered and said: "Because thou hast been evil and stubborn of conditions and would never be ruled after my counsel, I have neither land nor goods unbequeathed, but only a little vacant ground where a gallows standeth, which now I give and bequeath to thee—and God's curse withal." To whom the son answered as his brethern did and said: "Nay, father, I trust ye shall live and be in good health and have it and occupy it yourself by God's grace."

But after that, the father died, and this third son continued still his unthrifty [3] conditions, wherefore it was his fortune afterward (for his deserving [4]) to be hanged on the same gallows.

By this tale, men may well perceive that young people that will not be ruled by their friends' counsel in youth, in time come to a shameful end.

6.

Two gentlemen of acquaintance were appointed to lie with a gentlewoman in one night (the one not knowing of the other) at divers times. This first at his hour appointed came, and in the bed there he fortuned to lose a ring. The second gentleman (when he was gone) came and fortuned to find the same ring, and when he had sped his business, departed. And two or three

---

[2] *goods:* property
[3] *unthrifty:* prodigal
[4] *for his deserving:* i.e., he deserved it

days after, the first gentleman—seeing his ring on the other's finger—challenged it of him, and he denied it him and bad him tell where he had lost it. And he said in such-a-gentlewoman's bed. Then quod the other: "And there found I it."

And the one said he would have it. The other said he should not. Then they agreed to be judged by the next man that they met. And it fortuned them to meet with the husband of the said gentlewoman, and desired him of his best judgement—showing him all the whole matter. Then quod he: "By my judgement, he that owned the sheets should have the ring." Then quod they: "And for your good judgement you shall have the ring."

7.

In a village in Sussex there dwelled a husbandman whose wife fortuned to fall sick. This husbandman came to the priest of the church and desired his counsel what thing was best to help his wife, which answered him and said that in Bread Street in London there was a cunning physician whose name is called Master Jordayn. "Go to him and show him that thy wife is sick and impotent and not able to go. And show him her water and beseech him to be good master to thee, and pray him to do his cure upon her. And I warrent he will teach thee some medicine that shall help her."

This husbandman, following his counsel, came to London and asked of divers men which was the way to Good Ale Street, so that every man that heard him laughed him to scorn. At the last, one that heard him asked him whether it were not Bread Street that he would have. "By God," quod the husbandman, "ye say truth—for I wist well it was either bread or drink."

So when they had taught him the way to Bread Street and he was entered into that street, he asked of divers men where one Master Pispot dwelled—which said they knew of no such man and laughed at him apace. At last, one asked him whether it were not Master Jordayn the physician. "Ye, the same," quod the husbandman, "for I wot well a jordayn and a pispot is all one."

So when they had showed him his house he went thither and came to him and did his errand thus, and said: "Sir, if it please your maship, I understand ye are called a cunning confusion. So it is my wife is sick and omnipotent and may not go, and here I have brought you her water. I beseech you, do your courage [1] upon her and I shall give your maship a good reward."

The physician, perceiving by the water that she was weak of nature, bad him get her meat that were restorative and specially, if he could, let her have a poundgarnet [2] and to let her not overcome her stomach with much meat till she have an appetite. This husbandman, heard him speak of a poundgarnet and an appetite, had weened he had spoken of a pound of garlic and of an ape—and shortly bought a pound of garlic and, after, went to the Stylyard and bought an ape of one of the merchants and brought both home to his wife, and tied the ape with a chain at his bed's feet, and made his wife to eat the pound of garlic whether she would or no.

Whereby she fell in so great a task that it purged all the corruption out of her body. And by reason that the ape that was tied there made so many mocks, skips, and knacks that made her oftimes to be merry and laugh that (thanked be God) she was shortly restored to health.

By this tale ye may see that oft times medicines taken at adventure [3] do as much good to the patient as medicines given by the solemn counsel of cunning physicians.

8.

In the University of Oxenford there was a scholar that delighted much to speak eloquent English and curious terms, and

---

[1] *courage:* a malapropism, used here to mean "take your lust of her."
[2] *poundgarnet:* pomegranate
[3] *adventure:* chance

came to the cobbler with his shoes which were peaked before—
as they used that season—to have them clouted [1] and said this
wise: "Cobbler, I pray thee set me two triangles and two semi-
circles upon my subpeditals and I shall give thee for thy labor."
This cobbler because he understood him not half well answered
shortly and said: "Sir, your eloquence passeth mine intelligence
but I promise you if ye meddle with me, the clouting of your
shoon shall cost you three pence."

By this tale men may learn that it is folly to study to speak
eloquently before them that be rude and unlearned.

9.

A certain artificer in London there was which was sore sick,
that could not well digest his meat, to whom a physician came
to give him counsel and said that he must vie to eat meats that
be light of digestion, as small birds—as sparrows or swallows—
and especially that bird that is called a wagtail—whose flesh is
marvelous light of digestion because that bird is ever moving and
flying. The sick man, hearing the physician say so, answered him
and said: "Sir, if that be the cause that those birds be light of
digestion then I know a meat much lighter of digestion than
either sparrow, swallow, or wagtail and that is my wife's tongue,
for it is never in rest but ever moving and stirring."

By this tale ye may learn a good general rule of physic.

10.

A woman there was which had four husbands. It fortuned
also that this fourth husband died and was brought to church

[1] *clouted:* cleated

upon the bier—whom this woman followed and made great moan and waxed very sorry, insomuch that her neighbors thought she would swoon and die for sorrow. Wherefore one of her gossips [1] came to her and spake to her in her ear and bad her for God's sake to comfort herself and refrain that lamentation or else it would hurt her greatly and p'aventure [2] put her in jeopardy of her life. To whom this woman answered and said: "I wis, good gossip, I have great cause to moan—if ye knew all— for I have buried three husbands besides this man, but I was never in the case I am now—for there was not one of them but when that I followed the corpse to church yet I was sure always of another husband before that the corpse came out of my house —and now I am sure of no other husband and therefore ye may be sure I have great cause to be sad and heavy.

By this tale ye may see that the old proverb is true that it is as great pity to see a woman weep as a goose to go barefoot.

11.

Another woman there was that kneeled at the mass of requiem while the corpse of her husband lay on the bier in the church. To whom a young man came to speak with her in her ear as though it had been for some matter concerning the funeral. Howbeit, he spoke of no such matter but only wooed her that he might be her husband. To whom she answered and said thus: "Sir, by my troth, I am sorry that ye come so late, for I am sped already—for I was made sure [1] yesterday to another man."

By this tale ye may perceive that women oft times be wise and loath to lose any time.

[1] *gossips:* cousins
[2] *p'aventure:* per adventure, i.e., perchance
[1] *made sure:* engaged

12.

A merchant that thought to deride a miller said unto that miller sitting among company: "Sir, I have heard say that every true miller that tolleth [1] truly hath a golden thumb."

The miller answered and said it was truth.

Then quod the merchant: "I pray thee let me see thy thumb." And when the miller showed his thumb, the merchant said: "I cannot perceive that thy thumb is gilt, but it is but as all other men's thumbs be."

To whom the miller answered and said: "Sir, truth it is that my thumb is gilt, howbeit ye have no power to see it—for there is a property ever incident thereto that he that is a cuckold shall never have power to see it."

13.

One called Oconer, an Irish lord, took an horseman prisoner that was one of his great enemies—which, for any request or entreaty that the horseman made, gave judgement that he should incontinent [1] be hanged, and made a friar to shrive him and bad him make him ready to die. This friar that shrove him examined him of divers sins and asked him among others which were the greatest sins that ever he did.

This horseman answered and said: "One of the greatest acts that ever I did which I now most repent is that when I took Oconer the last week in a church and there I might have burned him, church and all—and because I had conscience and pity of burning of the church, I tarried that time so long that Oconer

---

[1] *tolleth:* counts, measures
[1] *incontinent:* immediately

escaped—that same deferring of burning of the church, and so long tarrying of that time, is one of the worst acts that ever I did whereof I most repent."

This friar, perceiving him in that mind, said: "Peace, man. In the name of God, change your mind and die in charity or else thou shalt never come in heaven."

"Nay," quod the horseman, "I will never change that mind whatsoever shall come to my soul."

This friar, perceiving him thus still to continue his mind, came to Oconer and said: "Sir, in the name of God, have some pity upon this man's soul and let him not die now till he be in a better mind. For if he die now he is so far out of charity that utterly his soul shall be damned—" and showed him what mind he was in and all the whole matter as is before showed.

This horseman, hearing the friar thus entreat for him, said to Oconer thus: "Oconer, thou seest well by this man's report that if I die now I am out of charity and not ready to go to heaven. And so it is that I am now out of charity indeed. But thou seest well that this friar is a good man. He is now well disposed and in charity, and he is ready to go to heaven—and so am not I. Therefore I pray thee hang up this friar while that he is ready to go to heaven, and let me tarry till another time that I may be in charity and ready and mete to go to heaven."

This Oconer, hearing this mad answer of him, spared the man and forgave him his life at that season.

By this, ye may see that he that is in danger of his enemy that hath no pity, he can do no better than show to him the uttermost of his malicious mind which that he beareth toward him.

14.

The Archdeacon of Essex, that had been long in authority, in a time of visitation when all the priests appeared before him, called aside three of the young priests which were accused that they could not well say their divine service. And he asked of them, when they said mass whether they said corpus meus or corpum meum. The first priest said that he said corpus meus. The second said that he said corpum meum. And then he asked of the third how he said, which answered and said thus: "Sir, because it is so great a doubt and divers men be in divers opinions thereto, and because I would be sure I would not offend, when I come to that place I leave it clean out and say nothing therefore." Wherefore he then openly rebuked them all three.

But divers that were present thought more default in him because he himself before time had admitted them to be priests.

By this tale ye may see that one ought to take heed how he rebuketh another, lest it turn most to his own rebuke.

15.

Two friars sat at a gentleman's table which had before him on a fasting day an eel and cut the head of the eel and laid it upon one of the friars' trenchers.[1] But the friar, because he would have had of the middle part of the eel, said to the gentleman he loved no eel heads. This gentlemen also cut the tail of the eel and laid it on the other friar's trencher. He likewise, because he would have had of the middle part of that eel, said he loved no eel tails. This gentleman, perceiving that, gave the tail to the friar that said he loved not the head and gave the head to him that said he loved not the tail. And as for the middle part of the eel, he ate part himself and part he gave to other folks at the table. Wherefore, these friars for anger would eat never a morsel. And so they for all their craft and subtlety were

---

[1] *trencher:* dish

not only deceived of the best morsel of the eel, but thereof had no part at all.

By this ye see that they that covet the best part sometime therefore lose the mean part and all.

16.

A welchman dwelling in a wild place of Wales came to his curate in the time of Lent and was confessed. And when his confession was in manner at the end, the curate asked whether he had any other thing to say that grieved his conscience—which, sore abashed, answered no word a great while. At last, by exhortation of his ghostly father, he said that there was one thing in his mind that greatly grieved his conscience, which he was ashamed to utter for it was so grievous that he trowed [1] God would never forgive him.

To whom the curate answered and said that God's mercy was above all, and bad him not despair in the mercy of God; for whatsoever it was, if he were repentant that God would forgive him. And so, by long exhortation, at the last he showed it and said thus: "Sir, it happened once that as my wife was making a cheese upon a Friday, I would have 'ssayed [2] whether it had been salt or fresh, and took a little of the whey in my hand and put it in my mouth, and ere I was 'ware, part of it went down my throat against my will—and so I brake my fast." To whom the curate said: "And if there be no other thing, I warrant God shall forgive thee."

So when he had well comforted him with the mercy of God, the curate prayed him to answer a question and to tell him truth. And when the welchman had promised to tell the truth, the curate said that there were robberies and murders done nigh the

[1] *trowed:* believed
[2] *'ssayed:* assayed, tried

place where he dwelt, and divers men found slain—and asked him whether he were consenting [3] to any of them. To whom he answered and said yes and said he was party to many of them, and did help to rob and to slay divers of them.

Then the curate asked him why he did not confess him thereof. The welchman answered and said he took that for no sin, for it was a custom among them that when any booty came of any rich merchant riding, that it was but a good neighbor's deed one to help another when one called another. And so they took that but for good fellowship and neighborhood.

Here ye may see that some have remorse of conscience of small venial sins and fear not to do great offenses without shame of the world or dread of God—and as the common proverb is: they stumble at a straw and leap over a block.

17.

A rich covetous merchant there was that dwelled in London which ever gathered money and could never find in his heart to spend nought upon himself nor upon no man else, which fell sore sick—and as he lay on his death bed had his purse lying at his bed's head—and had such a love to his money that he put his hand in his purse and took out thereof ten or twelve pounds in nobles and put them in his mouth.

And because his wife and others perceived him very sick and like to die, they exhorted him to be confessed and brought the curate unto him—which, when they had caused him to say Benedicite, the curate bad him cry God mercy, and show his sins. Then the sick man began to say: "I cry God mercy. I have offended in the seven deadly sins and broken the ten commandments" and because of the gold in his mouth, he muffled so in his speech that the curate could not well understand him.

[3] *consenting:* involved in

Wherefore the curate asked him what he had in his mouth that letted [1] his speech.

"I wis, master parson," quod the sick man muffling, "I have nothing in my mouth but a little money because I wot not whither I shall go. I thought I would take some spending money with me, for I wot not what need I shall have thereof." And incontinent [2] after that saying, he died before he was confessed or repentant that any man could perceive, and so by likelihood went to the devil.

By this tale ye may see that they that all their lives will never do charity to their neighbors, that God in time of their death will not suffer them to have grace of repentance.

18.

There was a certain rich husbandman in a village which loved nuts marvelously well, and set trees of filberts and other nut trees in his orchard and nourished them well all his life. And when he died, he made his executors to make promise to bury with him in his grave a bag of nuts or else they should not be his executors—which executors, for fear of losing their rooms,[1] fulfilled his will and did so.

It happened that the same night after that he was buried, there was a miller in a white coat came to this man's garden to th'intent to steal a bag of nuts. And in the way he met with a tailor in a black coat—an unthrift [2] of his acquaintance—and showed him his intent. This tailor likewise showed him that he intended the same time to steal a sheep. And so they both there agreed to go forthward every man severally with his purpose, and after that

---

[1] *letted:* impeded
[2] *incontinent:* immediately
[1] *rooms:* places, offices
[2] *unthrift:* ne'er-do-well

(they appointed [3]) to make good cheer each with the other, and to meet again in the church porch—and he that came first to tarry for the other.

This miller, when he had sped of [4] his nuts, came first to the church porch and there tarried for his fellow—and the meanwhile sat still there and knakked nuts.

It fortuned then the sexton of the church, because it was about nine of the clock, came to ring curfew. And when he looked in the porch and saw one all in white knakking nuts, he had weened [5] it had been the dead man risen out of his grave knakking the nuts that were buried with him—and ran home again in all haste and told to a cripple that was in his house what he had seen.

This cripple, thus hearing, rebuked the sexton and said that if he were able to go he would go thither and conjure that spirit. "By my troth," quod the sexton, "and if thou darest do it I will bear thee on my neck—" and so they both agreed. The sexton took the cripple on his neck and came into the church-yard again.

And the miller in the porch saw one coming bearing a thing on his back and weened it had been the tailor coming with the sheep, and rose up to meet them. And as he came towards them, he asked and said: "Is he fat? Is he fat?" And the sexton, hearing him say so, for fear cast the cripple down and said: "Fat or lean, take him there for me—" and ran away. And the cripple by miracle was made whole and ran away as fast as he or faster.

This miller, perceiving that they were two, and that one ran after another—supposing that one had spied the tailor stealing the sheep and that he had run after him to have taken him—and afraid that somebody also had spied him stealing nuts, he for fear left his nuts behind him and, as secretly as he could, ran home to his mill.

And anon after he was gone the tailor came with the stolen

[3] *appointed:* made an appointment
[4] *sped of:* succeeded with
[5] *weened:* imagined

sheep upon his neck to the church porch to seek the miller. And when he found there the nut shells, he supposed that his fellow had been there and gone home—as he was indeed. Wherefore he took up the sheep again on his neck and went toward the mill.

But yet, during this while, the sexton which ran away went not to his own house but went to the parish priest's chamber, and showed him how the spirit of the man was risen out of his grave knakking nuts (as ye have heard before). Wherefore the priest said that he would go conjure him if the sexton would go with him—and so they both agreed.

The priest did on [6] his surplice and a stole about his neck, and took holy water with him, and came with the sexton toward the church. And as soon as he entered into the churchyard, the tailor with the white sheep on his neck, intending (as I before have showed you) to go down to the mill, met with them and had weened that the priest in his surplice had been the miller in his white coat, and said to him: "By God, I have him! I have him—" meaning the sheep that he had stolen.

The priest, perceiving the tailor all in black and a white thing on his neck, weened it had been the devil bearing away the spirit of the dead man that was buried, and ran away as fast as he could—taking the way down toward the mill—and the sexton running after him.

This tailor, seeing one following him, had weened that one had followed the miller to have done him some hurt, and thought he would follow if need were to help the miller; and went forth till he came to the mill and knocked at the mill door.

The miller, being within, asked who was there. The tailor answered and said: "By God, I have caught one of them and made him sure [7] and tied him fast by the legs—" meaning the sheep that he had stolen and had then on his neck tied fast by the legs.

But the miller, hearing him say that he had him tied fast by the legs, had weened it had been the constable that had taken the tailor for stealing of the sheep, and had tied him by the legs.

[6] *did on:* put on
[7] *sure:* secure

And afraid that he had come to have taken him also for stealing of the nuts, wherefore the miller opened a back door and ran away as fast as he could.

The tailor, hearing the back door opening, went on the other side of the mill and there saw the miller running away—and stood there a little while musing, with the sheep on his neck. Then was the parish priest and the sexton standing there under the millhouse, hiding them for fear—and saw the tailor again with the sheep on his neck and had weened still it had been the devil with the spirit of the dead man on his neck—and for fear ran away.

But because they knew not the ground well, the priest leaped into a ditch almost over the head, like to be drowned, and he cried with a loud voice: "Help! Help!" Then the tailor looked about and saw the miller running away and the sexton another way, and heard the priest cry "Help!"—had weened it had been the constable with a great company crying for help to take him and bring him to prison for stealing of the sheep—wherefore he threw down the sheep, and ran away another way as fast as he could. And so every man was afraid of the other without cause.

By this ye may see well it is folly for any man to fear a thing too much till that he see some proof or cause.

19.

In the old world when all things could speak, the four elements met together for many things which they had to do because they must meddle always one with another, and had communication together of divers matters. And because they could not conclude all their matters at that season, they appointed to break communication for that time and to meet again another time. Therefore, each one of them showed to the others where their most abiding was and where their fellows should find them if need should require.

And first the earth said: "Brethern, ye know well, as for me I am permanent always and not removable. Therefore, ye may be sure to have me always when ye list."

The water said: "If ye list to seek me, ye shall be sure ever to have me under a tuft of green rushes or else a woman's eye."

The wind said: "If ye list to seek me, ye shall be sure ever to have me among aspen leaves or else in a woman's tongue."

Then quod the fire: "If any of you list to seek me, ye shall ever be sure to find me in a flintstone or else in a woman's heart."

By this tale ye may learn as well the properties of the four elements as the properties of a woman.

20.

There was a justice but late in the realm of England called Master Vavasour—a very homely man and rude of conditions [1] and loved never to spend much money. This Master Vavasour rode on a time in his circuit in a place of the north country where he had agreed with the sheriff for a certain sum of money for his charges through the shire, so that at every inn and lodging this Master Vavasour paid for his own costs.

It fortuned so that when he came to a certain lodging, he commanded one Torpin his servant to see that he used good husbandry and to save such things as were left, and to carry it with him to serve him at the next 'bating.[2] This Torpin, doing his master's commandment, took the broken bread, broken meat and all such things that was left and put it in his male.[3]

The wife of the house, perceiving that he took all such fragments and vittles with him that was left and put it in his male, she brought up the pottage that was left in the pot and when Torpin had turned his back a little aside, she poured the pot-

---

[1] *conditions:* behavior
[2] *'bating:* abating, stopping place
[3] *male:* traveling pouch, bag

tage into the male—which ran upon his robe of scarlet and other his garments, and rayed⁴ them very evil that they were much hurt therewith.

This Torpin suddenly turned and saw it, reviled the wife therefore, and ran to his master and told him what she had done. Wherefore Master Vavasour incontinent⁵ called the wife and said to her thus: "Thou drab (quod he), what hast thou done? Why hast thou poured this pottage in my male and marred my raiment and gear?"

"Oh, sir," quod the wife, "I know well ye are a judge of the realm, and I perceive by you, your mind is to do right and to have that that is your own, and your mind is to have all things with you that ye have paid for—both broken bread, meat, and other things that is left. And so it is reason that ye have. And therefore, because your servant hath taken the bread and the meat and put it in your male, I have therefore put in your male the pottage that he left because ye have well and truly paid for them. For if I should keep any thing from you that ye have paid for, peradventure ye would trouble me in the law another time."

Here ye may see that he that playeth the niggard too much sometime it turneth him to his own loss.

21.

A certain wedded man there was which, when he was dead, came to heaven gates to Saint Peter and said he came to claim his heritage which he had deserved. Saint Peter asked him what he was and he said, "A wedded man." Anon, Saint Peter opened the gates and bad him come in and said he was worthy to have his heritage because he had had much trouble, and was worthy to have a crown of glory.

Anon after that, there came another man that claimed heaven

⁴ *rayed:* streaked
⁵ *incontinent:* immediately

and said to Saint Peter he had had two wives, to whom Saint Peter answered and said: "Come in, for thou art worthy to have a double crown of glory, for thou hast had double trouble."

At the last there came a third claiming heaven and said to Saint Peter that he had had three wives, and desired to come in. "What!" quod Saint Peter, "thou hast been once in trouble and thereof delivered, and then willingly wouldst be troubled again and yet again thereof delivered, and for all that couldst not beware the third time—but enterest willingly in trouble again! Therefore go thy way to hell, for thou shalt never come in heaven for thou art not worthy."

This tale is a warning to them that have been twice in peril, to beware how they come therein the third time.

22.

A rich merchant of London there was which had but one son that was somewhat unthrifty.[1] Therefore his father upon his deathbed called him to him and said he knew well that he had been unthrifty. Howbeit, if he knew he would amend his conditions,[2] he would make him his executor and leave him his goods [3] so that he would promise to pray for his soul and find one daily to sing for him—which thing to perform, his son there made a faithful promise.

After that, this man made him his executor and died. But after that, his son kept such riot that in short time he had wasted and spent all and had nothing left but a hen and a cock that was his father's. It fortuned then that one of his friends came to him and said he was sorry that he had wasted so much, and asked him how he would perform his promise made to his father that he would keep one to sing for him.

[1] *unthrifty:* profligate
[2] *conditions:* behavior
[3] *goods:* property

This young man answered and said: "By God, yet I will perform my promise, for I will keep this same cock alive still and he will crow every day and so he shall sing every day for my father's soul—and so I will perform my promise well enough."

By this, ye may see that it is wisdom for a man to do good deeds himself while he is here, and not to trust to the prayer and promise of his executors.

23.

There was a maid stood by a river's side in her smock, washing clothes. And as she stooped, oft times her smock cleaved between her buttocks. By whom there came a friar, seeing her, and said in sport: "Maid, maid, take heed—for Bayard bites on the bridle!" "Nay, wis,[1] master friar (quod the maiden), he doth but wipe his mouth and weeneth ye will come and kiss him."

By this ye may see that a woman's answer is never to seek.

24.

A certain man there was dwelling in a town called Gotham which went to a fair three miles off to buy sheep. And as he came over a bridge, he met with one of his neighbors and told him whither he went. And he asked him which way he would bring them, which said he would bring them over the same bridge. "Nay," quod the other man, "but thou shalt not!"

"By God," quod he, "but I will." The other again said he should not, and he again said he would bring them over, spite of his teeth. And so they fell at words and at the last to buffets, that each one knocked the other well about the head with their fists.

---

[1] *wis:* I wis, i.e., I know

To whom there came a third man which was a miller, with a sack of meal upon a horse—a neighbor of theirs—and parted them, and asked them what was the cause of their variance. Which then showed him the matter and cause as ye have heard. This third man, the miller, thought to rebuke their foolishness with a familiar example and took his sack of meal from his horse's back and opened it and poured all the meal in the sack over the bridge into the running river—whereby all the meal was lost—and said thus:

"By my troth, neighbors, because ye strive for driving over the bridge those sheep which be not yet bought nor wot [1] not where they be, me thinketh therefore there is even as much wit in your heads as there is meal in my sack."

This tale showeth you that some man taketh upon him to show other men wisdom when he is but a fool himself.

25.

A man there was that came to confess himself to a gray friar and shrove [1] him that he had lain with a young gentlewoman. The friar then asked him in what place, and he said it was in a goodly chamber all night long in a soft warm bed. The friar, hearing that, shrugged in his clothes and said: "Now, by sweet Saint Francis, then wast thou very well at ease."

26.

A chandler, being a widower dwelling at Holborne Bridge in London, had a fair daughter whom a young gentleman of

---

[1] *wot:* know
[1] *shrove:* confessed

Davy's Inn wooed greatly to have his pleasure of her—which, by long suit to her made, at the last granted him and 'pointed [1] him to come upon a night to her father's house in the evening and she would convey him into her chamber secretly, which was an inner chamber within her father's chamber.

So, according to the 'pointment, all thing was performed so that he lay with her all night and made good cheer till about four a-clock in the morning—at which time it fortuned this young gentleman fell a-coughing, which came upon him so sore that he could not refrain.

This young wench, then fearing her father that lay in the next chamber, bad him go put his head in the draught [2] lest that her father should hear him—which, after her counsel, rose in his shift [3] and so did. But then, because of the savor of the draught, it caused him to cough much more and louder, that the wench's father heard him and asked of his daughter what man was that that coughed in her chamber.

She answered and said, "Nobody." But ever this young man coughed still more and more, whom the father hearing said: "By God's body, whore, thou liest. I will see who is there—" and rose out of his bed.

This wench, perceiving her father rising, came to the gentleman and said: "Take heed, sir, to yourself. My father cometh." This gentleman, suddenly therewith abashed, would have pulled his head out of the draught hole—which was so very strait [4] for his head that he pulled the siege board [5] up therewith. And with it hanging about his neck, he ran upon the father (being an old man, gave him a great fall and bare him down and hurt his arm) and opened the doors and ran into the street with the draught board about his neck towards Davy's Inn as fast as he could.

This wench for fear ran out of her father's house and came not there a month after.

[1] *'pointed:* appointed, made an appointment
[2] *draught:* privy
[3] *shift:* undershirt
[4] *strait:* tight
[5] *siege board:* toilet seat

This gentleman, as he came upon Holborne Bridge, met with a collier's cart laden with coals, where there was two or three skittish horses—which, when they saw this gentleman running, started aside and threw down the cart with the coals and drew it aside and brake the cart rope, whereby the coals fell out—some in one place, some in another.

And after, the horses brake their traces and ran—some toward Smithfield and some toward Newgate, that the collier ran after them and was an hour or more ere he could get his horses together again. By which time, the people of the street were risen and came to that street and saw it strewed with coals. Every one for his part gathered up the coals—that the most part of the coals were gone ere the collier had got his horses.

But during this while, the gentleman went through Saint Andrew's Churchyard toward Davy's Inn, and there met with the sexton coming to church to ring to morrow mass—which, when he saw the gentleman in the churchyard in his shift with the draught board about his neck, had weened it had been a spirit and cried, "Alas, alas, a sprite!" and ran back again to his house almost at the barrys,[6] and for fear was almost out of his wits that he was the worse half a year after.

This gentleman then, because Davy's Inn gates were not open, went on the back side and leaped over the garden wall. But in leaping, the siege board so troubled him that he fell down into the garden and had almost broken his neck—and there lay still till the principal came into the garden, which when he saw him lie there had weened [7] some man had been slain and there cast over the wall, and durst not come nigh him till he had called up his company—which, when many of the gentlemen were come together, looked well upon him and knew him and after relieved him. But the board that was about his neck caused his head so to swell that they could not get it off till they were fain to cut it off with hatchets.

Thus was the wench well japed [8] and for fear she ran from

---

[6] *at the barrys:* losing control of himself
[7] *weened:* imagined
[8] *japed:* mocked, made jest of

her father; her father's arm was hurt; the collier lost his coals; the sexton was almost out of his wit; and the gentleman had almost broke his neck.

27.

A merchant's wife there was in Bowe Parish in London, somewhat steeped in age, to whom her maid came on a Sunday in Lent after dinner and said: "Mistress (quod she), they ring at Saint Thomas of Acres, for there shall be a sermon preached anon." To whom the mistress answered and said: "Marry, God's blessing on thy heart for warning me thereof. And because I slept not well all this night, I pray thee bring my stole with me, for I will go thither to look whether I can take a nap there while the priest is preaching."

By this, ye may see that many one goeth to church as much for other things as for devotion.

28.

There was a certain company of women gathered together in communication. One happened thus to say her pigs, after they were farrowed, died and would not live. And one old wife of her acquaintance, hearing her say so, bad her get a cuckold's hat and put the pigs therein a while after they were farrowed, and they should live. Which wife, intending to do after her counsel, came to one of her gossips [1] and showed her what medicine was thaugh her [2] for her pigs and prayed her to lend her her husband's hat—which answered her angrily and said: "I would thou knewest it, drab, I have none, for my husband is no cuckold, for I

[1] *gossips:* cousins
[2] *thaugh her:* i.e., she needed

am a good woman—" and so likewise every wife answered her in like manner, that she departed from many of them in anger and scolding.

But when she saw she could get none, she came again to her gossip's all angrily and said: "I have gone round about to borrow a cuckold's hat and I can get none—wherefore if I live another year I will have one of mine own and be out of my neighbor's danger." [3]

By this tale a man may learn that it is more wisdom for a man to trust more to his own store than to his neighbor's gentleness.

29.

A gentleman and a gentlewoman sat together talking—which gentleman had great pain in one of his teeth, and happened to say to the gentlewoman thus: "I wis,[1] mistress, I have a tooth in my head which grieveth me very sore, wherefore I would it were in your tail." She, hearing him saying so, answered thus: "In good faith, sir, if your tooth were in my tail, it could do it but little good—but if there be anything in my tail that can do your tooth good, I would it were in your tooth."

By this, ye may see that a woman's answer is seldom to seek.

30.

In the time of Lent a welchman came to be confessed of his curate—which in his confession said that he had killed a friar. To whom the curate said he could not absolve him. "Yes (quod the welchman), if thou knewest all, thou wouldst absolve me well enough."

[3] *danger:* i.e., dependence
[1] *wis:* know

And when the curate had commanded him to show him all the case, he said thus: "Marry, there were two friars and I might have slain them both if I had list, but I let the one 'scape. Therefore, master curate, set the one against th' other and then the offense is not so great but ye may absolve me well enough."

By this, ye may see that divers men have so evil and large consciences that they think if they do one good deed, or refrain from the doing of one evil sin, that it is a satisfaction for other sins and offenses.

31.

There was a company of gentlemen in Northamptonshire which went to hunt for deer in the purlieus in the gulley beside Stony Stratford. Among which gentlemen there was one which had a welchman to his servant, a good archer.

When they came to a place where they thought they should have game, they made a standing and 'pointed this welchman to stand by a tree nigh the highway and bad him in any wise to take heed that he shot at no rascal [1] nor meddle not without it were a male—and if it were a male, to spare not. "Well," quod this welchman, "let me alone."

And when this welchman had stand there a while, he saw much deer coming—as well of antlers [2] as of rascals. But ever he let them go and took no heed of them.

And within an hour after, he saw come riding in the highway a man of the country which had a budget [3] hanging at his saddle bow, and when this welchman had espied him, he bad him stand and began to draw his bow and bad him deliver "that little male" [4] that hung at his saddle bow. This man, for fear of his

[1] *rascal:* fawn
[2] *antlers:* antlered bucks
[3] *budget:* pouch, male (thus the pun)
[4] *male:* wallet

life, was glad to deliver him his budget and so did, and then rode his way and was glad he was so escaped.

And when this man of the country was gone, the welchman was very glad and went incontinent [5] to seek his master, and at last found him with his company. And when he saw him, he came to him and said thus: "Master, by Cot's bloot and her nail I have stand yonder this two hours and I could see never a male but a little male that a man had hanging at his saddle bow— and that I have gotten, and, lo, here it is—" and took his master the budget which he had taken away from the foresaid man. For the which deed, both the master and the servant were afterward in great trouble.

By this ye may learn it is great folly for a master to put a servant to that business wherof he can nothing skill [6] and wherein he hath not been used.

32.

A young gentleman of the age of twenty years, somewhat disposed to mirth and game, on a time talked with a gentlewoman which was right wise and also merry. This gentlewoman, as she talked with him, happened to look upon his beard (which was but young and grown somewhat upon the overlip and but little grown beneath—as all young men's beards commonly use to grow) said to him thus: "Sir, ye have a beard above and none beneath."

And he, hearing her say so, said in sport: "Mistress, ye have a beard beneath and none above."

"Marry," quod she, "then set the one against the t'other—" which answer made the gentleman so abashed that he had not one word to answer.

[5] *incontinent:* immediately
[6] *can nothing skill:* has no skill at all

33.

There was a certain white friar [1] which was a very glutton and a great niggin,[2] which had an ungracious boy that ever followed him and bare his cloak. And, what for the friar's gluttony and for his churlishness, the boy wherever he went could scant get meat enough, for the friar would eat almost all himself.

But on a time, the friar made a sermon in the country wherein he touched very many miracles which Christ did afore his passion, among which he specially rehearsed the miracle that Christ did in feeding five thousand people with five loaves of bread and with three little fishes.

And this friar's boy which cared not greatly for his master, hearing him say so and considering that his master was so great a churl and glutton, answered with a loud voice that all the church heard, and said: "By my troth, master, then there were no friars there—" which answer made all the people to fall on such a laughing that for shame the friar went out of the pulpit. And as for the friar's boy, he then departed out of the church that the friar never saw him after.

By this, ye may see that it is honesty for a man that is at meat to depart with such as he hath [3] to them that be present.

34.

A rich franklin [1] dwelling in the country had a friar using [2] to his house of whom he could never be rid, and had tarried with

---

[1] *white friar:* Carmelite friar
[2] *niggin:* niggard
[3] *depart . . . hath:* share what he has
[1] *franklin:* freeholder, wealthy farmer, country gentleman
[2] *using:* visiting

him the space of a se'nnight and never departed. Wherefore the franklin, being weary of him, on a time as he and his wife and this friar sat together at supper feigned himself very angry with his wife, insomuch (he said) he would beat her.

This friar, perceiving well what they meant, said thus: "Master Franklin, I have been here this sevennight when ye were friends and I will tarry here this fortnight longer but I will see you friends again ere I go."

This man, perceiving that he could no good nor would not depart by no honest means, answered him shortly and said: "By God, friar, but thou shalt abide here no longer—" and took him by the shoulders and thrust him out of the doors by violence.

By this, ye may see that he that will learn no good by example nor good manners to him showed, is worthy to be taught with open rebukes.

35.

A friar limitor [1] came into a poor man's house in the country and because this poor man thought this friar might do him some good he therefore thought to make him good cheer. But because his wife would dress him no good meat for cost, [2] he therefore at dinner time said thus: "By God, wife, because thou did'st dress me no good meat to my dinner, were it not for master friar thou should have half a dozen stripes."

"Nay, sir," quod the friar, "I pray you spare not for me—" wherewith the wife was angry, and therefore at supper caused them to fare worse.

By this ye may see it is good policy for guests if they will have any good cheer to please always the wife of the house.

[1] *friar limitor:* a mendicant friar limited to a given territory
[2] *for cost:* because of the expense

36.

There was a friar which, though he were well learned yet he was called wicked of conditions,[1] which had a gentleman's son to wait upon him and to teach him to speak Latin. This friar came to this child's father dwelling in the country. And because this friar would have this gentleman to know that this child had metely well spent his time for the while he had been with him, he bad this child to make in Latin shortly: "Friars walk in the cloister." This child, half-astonished because his master bad him make this Latin so shortly, answered at all adventures[2] and said: "In circuitu impu ambulant."[3]

37.

In the term time, a good old gentleman being a lawyer came to London to the term. And as he came, he happened to overtake a friar which was some unthrift[1] and went along without his beaver.[2] Wherefore this gentleman asked this friar where was his beaver that should keep him company—and said it was contrary to his religion to go alone, and it would cause people to suppose him to be some apostate or some unthrift. "By God, sir," quod the friar, "my fellow commendeth him unto your mastership." "Who?" quod the gentleman. "I know him not." Then quod the friar to the gentleman: "Ye are the more to blame to ask for him."

[1] *conditions:* habits, manners
[2] *at all adventures:* by chance
[3] *"In . . . ambulant":* i.e., "The imps walk around in circles."
[1] *unthrift:* ne'er-do-well
[2] *beaver:* ?servingboy

By this tale ye may see that he that giveth counsel to an unthrift and teacheth him his duty shall have oftentimes but a mock for his labor.

38.

Three gentlemen came into an inn where a fair woman was tapster. Wherefore, as these three sat there making merry, each one of them kissed her and made good pastime and pleasure. Howbeit, one spake merrily and said: "I cannot see how this gentlewoman is able to make pastime and pleasure to us all except that she were departed [1] in three parts." "By my troth," quod one of them, "if that she might be so departed then I would choose for my part her head and her fair face that I might always kiss her."

The quod the second: "I would have the breast and heart for there lieth her love."

The quod the third: "Then there is nothing left for me but the loins, buttocks, and legs, and I am content to have it for my part."

And when these gentlemen had passed the time there by the space of one hour or two, they took their leave and were going away. But ere they went the third man that had chosen the belly and the buttocks did kiss the tapster and bad her farewell.

"What!" quod the first man, that had chosen the face and the mouth, "why dost thou so? Thou dost me wrong to kiss my part that I have chosen of her."

"O," quod the other, "I pray thee be not angry, for I would content that thou shalt kiss my part for it."

[1] *departed:* shared

39.

In Essex there dwelled a merry gentleman which had a cook called Thomas that was greatly diseased with the toothache and complained to his master thereof. Which said he had a book of medicines and said he would look up his book to see whether he could find any medicine there for it. And so sent he one of his daughters to his study for his book, and incontinent [1] looked upon it a long season and then said thus to his cook: "Thomas (quod he), here is a medicine for thy toothache and it is a charm. But it will do you no good except ye kneel on your knee and ask it for Saint Charity."

This man, glad to be released of his pain, kneeled and said: "Master, for Saint Charity, let me have that medicine." Then quod this gentleman: "Kneel on your knees and say after me . . ."—which kneeled down and said after him as he bad him.

This gentleman began and said thus: "The sun on the Sunday."

"The sun on the Sunday," quod Thomas.

"The moon on the Monday."

"The moon on the Monday."

"The Trinity on the Tuesday."

"The Trinity on the Tuesday."

"The wit on the Wednesday."

"The wit on the Wednesday."

"The holy, holy Thursday."

"The holy, holy Thursday."

"And all that fast on Friday."

"And all that fast on Friday."

"Shite in thy mouth on Saturday."

This Thomas cook, hearing his master thus mocking him, in

[1] *incontinent:* intently

an anger started up and said: "By God's body, mocking churl, I will never do thee service more—" and went forth to his chamber to get his gear together to th'intent to go thence by-and-by.

But—what for the anger that he took with his master for the mock that he gave him, and what for labor that he took to gather his gear—so shortly together the pain of the toothache went from him incontinent [2] that his master came to him and made him tarry still, and told him that his charm was the cause of the ease of the pain of his toothache.

By this tale ye may see that anger oftimes putteth away bodily pain.

40.

A scholar of Oxford lately made master of arts came to the city of London and in Paul's [1] met with the said merry gentleman of Essex (which was ever disposed to play many merry pageants [2]) with whom before he had been of familiar acquaintance, and prayed him to give him a sarcenet typet. [3]

This gentleman, more liberal of promise than of gift, granted him he should have one if he would come to his lodging to the sign of the bull without Bishopsgate in the next morning at six of the clock. This scholar thanked him and for that night departed to his lodging in Fleet Street, and in the morning early as he 'pointed, came to him to the sign of the bull.

Anon as this gentleman saw him, he bad him go with him into the City and he should be sped [4] anon. Incontinent [5] they went together till they came into Saint Laurence Church in the Jury,

---

[2] *incontinent:* immediately
[1] *Paul's:* St. Paul's churchyard
[2] *pageants:* elaborate practical jokes (as described in this tale)
[3] *sarcenet typet:* a tippet, or scarf, of very fine, soft material
[4] *sped:* taken care of
[5] *incontinent:* immediately

where the gentleman espied a priest ravished [6] to mass, and told the scholar: "That yonder is the priest that hath the typet for you—" and bad him kneel down in the pew and he would speak to him for it.

And incontinent this gentleman went to the priest and said: "Sir, here is a scholar and kinsman of mine greatly diseased with the chincough.[7] I pray you when mass is done, give him three draughts of your chalice."

The priest granted him and turned him to the scholar and said: "Sir, I shall serve you as soon as I have said mass." The scholar then tarried still and heard the mass, trusting then when the mass was done that the priest would give him his typet of sarcenet. This gentleman in the meanwhile departed out of the church.

This priest when mass was done put wine in the chalice and came to the scholar kneeling in the pew, proffering him to drink of the chalice. This scholar looked upon him and mused and said: "Master Parson, wherefore proffer ye me the chalice?"

"Marry," quod the priest, "for the gentleman told me ye were diseased with the chincough and prayed me therefore that for a medicine ye might drink of the chalice."

"Nay, by Saint Mary," quod the scholar, "he promised me ye should deliver me a typet of sarcenet."

"Nay," said the priest, "he spake to me of no typet, but he desired me to give you drink of the chalice for the chincough."

"By God's body," quod the scholar, "he is as he was ever wont to be, but a mocking wretch, and ever I live I shall quit it him [8]—" and so departed out of the church in great anger.

By this tale ye may perceive it were no wisdom for a man to trust to a man to do a thing that is contrary to his old accustomed conditions.[9]

[6] *ravished:* dressed in ecclesiastical garments
[7] *chincough:* whooping cough
[8] *quit it him:* get even with him
[9] *conditions:* habits

41.

It fortuned there was a great variance between the Bishop of Norwich and one Master Skelton a poet laureat, insomuch that the Bishop commanded him that he should not come in at his gates. This Master Skelton did absent himself for a long season, but at the last he thought to do his duty to him, and studied ways how he might obtain the Bishop's favor—and determined himself that he would come to him with some present and humble himself to the Bishop. And he gat a couple of pheasants and came to the Bishop's palace and required the porter he might come in and speak with my lord.

This porter, knowing his lord's pleasure, would not suffer him to come in at the gates—wherefore this Master Skelton went on the backside to seek some other way to come into the palace. But the palace was moated that he could see no way to come over except in one place where there lay a long tree over the moat (in manner of a bridge) that was fallen down with wind. Wherefore this Master Skelton went along upon the tree to come over. And when he was almost over, his foot slipped for lack of sure footing and fell into the moat up to the middle.

But at the last, he recovered himself and, as well as he could, dried himself again and soddenly [1] came to the Bishop—being in his hall then lately risen from dinner—which, when he saw Skelton coming soddenly, said to him: "Why! thou caitiff, I warned thee thou shouldst never come in at my gates, and charged my porter to keep thee out!"

"Forsooth, my lord," quod Skelton, "though ye gave such charge and though your gates be never so surely kept, yet it is not more possible to keep me out of your doors than to keep out crows or pies. For I came not in at your gates, but I came over the moat that I have been almost drowned for my labor—"

[1] *soddenly:* soaking wet

and showed his clothes, how evil he was arrayed, which caused many that stood thereby to laugh apace.

Then quod Skelton: "If it like your lordship, I have brought you a dish to your supper, a couple of pheasants."

"Nay," quod the Bishop, "I defy thee and thy pheasants also—and, wretch as thou art, pick thee [2] out of my house, for I will none of thy gift."

Howbeit, with as humble words as he could, this Skelton desired the Bishop to be his good lord and to take his little gift of him. But the Bishop called him "daw" and "fool" oftentimes, and in no wise would receive that gift. This Skelton, then considering that the Bishop called him fool so oft, said to one of his familiars thereby that, though it were evil to be christened a fool, yet it was much worse to be confirmed a fool of such a Bishop, for the name of confirmation must needs abide.

Therefore he imagined how he might avoid that confirmation, and mused a while. And at the last, he said to the Bishop thus: "If your lordship knew the names of these pheasants, ye would be content to take them."

"Why, caitiff?" quod the Bishop hastily and angrily. "What be their names?"

"I wis, my lord," quod Skelton, "this pheasant is called 'alpha' (viz. primus, the first), and this is called 'omega' (viz. novissimus, the last). And for the more plain understanding of my mind: If it please your lordship to take them I promise you this 'alpha' is the first that ever I gave you, and this 'omega' is the last that ever I will give you while I live." At the which answer, all that were by made great laughter and all they desired the Bishop to be good lord to him for his merry conceits—at whose request ere they went the Bishop was content to take him unto his favor again.

By this, ye may see that merry conceits doth a man more good than to fret himself with anger and melancholy.

[2] *pick thee:* throw thee

42.

A yeoman of the king's guard dwelling in a village beside London had a very fair young wife to whom a carter of the town, a tall fellow, resorted and lay with her divers times when her husband was from home—and so openly known that all the town spake thereof. Wherefore there was a young man of the town well acquainted with this yeoman of guard that told him that such a carter had lain by his wife. To whom this yeoman of guard said and swore: "By God's body," that if he met him it should cost him his life.

"Marry," quod the young man, "if ye go straight even now the highway, ye shall overtake him driving of a cart laden with hay toward London."

Wherefore this yeoman of guard incontinent [1] rode after this carter and within short space overtook him and knew him well enough, and incontinent called the carter to him, and said thus: "Sirra, I understand that thou dost lie every night with my wife when I am from home."

This carter, being nothing afraid of the other, answered: "Ye, marry, what then?"

"What then?" quod the yeoman of guard. "By God's heart, haddest thou not told me the truth I would have broken thy head." And so the yeoman of guard returned and no hurt done nor stroke stricken nor proffered.

By this ye may see that the greatest crakers [2] sometime when it cometh to the proof be most cowards.

[1] *incontinent:* immediately
[2] *crakers:* boasters

43.

In the town of Bottelley dwelled a miller which had a good homely wench to his daughter, whom a curate of the next town loved and—as the fame went—had her at his pleasure. But on a time this curate preached of these curious [1] wives nowadays. And whether it were for the nonce or whether it came out at all adventures,[2] he happened to say thus in his sermon:

"Ye wives, ye be so curious in all your works that ye wote not what ye mean.[3] But ye should follow Our Lady. For Our Lady was nothing so curious as ye be, but she was a good homely wench like the miller's daughter of Bottelley." At which saying all the parishioners made great laughing, and specially they that knew that he loved the same wench.

By this ye may see it is great folly for a man that is suspected with any person to praise or to name the same person openly, lest it bring him further in slander.

44.

A fool there was that dwelled with a gentleman in the country which was called a great tyrant and an extortioner. But this fool loved his master marvelously because he cherished [1] him so well. It happened upon a season, one of the gentleman's servants said to the fool, as they talked of sermon matters: "By my troth, Jack (quod he), would to God that thou and I were both of us in heaven."

---

[1] *curious:* fastidious
[2] *for the nonce . . . adventures:* on purpose or by chance
[3] *ye wote not . . . mean:* you don't know what you're doing
[1] *cherished:* took care of

"Nay, by lady," quod the fool, "I will not go to heaven for I had lever [2] go to hell."

Then the other asked him why he had lever go to hell. "By my troth," quod the fool, "for I will go with my master, and I am sure my master shall go to hell—for every man sayeth he shall go to the devil of hell. Therefore I will go thither with him."

45·

There was a certain ploughman's son of the country, of the age of sixteen years, that never came much among company but always went to plough and husbandry. On a time, this young lad went to a wedding with his father where he saw one lute upon a lute. And when he came home again at night, his mother asked him what sport he had at the wedding. This lad answered and said: "By my troth, mother (quod he), there was one that brought in a goose between his arms and tickled her so upon the neck that she creaked the sweetest that ever I heard goose creak in my life."

46.

In a merchant's house in London there was a maid which was gotten with child, to whom the mistress of the house came and charged her to tell her who was the father of the child. To whom the maiden answered: "Forsooth, nobody."

"Why!" quod the mistress, "it is not possible but some man must be the father thereof." To whom the maid said: "Why, mistress? Why may not I have a child without a man as well as a hen to lay eggs without a cock?"

Here ye may see it is hard to find a woman without an excuse.

[2] *lever:* rather

47.

A gentleman there was dwelling nigh Kingston upon Thames, riding in the country with his servant—which was not the most quickest [1] fellow, but rode always sadly [2] by his master and had very few words. His master said to him: "John (quod he), why ridest so sadly? I would have thee tell me some merry tales to pass the time with."

"By my troth, master," quod he, "I can tell no tales."

"Why," quod the master, "canst not sing?"

"No, by my troth," quod his servant, "I could never sing in all my life."

"Why," quod the master, "canst thou rhyme then?"

"By my troth, master," quod he, "I cannot tell. But if ye will begin to rhyme, I will follow as well as I can."

"By my troth," quod the master, "that is well said. Then I will begin to make a rhyme. Let me see how well thou canst follow." So the master mused a while and then began to rhyme thus:

> Many men's swans swims in Thames
> And so do mine

Then quod the servant:

> And many men lie by other men's wives
> And so do I by thine

"What dost, whoreson!" quod the master.

"By my troth, master, nothing (quod he), but make up the rhyme."

"But," quod the master, "I charge thee tell me why thou sayest so."

---

[1] *quickest:* liveliest
[2] *sadly:* quietly

"Forsooth, master," quod he, "for nothing in the world but to make up your rhyme."

Then quod the master: "If thou do it for nothing else, I am content." So the master forgave him his saying—although he had said truth.

48.

A knight in Middlesex had a servant which had committed a felony, whereof he was indicted, and because the term drew nigh he feared he should be shortly arraigned thereof and in jeopardy of his life. Wherefore in all haste he sent a letter by a welchman, a servant of his, unto the King's Justice of the King's Bench— requiring [1] him to owe his lawful favor to his servant—and commanded his servant shortly to bring him an answer.

This welchman came to the Chief Justice's palace, and at the gate saw an ape sitting there in a coat made for him, as they used to apparel apes for disport. This welchman did off [2] his cap and made courtesy to the ape and said: "My master recommendeth him to my lord your father and sendeth him here a letter."

This ape took the letter and opened it and looked thereon, and, after, looked upon the man, making many mocks and moves as the property of apes is to do. This welchman because he understood him not, came again to his master according to his commandment and said he had delivered the letter unto my Lord Chief Justice's son which sat at the gate in a furred coat.

Anon his master asked him what answer he had, which said he gave him an answer but it was either French or Latin, for he understood him not. "But, sir," quod he, "ye need not to fear for I saw by his countenance so much that I warrant you he will do your errand surely to my lord his father." This gentleman in

[1] *requiring:* petitioning, asking
[2] *did off:* took off

trust thereof made none other labor—for lack whereof his servant that had done the felony, within two days after was 'raigned at the King's Bench and cast and afterward hanged.

By this, ye may see that every wise man ought to take heed that he send no foolish servant upon a hasty message that is a matter of weight.

49.

A certain fellow there was which proffered a dagger to sell to a fellow of his which answered him and said that he had right nought to give him therefore. Wherefore the other said that he should have his dagger upon condition that he should give and deliver unto him therefore within six days after, right nought or else 40 shillings in money. Whereto this other was content.

This bargain thus agreed, he that should deliver this "right nought" took no thought until such time that the day appointed drew nigh. At the which time he began to imagine how he might give him right nought. And first of all, he thought on a feather, a straw, a pin's point, and such other. But nothing could he devise but that it was somewhat. Wherefore he came home all sad and pensive for sorrow of losing of his 40 shillings, and could neither sleep nor take rest.

Whereof his wife, being aggrieved, demanded the cause of his heaviness—which at the last after many denies told her all. "Well, sire," quod she, "let me herewith alone and get ye forth a-town, and I shall handle this well enough." This man following his wife's counsel went forth of the town and let his wife shift.

This woman then hung up an earthen pot, whereof the bottom was out, upon the wall by a cord. And when this other man came and asked for the good man, she said that he was not within: "But, sir (quod she), I know your errand well enough, for I wote well ye would have of mine husband 40 shillings because he can not deliver to you this day right nought. Therefore, sir (quod she), put your hand into yonder pot and take your money."

This man, being glad, thrust his hand in, supposing to have taken 40 shillings of money and thrust his hand up through up to the elbow. Quod the wife then: "Sir, what have ye there?"

"Marry," quod he, "right nought."

"Sir," quod she, "then have ye your bargain, and then my husband hath contented you for his dagger according to his promise."

By this, ye may see that oftentimes a woman's wit at an extremity is much better than a man's.

50.

There was a certain limitor [1] which went a-limiting to a certain village wherein dwelled a certain rich man of whom he never could get the value of an halfpenny. Yet he thought he would go thither again to assay [2] them. And as he went thitherward, the wife—standing at the door, perceiving him coming afar off— thought that he would come thither, and by-and-by ran in and bad her children standing at the door that if the friar asked for her, say she was not within.

The friar saw her run in and suspected the cause, and came to the door and asked for the wife. The children as they were bidden said that she was not within. Then stood he still, looking on the children. And at the last he called to him the eldest and bad him let him see his hand. And when he had seen his hand: "O Jesu!" quod he, "what fortune for thee is ordained!"

Then called he the second son to see his hand, and, his hand seen, the friar said: "O, lord, what a destiny is for thee prepared!"

Then looked he in the third son's hand: "Surely," quod he,

[1] *limitor:* friar licensed to beg within a certain territory
[2] *assay:* try

"thy destiny is hardest of all." And therewith went he his way.

The wife, hearing these things, suddenly ran out and called the friar again. And first she made him to come in, and after to sit down, and set before him the best meat that she had. And when he had well eaten and drunken, she besought him to tell her the destinies of her children—which, at the last, after many denies, told her that the first should be a beggar; the second a thief; the third an homicide. Which she hearing, fell down in a swoon and took it grievously.

The friar comforted her and said that though these were their fortune, yet there might be remedy had. Then she besought him of his counsel. Then said the friar: "Ye must make the eldest that shall be a beggar, a friar; and the second that shall be a thief, a man of law; and the third that shall be an homicide, a physician."

By this, ye may learn that they that will come to the speech or presence of any person, for their own cause, they must first endeavor themselves to show such matters as those persons most delight in.

51.

A certain friar had a boy that ever was wont to bear this friar's money. And on a time when the boy was far behind his master as they two walked together by the way, there met a man the friar which knew that the boy bare the friar's money and said: "How, master friar, shall I bid thy boy hie him apace after thee?"

"Ye," quod the friar.

Then went the man to the boy and said: "Sir, thy master biddeth ye giveth me 40 pence."

"I will not," quod the boy.

Then called the man with an high [1] voice to the friar and said: "Sir, he sayeth he will not."

[1] *high:* loud

"Then," quod the friar, "beat him." And when the boy heard his master say so, he gave the man 40 pence.

By this, ye may see it is folly for a man to say ye or nay to a matter except he know surely what the matter is.

52.

A certain butcher dwelling in Saint Nicholas Fleshambles in London, called Paul, had a servant called Peter. This Peter on a Sunday was at the church hearing mass, and one of his fellows —whose name was Philip Spencer—was sent to call him at the commandment of his master.

So it happened at the time that the curate preached. And in his sermon he touched many authorities of the Holy Scripture— among all, the words of the 'pistle of Saint Paul ad Philippenses: that we be not only bound to believe in Christ but also to suffer for Christ's sake—and said these words in the pulpit: "What say- eth Paul ad Philippenses to this?"

This young man that was called Philip Spencer had weened he had spoken of him, answered shortly and said: "Marry, sir, he bad Peter come home and take his part of a pudding, for he should go for a calf anon." The curate hearing this was abashed, and all the audience made great laughter.

By this tale ye may learn that it is no token of a wise man to give a sudden answer to a question before that he know surely what the matter is.

53.

There came a courtier by a carter, the which in derision praised the carter's back, legs, and other members of his body marvelously—whose jesting the carter perceived and said he had another property than the courtier espied in him. And when the courtier had demanded what it should be, he looked aside over his shoulder upon the courtier and said thus: "Lo, sir, this is my property. I have a wall eye in my head, for I never look over my shoulder this wise but I lightly espy a knave."

By this tale a man may see that he that used to deride and mock other folks is sometimes himself more derided and mocked.

54·

A young man of the age of 20 years, rude and unlearned, in the time of Lent came to his curate to be confessed—which, when he was of his life searched and examined, could not say his Pater Noster. Wherefore his confessor exhorted him to learn his Pater Noster and showed him what an holy and goodly prayer it was and the effect thereof and the seven petitions therein contained:

"The first petition beginneth, Pater Noster, etc., that is to say—'O Father hallowed by Thy name among men in earth as among angels in heaven.' The second, Adveniat, etc., 'Let Thy kingdom come and reign Thou among us men in earth as among angels in heaven.' The third, Fiat, etc., 'Make us to fulfill Thy will here in earth as Thy angels in heaven.' The fourth, Panem nostrum, etc., 'Give us our daily sustenance always and help us as we give and help them that have need of us.' The fifth, Dimitte, etc., 'Forgive us our sins done to Thee as we forgive them that trespass against us.' The sixth, Et ne nos, 'Let us not be overcome with evil temptation.' The seventh, Sed libera, etc., 'But deliver us from all evil—Amen.' "

And then his confessor after this exposition to him made, enjoined him in penance to fast every Friday on bread and water till he had his Pater Noster well and sufficiently learned.

This young man meekly accepting his penance so departed and

came home to one of his companions and said to his fellow: "So it is that my ghostly father hath given me in penance to fast every Friday on bread and water till I can say my Pater Noster. Therefore I pray ye teach me my Pater Noster and, by my troth, I shall therefore teach thee a song of Robin Hood that shall be worth 20 of it."

By this tale ye may learn to know the effect of the holy prayer of the Pater Noster.

55.

A certain friar there was which upon Our Lady day, the Annunciation, made a sermon in the White Friars in London and began his antetheme [1] this wise: "Ave Maria gracia plena dominus tecum, etc. These words (quod the friar), were spoken by the angel Gabriel to Our Lady when she conceived Christ, which is as much to say in our mother tongue as—'All hail, Mary, well thou be, the Son of God is with thee.' 'And furthermore,' the angel said, 'thou shalt conceive and bear a son, and thou shalt call his name Jesum. And Elizabeth thy sweet cousin, she shall conceive the sweet Saint John.' "

And so he proceeded still in his sermon in such fond rhyme that divers and many gentlemen of the court that were there began to smile and laugh. The friar, that perceiving, said thus: "Masters, I pray you hark. I shall tell you a narration:

"There was once a young priest, that was not all the best clerk,[2] said mass and read a collect thus: 'Deus qui vigenti/filii tui, etc.'—where he should have said 'unigenti filii tui, etc.'—and after when mass was done there was such a gentleman (as one of you are now) that had heard his mass, came to the priest and said thus: 'Sir, I pray you tell me how many sons had God almighty?'

[1] *antetheme:* text of sermon
[2] *clerk:* i.e., scholar

"Quod the priest: 'Why ask you that?'

" 'Marry, sir,' quod the gentleman, 'I suppose he had twenty sons, for ye said right now—"Deus qui vigenti filii tui!" '

"The priest perceiving how that he derided him, answered him shortly and said thus: 'How many sons soever God almighty had, I am sure that thou art none of them, for ye scornest the word of God.' "

And so said the friar in the pulpit: "No more are ye none of the children of God. For ye scorn and laugh at me now, that preach to you the word of God"—which words made the gentlemen and all the other people laugh much more than they did before.

By this tale a man may learn to perceive well that the best, the wisest, and the most holy matter that is, by found [3] pronunciation and utterance may be marred, nor shall not edify to the audience. Therefore every process would be uttered with words and countenance convenient to the matter.

Also yet by this tale, they that be unlearned in the Latin tongue may know the sentence [4] of the Ave Maria.

56.

In a village in Warwickshire there was a parish priest, and though he were no great clerk nor graduate of the university, yet he preached to his parishioners upon a Sunday, declaring to them the twelve articles of the Creed, showing them that the first article was to believe in God the Father almighty maker of heaven and earth; the second, to believe in Jesu Christ his only son, our Lord coequal with the Father in all things pertaining to the deity; the third, that he was conceived of the Holy Ghost, born of the Virgin Mary; the fourth, that He suffered death under Pontius Pilate, and that he was crucified dead and buried; the fifth, that he descended to hell and set out the good souls

[3] *found:* confounded
[4] *sentence:* i.e., meaning

that were in faith and hope, and that he the third day rose from death to life.

The sixth, he ascended into heaven to the right side of God the Father where he sitteth; the seventh, that he shall come at the day of doom to judge both us that be quick and them that be dead; the eighth, to believe in the Holy Ghost equal God with the Father and the Son; the ninth, in Holy Church Catholic, and in holy communion of saints; the tenth, in the remission of sins; the eleventh, in the resurrection general of the body and soul; the twelfth, in everlasting life, that God shall reward them that be good.

And he said to his parishioners further that "these articles ye be bound to believe, for they be true and of authority. And if you believe not me then for a more sure and sufficient authority, go your way to Coventry and there ye shall see them all played in Corpus Christi play."

By reading of this tale, they that understand no Latin may learn to know the twelve articles of the faith.

57.

A limitor [1] of the gray friars in London which preached in a certain village in the country in the time of his limitation, had but one sermon which he had learned by heart, that was of the declaring of the ten commandments. The first, to believe in one God and to honor Him above all things; the second, to swear not in vain by Him nor none other of His creatures; the third, to abstain from worldly operation on the holy day—thou and all thy servants of whom thou hast charge; the fourth, to honor thy parents and help them in their necessity.

The fifth, to slay no man in deed nor will, nor for no hatred hurt his body nor good name; the sixth, do no fornication actual, nor by no unlawful thought to desire no fleshly delectation; the

[1] *limitor:* friar licensed to beg within limited territory

seventh, to steal nor deprive no man's goods by theft, robbery, extortion, usury, nor deceit; the eighth, to bear no false witness to hurt another, nor to tell no lies, nor to say nothing against truth; the ninth, to covet nor desire no man's goods unlawful; the tenth, to covet nor to desire thy neighbor's wife for thine own appetite unlawfully.

And because this friar had preached this sermon so often, one that had heard it before told the friar's servant that his master was called Friar John Ten Commandments. Wherefore this servant showed the friar his master thereof, and advised him to preach some sermon of some other matter—for it grieved him to hear his master so derided and to be called Friar John Ten Commandments. "For every man knoweth what ye will say as soon as ever ye begin, because ye have preached it so oft."

"Why, then," quod the friar, "I am sure thou knowest well which be the ten commandments that hast heard them so oft declared."

"Ye, sir," quod the servant, "that I do."

"Then," quod the friar, "I pray thee rehearse them unto me now."

"Marry," quod the servant, "these be they: pride, covetousness, sloth, envy, wrath, gluttony, and lechery."

By reading this tale ye may learn to know the ten commandments and the seven deadly sins.

58.

The husband said to his wife thus: "Wife, by this candle, I dreamed this night that I was a cuckold." To whom she answered and said: "Husband, by this bread, ye are none."

Then said he: "Wife, eat the bread." She answered and said to her husband: "Then eat you the candle, for you sware first."

By this a man may see that a woman's answer is never to seek.

59.

A woman demanded a question of a young child, son unto a man of law, of what craft his father was—which child said his father was "a crafty man of law."

By this tale a man may perceive that sometime peradventure young innocents speak truly unadvised.

60.

In a certain parish church in London, after the old laudable and accustomed manner, there was a friar minor.[1] Although he were not the best clerk [2] nor could not make the best sermon, yet by the license of the curate he there preached to the parishioners. Among the which audience there was a wife at that time, little disposed to contemplation, talked with a gossip [3] of hers of other feminine tales—so loud that the friar heard and somewhat was perturbed therewith. To whom therefore openly the friar spake and said: "Thou woman, there in the tawny gown—hold thy peace and leave thy babbling. Thou troublest the word of God."

This woman therewith suddenly abashed because the friar spake to her so openly that all the people her beheld, answered shortly and said: "I beshrew thee hard, that babbleth more of us two." At which saying, the people did laugh because they felt but little fruit in his sermon.

By this tale a man may learn to beware how he openly rebuketh any other and in what audience, lest it turn to his own reproof.

[1] *friar minor:* a Franciscan
[2] *clerk:* scholar
[3] *gossip:* friend

61.

In the reign of the most mighty and victorious Prince, King Henry VIII, cruel war began between Englishmen, Frenchmen, and Scots. The Englishmen were so mighty upon the sea that none other people of other realms were able to resist them, wherefore they took many great enterprises and many ships and many prisoners of other realms that were their enemies. Among the which, they happened on a season to take a scots ship, and divers scots they slew, and took prisoners. Among whom there was a welchman that had one of the scots prisoner and bad him that he should do off[1] his harness. Which to do, the scot was very loath.

Howbeit, for fear at the last he pulled it off with an evil will and said to the welchman: "If thou wilt needs have my harness, take it there—" and cast it over the board into the sea. The welchman, seeing that, said: "By Cot's blut and her nail, I shall make her fet[2] it again—" and took him by the legs and cast him after over the board into the sea.

By this tale a man may learn that he that is subject to another ought to forsake his own will and follow his will and commandment that so hath subjection over him—lest it turn to his greater hurt and damage.

62.

There was a man that married a woman which had great riches and beauty. Howbeit, she had such an impediment of nature that she was dumb and could not speak, which thing made him full oft to be right pensive and sad. Wherefore upon

---

[1] *do off:* doff
[2] *fet it:* fetch it

a day as he walked alone right heavy in heart, thinking upon his wife, there came one to him and asked him what was the cause of his heaviness—which answered that it was only because his wife was born dumb. To whom this other said: "I shall show ye soon a remedy and a medicine therefore that is thus— Go take an aspen leaf and lay it under her tongue this night, she being asleep, and I warrant thee that she shall speak on the morrow."

Which man, being glad of this medicine, prepared therefore and gathered aspen leaves whereof he laid three of them under her tongue when she was asleep. And upon the morrow when he himself waked, he—desirous to know how his medicine wrought—being in bed with her, demanded [1] of her how she did. And suddenly she answered and said: "I beshrew your heart for waking me so early!" And so by virtue of that medicine she was restored to her speech.

But, in conclusion, her speech so increased day by day, and she was so cursed of conditions [2] that every day she brawled and chided with her husband so much that at the last he was more vexed and had much more trouble and disease [3] with her shrewd words than he had before when she was dumb. Wherefore, as he walked another time alone, he happened to meet again with the same person that taught him the said medicine, and said to him this wise:

"Sir, ye taught me a medicine but late to make my dumb wife to speak, bidding me lay an aspen leaf under her tongue when she slept. And I laid three aspen leaves there—wherefore, now she speaketh. But yet she speaketh so much and so shrewdly that I am more weary of her now than I was before when she was dumb. Wherefore, I pray you teach me a medicine to modify her that she speak not so much."

This other answered and said thus: "Sir, I am a devil of hell, but I am one of them that have least power there, albeit yet

---

[1] *demanded:* asked
[2] *conditions:* behavior
[3] *disease:* discomfort

I have power to make a woman to speak. But yet if a woman begin once to speak, I nor all the devils in hell that have the most power be not able to make a woman to be still, nor to cause her to leave her speaking."

By this tale ye may note that a man oftimes desireth and coveteth too much that thing that oft turneth to his displeasure.

63.

One asked a proctor of the Arches, lately before married, why he chose him so little a wife—which answered, because he had a text saying thus: "Ex duobus malis minus malum est eliendum —" that is to say in English: "Among evil things, the least is to be chosen."

64.

In the time of Lent, there came two nuns to Saint Johns in London because of the great pardon there to be confessed. Of the which nuns, the one was a young lady and the other was old. This young lady chose first her confessor and confessed her that she had sinned in lechery. The confessor asked with whom it was. She said it was with a lusty gallant. He demanded where it was. She said in a pleasant green arbor. He asked further when it was. She said in the merry month of May.

Then said the confessor this wise: "A fair young lady with a lusty gallant in a pleasant arbor in the merry month of May —ye did but your kind.[1] Now, by my troth, God forgive you and I do."

And so she departed, and incontinent [2] the old nun met with

[1] *ye did but your kind:* you acted only natural
[2] *incontinent:* immediately

her, asking her how she liked her confessor—which said that he was the best ghostly father that ever she had, and the most easiest in penance-giving.

For comfort whereof, this other nun went to the same confessor, and shrove her likewise that she had sinned in lechery. And he demanded with whom, which said with an old friar. He asked where. She said in her old cloister. He asked what season. She said in Lent. Then the confessor said thus: "An old whore to lie with an old friar in the old cloister in the holy time of Lent—By cock's body! if God forgive thee, yet will I never forgive thee—" which words caused her to depart all sad and sore abashed.

By this tale men may learn that a vicious act is more abominable in one person than in another, in one season than in another, and in one place than in another.

65.

The most noble and fortunate prince King Edward of England made war in France with a great puissance [1] and army of people, whom the French king with another great host encountered. And when both the hosts should join and the trumpets began to blow, a young squire of England was riding on a lusty courser—of which horse the noise of the trumpets so pricked the courage [2] that the squire could not him retain, so that against his will he ran upon his enemies.

Which squire, seeing none other remedy, set his spear in the rest and rode through the thickest of his enemies, and—in conclusion—had good fortune and saved himself alive without hurt. And the English host followed and had the victory.

And after, when the field was done, this King Edward called the squire and bad him kneel down, for he would make him

[1] *puissance:* force
[2] *pricked the courage:* stimulated

knight because that he valiantly was the man that day which, with the most courageous stomach, adventured first upon their enemies. To whom the squire thus answered: "If it like your grace to make anybody knight therefore, I beseech you to make my horse knight and not me, for certes it was his deed and not mine, and full sore against my will—" which answer the King hearing refrained to promote him to the order of knighthood, reputing him in manner but a coward—and ever after favored him the less.

By this tale a man may learn how it is wisdom for one that is in good credence to keep him therein and in no wise to disable himself too much.

66.

A young man lately married to a wife thought it was good policy to get the mastery of her in the beginning, and came to her when the pot was seething over the fire. Although the meat therein were not enough,[1] he suddenly commanded her to take the pot from the fire—which answered and said that the meat was not ready to eat. And he said again: "I will have it taken off for my pleasure."

This good woman, loath yet to offend him, set the pot beside the fire as he bad. And, anon after, he commanded her to set the pot behind the door. And she said thereto again: "Ye be not wise therein."

But he precisely said it should be so as he bad, and she genteely again did his commandment. This man yet not satisfied, commanded her to set the pot ahigh upon the hen roost. "What!" quod the wife again, "I trow[2] ye be mad."

And he fiercely then commanded her to set it there or else, he said, she should repent. She somewhat afraid to move his

---

[1] *enough:* cooked enough
[2] *I trow:* I believe

patience, took a ladder and set it to the roost, and went herself up the ladder, and took the pot in her hand—praying her husband then to hold the ladder fast for sliding, which he so did.

And when the husband looked up and saw the pot stand there on high, he said thus: "Lo, now standeth the pot there as I would have it." This wife, hearing that, suddenly poured the hot pottage [3] on his head and said thus: "And now been the pottage there as I would have them."

By this tale men may see it is no wisdom for a man to attempt a meek woman's patience too far, lest it turn to his own hurt and damage.

67.

A certain confessor in the holy time of Lent enjoined his penitent to say daily for his penance this prayer: "Agnus dei miserere mei," which was as much to say in English as "The Lamb of God have mercy upon me." This penitent, accepting his penance, departed and that time twelve-month after, came again to be confessed of the same confessor, which demanded of him whether he had fulfilled his penance that he him enjoined the last year. And he said thus: "Ye, sir, I thank God, I have fulfilled it—for I have said thus today morning and so daily: 'The Sheep of God have mercy upon me.'"

To whom the confessor said: "Nay, I bad ye say—'Agnus dei miserere mei'—that is, 'The Lamb of God have mercy upon me!'"

"Ye, sir," quod the penitent, "ye say truth. That was the last year, but now it is at twelve month sith [1] and it is a sheep by this time. Therefore I must needs say now—'The Sheep of God have mercy upon me.'"

By this tale ye may perceive that if holy scripture be expounded

---

[3] *pottage:* the stew, or contents of the pot
[1] *sith:* since

to rude lay people only in the literal sense, peradventure it shall do but little good.

68.

It fortuned divers to be in communication, among whom there was a curate, or a parish priest, and one John Daw, a parishioner of his—which two had communication more busy than others, in this manner: This priest thought that one might not by feeling know one from another in the dark. John Daw, his parishioner, of contrary opinion, laid with his curate for a wager 40 pence.

Whereupon, the parish priest, willing to prove his wager, went to this John Daw's house in the evening and suddenly got him to bed with his wife—where, when he began to be somewhat busy, she feeling his crown said shortly with a loud voice: "By God, thou art not John Daw!"

That hearing, her husband answered: "Thou sayest truth, wife—I am here, John Daw. Therefore, Master Parson, give me the money for ye have lost your 40 pence."

By this tale ye may learn to perceive that it is no wisdom for a man, for the covetous of winning of any wager, to put in jeopardy a thing that may turn him to greater displeasure.

69.

A rich franklin [1] in the country, having by his wife but one child and no more, for the great affection that he had to his said child founded him [2] at Oxford to school by the space of

---

[1] *franklin:* freeholder, country gentleman
[2] *founded him:* supported him

two or three years. This young scholar in a vacation time, for his disport, came home to his father.

It fortuned afterward in a night, the father, the mother, and the said young scholar sitting at supper, having before them no more meat but only a couple of chickens, the father said this wise: "Son, so it is that I have spent much money upon thee to find thee to school—wherefore I have great desire to know what hast learned."

To whom the son answered and said: "Father, I have studied sophistry, and by that science I can prove that these two chickens in the dish be three chickens."

"Marry," said the father, "that would I fain see."

The scholar took one of the chickens in his hand and said: "Lo, here is one chicken." And incontinent ³ he took both the chickens in his hand jointly and said: "Here is two chickens— and one and two maketh three. Ergo, here is three chickens!"

Then the father took one of the chickens to himself and gave another to his wife, and said thus: "Lo, I will have one of the chickens to my part, and thy mother shall have another. And because of thy good argument, thou shalt have the third to thy supper—for thou gettest no more meat here at this time—" which promise the father kept, and so the scholar went without his supper.

By this tale men may see that it is great folly to put one to school to learn any subtle science which hath no natural wit.

70.

A friar of London there was that on a Sunday morning early in the summer season, came from London to Barnet to make a collation, and was there an hour before high mass began. And because he would come to church honestly,¹ he went first to

³ *incontinent:* immediately
¹ *honestly:* decently

an alehouse there to wipe his shoes and to make himself cleanly.

In the which house there were puddings to sell and divers folks there breaking their fast and eating puddings. But the friar brake his fast in a secret place in the same house.

This friar soon after came to the church and, by license of the curate, entered into the pulpit to make a collation, or sermon. And in his sermon there, he rebuked sore the manner of them that used to break their fast on the Sunday before high mass, and said it was called the devil's black breakfast.

And with that word speaking, as he did cast his arms out to make his countenance,[2] there fell a pudding out of his sleeve—which he himself had stolen a little before in the same alehouse. And when the people saw that—and specially they that brake their fast there the same morning, and knew well that the wife had complained how she had one of her puddings stolen—they laughed so much at the friar that he incontinent [3] went down of the pulpit for shame.

By this tale a man may see that when a preacher doth rebuke any sin or vice wherein he is known openly to be guilty himself, such preaching shall little edify to the people.

71.

A certain scholar there was, intending to be made priest, which had neither great wit nor learning and came to the bishop to take orders, whose foolishness the bishop perceiving—because he was a rich man's son—would not very strongly oppose him but asked him this small question: "Noah had three sons—Sem, Cham, and Japhet. Now, tell me (quod the bishop), who was Japhet's father and thou shalt have orders."

Then said the scholar: "By my troth, my lord, I pray you pardon me, for I never learned but little of the Bible."

[2] *countenance:* i.e., make his point more emphatic
[3] *incontinent:* immediately

Then quod the bishop: "Go home and come again and solve me this question, and thou shalt have orders."

This scholar so departed and came home to his father and showed him the cause of the hindrance of his orders. His father, being angry at his foolishness, thought to teach him the solution of this question by a familiar example, and called his spaniels before him, and said thus: "Thou knowest well Coll my dog hath these three whelps—Ryg, Tryg, and Tryboll. Must not Coll my dog needs be sire to Tryboll?"

Then quod the scholar: "By God, father, ye say truth. Let me alone now. Ye shall see me do well enough the next time."

Wherefore, on the morrow he went to the bishop again and said he could solve his question. Then said the bishop: "Noah had three sons—Sem, Cham, and Japhet. Now tell me who was Japhet's father."

"Marry, sir," quod the scholar, "if it please your lordship— Coll, my father's dog."

By this tale a man may learn that it is but lost time to teach a fool anything, which hath no wit to perceive it.

72.

It fortuned so that a friar late in the evening desired lodging of a poor man of the country, the which (for lack of other lodging, glad to harbor the friar) lodged him in his own bed. And after, he and his wife (the friar being asleep) came and lay in the same bed. And in the morning, after the poor man rose and went to the market, leaving the friar in the bed with his wife—as he went, he smiled and laughed to himself. Wherefore his neighbors demanded of him why he so smiled. He answered and said: "I laugh to think how shamefast the friar shall be when he waketh, whom I left in bed with my wife."

By this tale a man may learn that he that overshooteth himself doth foolishly, yet he is more fool to show it openly.

73.

Sometime there dwelled a priest in Stratford-upon-Avon of small learning, which undevoutly sang mass, and oftentimes twice in one day. So it happened on a time, after his second mass was done in Shottery—not a mile from Stratford, there met with him divers merchantmen which would have heard mass, and desired him to sing mass and he should have a groat. Which answered them and said: "Sirs, I will say mass no more this day, but I will say you two gospels for one groat, and that is dog cheap a mass in any place in England."

By this tale a man may see that they that be rude and unlearned regard but little the merit and goodness of holy prayer.

74.

A courtier and a friar happened to meet together in a ferry boat, and in communication between them, fell at words angry —and, displeased each with other—fought and struggled together so that at the last the courtier cast the friar over the boat. So was the friar drowned.

The ferryman, which had been a man of war the most part of his life before and seeing the friar was so drowned and gone, said thus to the courtier: "I beshrew thy heart. Thou shouldest have tarried and fought with him a-land, for now thou hast caused me to lose an half-penny for my fare."

By this tale a man may see that he that is accustomed in vicious and cruel company shall lose that noble virtue to have pity and compassion upon his neighbor.

75.

A preacher in the pulpit which preached the word of God, among other matters spake of men's souls and said they were so marvelous and so subtle that a thousand souls might dance in the space of a nail of a man's finger. Among his audience there was a merry conceited fellow of small devotion that answered and said thus: "Master doctor, if that a thousand souls may dance on a man's nail, I pray you tell then where shall the piper stand?"

By this tale a man may see that it is but folly to show or to teach virtue to them that have no pleasure nor mind thereto.

76.

In London there was a certain artificer having a fair wife, to whom a lusty gallant made pursuit to accomplish his pleasure. This woman, denying, showed the matter unto her husband which, moved therewith, bad his wife to appoint him a time to come secretly to lie with her all night. And with great crakes [1] and oaths, he swore against his life that he would be ready harnessed against his coming and would put him in jeopardy except he would make him great amends.

This night was then appointed, at which time this courtier came at his house and entered into the chamber, set his two-hand sword down, and said these words: "Stand thou there, thou sword, the death of three men."

This husband, lying under the bed in harness, hearing these words lay still for fear. The courtier anon got him to bed with the wife, about his prepensed [2] business.

---

[1] *crakes:* boasts
[2] *prepensed:* planned

And within an hour or two, the husband—being weary of lying—began to remove himself. The courtier, that hearing, asked the wife what thing that was that removed under the bed —which, excusing the matter, said it was a little sheep that was wont daily to go about the house. And the husband, that hearing, anon cried "Ble," as it had been a sheep.

And so, in conclusion, when the courtier saw his time, he rose and kissed the wife and took his leave and departed. And as soon as he was gone, the husband arose. And when the wife looked on him somewhat abashed, she began to make a sad countenance and said: "Alas, sir, why did ye not rise and play the man as ye said ye would?"

He answered and said: "Why, dame, didst thou not hear him say that his sword had been the death of three men? I had been a fool then if I had put myself in jeopardy to have been the fourth."

Then said the wife thus: "But, sir, spake not I wisely then when I said ye were a sheep?"

"Yes," quod the husband. "But then did not I more wisely, dame, when that I cried 'Ble'?"

By this ye may see that he is not wise that will put his confidence too much upon these great crakers which oftimes will do but little when it cometh to the point.

77·

There was a shoemaker sitting in his shop that saw a collier come by, thought to deride him because he was so black, and asked him what tidings were in hell and how the devil fared. To whom the collier said: "The devil fared well when I saw him last, for he was riding for thee and tarried but for a sutor [1] to pluck on his boots."

---

[1] *sutor:* shoemaker

By this, ye may see that he that useth to deride other folks is sometime himself more derided and mocked.

78.

I find written among old gests, how God made Saint Peter porter of heaven, and that God of His goodness soon after His passion, suffered many men to come to the kingdom of heaven with small deserving—at which time there was in heaven a great company of welchmen, which with their craking [1] and babbling troubled all the others. Wherefore God said to Saint Peter that He was weary of them, and that He would fain have them out of heaven.

To whom Saint Peter said: "Good Lord, I warrant you that shall be shortly done."

Wherefore Saint Peter went out of heaven's gates and cried with a loud voice—"Cause bob!"—that is as much to say as "roasted cheese," which thing the welchmen hearing, ran out of heaven a great pace. And when Saint Peter saw them all out, he suddenly went into heaven and locked the door and so sparred [2] all the welchmen out.

By this, ye may see that it is no wisdom for a man to love or to set his mind too much upon any delicate or worldly pleasure whereby he shall lose the celestial and eternal joy.

79.

Two knights there were which went to a standing-field [1] with their prince. But [2] one of them was confessed before he went,

[1] *craking:* boasting
[2] *sparred:* barred
[1] *standing-field:* battlefield
[2] *But:* only

but the other went into the field without shrift or repentance. Afterward, this prince won the field and had the victory that day—wherefore he that was confessed came to the prince and asked an office and said he had deserved it, for he had done good service and adventured that day as far as any man in the field.

To whom the other, that was unconfessed, answered and said: "Nay, by the mass, I am more worthy to have a reward than he, for he adventured but his body for your sake—for he durst not go to the field till he was confessed—but as for me I did jeopard both body, life and soul for your sake, for I went to the field without confession or repentance."

80.

A certain miller there was which had divers ponds of eels wherein was good store of eels. Wherefore the parson of the town, which looked like a holy man, divers and many times stole many of them—insomuch that he had left few or none behind him. Wherefore this miller, seeing his eels stolen and wist [1] not by whom, came to the said parson and desired him to curse for them. The parson said he would, and the next Sunday came into the pulpit with book, bell and candle—and, perceiving there were none in the church that understood Latin, said thus: "He that stale the miller's eels, laudate damnum de celis,[2] but he that stale the greater [3] eels, gaudeat ipse in celis." [4]

Therewith—"Put out the candle, sir," quod the miller, "no more, for this sauce is sharp enough for him."

By this ye may see that some curates that look full holy be but dissemblers and hypocrites.

[1] *wist:* knew
[2] *laudate . . . celis:* i.e., praise his dominion under heaven
[3] *greater:* greater part
[4] *gaudeat . . . celis:* i.e., praise him in heaven

81.

A welchman on a time went to church to hear mass and happened to come in even at the sacring [1] time. When he had heard the mass to the end, he went home—where one of his fellows asked him whether he had seen God Almighty today, which answered and said: "Nay, but I saw one 40 shillings better than He."

By this ye may see that they that be evil brought up have but little devotion to prayer and virtue.

82.

Upon a time certain women in the country were appointed [1] to deride and mock a friar, a limitor [2] that used much to visit them. Whereupon one of them, a little before that the friar came, killed an hog and for disport laid it under the board [3] after the manner of a corpse—and told the friar it was her goodman and desired him to say "Dirige" [4] for his soul.

Wherefore, the friar and his fellow began "Placebo" and "Dirige" and so forth said the service full devoutly. Which the wives so hearing, could not refrain themselves from laughing and went into a little parlor to laugh more at their pleasure.

These friars somewhat suspected the cause and quickly, ere that the women were 'ware, looked under the board and spied that it was an hog, suddenly took it between them, and bare

[1] *sacring:* sacrament
[1] *appointed:* met together
[2] *limitor:* mendicant friar limited to an assigned territory
[3] *board:* table
[4] *"Dirige":* the funeral service

it homeward as fast they might. The women, seeing that, ran after the friar and cried: "Come again,[5] master friar, come again and let it alone!"

"Nay, by my faith," quod the friar, "he is a brother of ours and therefore he must needs be buried in our cloister." And so the friars got the hog.

By this, ye may see that they that use to deride and mock others, sometime it turneth to their own loss and damage.

83.

A certain priest there was that dwelled in the country, which was not very learned. Therefore, on Easter even he sent his boy to the priest of the next town that was two miles from thence, to know what mass he should sing on the morrow. This boy came to the said priest and did his master's errand to him. Then quod the priest: "Tell thy master that he must sing tomorrow of the Resurrection." And furthermore quod he: "If thou hap to forget it, tell thy master that it beginneth with a great 'R'—" and showed him the mass book where it was written "Resurrexi," etc.

This boy then went home again and all the way as he went he clattered still: "Resurrexi. Resurrexi." But at the last he happened to forget it clean and when he came home, his master asked him what mass he should sing on the morrow. "By my troth, master," quod the boy, "I have forgotten it—but he bad me tell you it began with a great 'R.'"

"By God," quod the priest, "I trow thou sayest truth, for now I remember well it must be 'requiem eternam,' for God almighty died as on yesterday, and now we must say mass for his soul."

By this ye may see that when one fool sendeth another fool on his errand, oftentimes the business is foolishly sped.

[5] *"Come again"*: "Come back"

84.

A scholar of Oxenford which had studied the indicals [1] of astronomy, on a time was riding by the way, which came by a herdsman and inquired of him how far it was to the next town. "Sir," quod the herdsman, "ye have nothid [2] past a mile and a half. But, sir, (quod he), ye need to ride apace, for ye shall have a shower of rain ere ye come thither."

"What!" quod the scholar. "It is not so, for here is no token of rain. For all the clouds be both fair and clear."

"By God, sir," quod the herdsman, "but ye shall find it so."

The scholar then rode forth his way, and ere he had ridden half a mile further, there fell a good shower of rain that the scholar was well washed and wet to the skin. The scholar then turned his horse and rode again to the herdsman, and desired him to teach him that cunning.

"Nay," quod the herdsman, "I will not teach you my cunning for nought." Then the scholar proffered him 40 shillings to teach him that cunning. The herdsman, after he had received his money, said thus: "Sir, see you not yonder dun cow with the white face?"

"Yes," quod the scholar.

"Surely," quod the herdsman, "when she danceth and holdeth up her tail it shall have a shower of rain within half an hour after."

By this, ye may see that the cunning of herdsmen and shepherds as touching alterations of weather is more sure than the indicals of astronomy.

[1] *indicals:* indexes, signs
[2] *nothid:* nothing

85.

In a certain town there was a rich man that lay on his death bed, at point of death, which charged his executors to dele [1] for his soul a certain sum of money in pence—and on this condition charged them ("as ye would answer afore God"): that every poor man that came to them and told a true tale should have a penny, and they that said a false thing should have none.

And in the dole time, there came one which said that God was a good man. Quod the executors: "Thou shalt have a penny, for thou sayest truth."

Anon came another and said the devil was a good man. Quod the executors: "There thou liest. Therefore, thou shalt have ne'er a penny."

At last came one to the executors and said thus: "Ye shall give me ne'er a penny—" which words made the executors amazed and took advisement whether they should give him the penny or no.

By this, ye may see it is wisdom for judges in doubtful matters of law to beware of hasty judgement.

86.

A man asked his neighbor which was but late married to a widow how he agreed with his wife—for he said that her first husband and she could never agree. "By God," quod the other, "we agree marvelous well." "I pray thee—how so?" "Marry," quod the other, "I shall tell thee: When I am merry, she is merry, and when I am sad, she is sad. For when I go out of

[1] *dele:* distribute

my doors I am merry to go from her, and so is she. And when I come in again, I am sad, and so is she."

87.

In the time of visitation, a bishop which was somewhat lecherous and had got many children, prepared to come to a priest's house to see what rule he kept—which priest had a leman [1] in his house called Ede, and by her had two or three small children in short space. But against the bishop's coming, the priest prepared a room to hide his leman and his children over in the roof of his hall.

And when the bishop was come and set at dinner in that same hall, having ten of his own children about him, this priest (which could speak little Latin or none) bad the bishop in Latin to eat, saying: "Comede episcope." This woman in the roof, hearing the priest say so, had weened he had called her—bidding her "Come, Edee"—and answered shortly: "Shall I bring my children with me also?"

This bishop, hearing this, said: "Uxor tua sicut vitis abundans in lateribus domus tuae." [2] The priest then, half amazed, answered shortly and said: "Filii tui sicut novellae olivarum in circuitu mensae tuae." [3]

By this ye may see that they that have but small learning, sometimes speak truly, unadvised.

[1] *leman:* mistress
[2] *"Uxor . . . tuae":* "Thy wife shall be as a fruitful vine by the sides of thine house . . ."
[3] *"Filii . . . tuae":* "Thy children like olive plants round about thy table."

88.

On Ash Wednesday in the morning was a curate of a church (which had made good cheer the night before and sitten up late) come to the church to hear confession, to whom there came a woman. And among other things, she confessed her that she had stolen a pot. But then because of great watch [1] that this priest had, he there suddenly fell asleep. And when this woman saw him not willing to hear her, she rose up and went her way.

And anon, another woman kneeled down to the same priest and began to say, "Benedicite." Wherewith this priest suddenly waked, weening she had been the other woman, and said all angrily: "What! art thou now at 'benedicite' again! Tell me what didst thou when thou hadst stolen the pot."

89.

Soon after one Master Whittinton had builded a college, on a night as he slept he dreamed that he sat in his church, and many folks there also. And further he dreamed that he saw Our Lady in the same church with a glass of goodly ointment in her hand—going to one, asking him what he had done for her sake, which said that he had said Our Lady's Psalter every day; wherefore she gave him a little of the oil.

And anon, she went to another, asking him what he had done for her sake, which said that he had said two Lady's Psalters every day—wherefore Our Lady gave him more of the ointment than she gave that other.

This Master Whittinton then thought that when Our Lady should come to him, she would give him all the whole glass be-

[1] *watch:* lack of sleep

cause that he had builded such a great college—and was very glad in his mind. But when Our Lady came to him, she asked him what he had suffered for her sake—which words made him greatly abashed because he had nothing to say for himself. And so he dreamed that for all the great deed of building of that said college, he had no part of that goodly ointment.

By this, ye may see that to suffer for God's sake is more meritorious than to give great goods.

90.

A certain bishop appointed [1] to go on visitation to a priest's house, and because he would have the priest do [2] but little cost upon him, he bad him dress but little meat—saying thus in Latin: "Preparas mihi modicum."

This priest, which understood him not half well, had a horse called Modicum, wherefore he thought to obtain the bishop's favor—and against the bishop's coming, killed his horse that was called Modicum, whereof the bishop and his servants ate it. Which when that bishop knew afterward, he was greatly displeased.

By this, ye may see that many a fool doth much cost which hath but little thank [3] for his labor.

91.

A certain maltman of Colbrook, which was a very covetous wretch and had no pleasure but only to get money, came to

[1] *appointed:* arranged
[2] *do:* spend
[3] *thank:* reward

London to sell his malt and brought with him four capons. And there he received four or five shillings for malt and put it in a little purse tied to his coat, and after went about the streets to sell his capons—whom a polling fellow [1] that was a dicer and an unthrift [2] had espied and imagined how he might beguile the man either of his capons or of his money.

And he came to this maltman in the street bearing these capons in his hand, and asked him how he would sell his capons. And when he had showed him the price of them, he bad him go with him to his master and he would show them to his master, and he would cause him to have money for them. Whereto he agreed.

This poller went to the Cardinal's Hat in Lombards Street, and when he came to the door he took the capons from the maltman and bad him tarry at the door till he had showed his master, and he would come again to him and bring him his money for them. This poller, when he had gotten the capons, went into the house and went through the other, back, entry into Cornhill, and so took the capons with him.

And when this maltman had stood there a good season, he asked one of the taverners where the man was that had the capons to show his master. "Marry," quod the taverner, "I can not tell thee. Here is neither master nor man in this house— for this entry here is a common highway and goeth into Cornhill. I am sure he is gone away with thy capons."

This maltman, hearing that, ran through the entry into Cornhill and asked for a fellow in a tawny coat that had capons in his hand. But no man could tell him which way he was gone. And so the maltman lost his capons and after, went into his inn all heavy and sad, and took his horse to th'intent to ride home.

This poller by that time had changed his raiment and borrowed a furred gown and came to the maltman sitting on horseback, and said thus: "Good man, methought I heard thee inquire even now for one in a tawny coat that had stolen from thee four capons. If thou wilt give me a quart of wine, go with me and

[1] *polling fellow, or poller:* i.e., a confidence man
[2] *unthrift:* ne'er-do-well

I shall bring ye to a place where he sitteth drinking with other fellows and had the capons in his hand."

This maltman, being glad thereof, granted him to give him the wine because he seemed to be an honest man, and went with him unto the Dagger in Cheap. This poller then said to him: "Go thy way straight to th'end of that long entry and there thou shalt see whether it be he or no. And I will hold thy horse here till thou come again."

This maltman, thinking to find the fellow with his capons, went in and left his horse with the other at the door. And as soon as he was gone into the house, this poller led the horse away into his own lodging.

This maltman inquired in the house for his fellow with the capons, but no man could tell him no tidings of such man. Wherefore he came again to the door all sad, and looked for him that had his horse to keep. And because he saw him not, he asked divers there for him. And some said they saw him, and some said they saw him not. But no man could tell which way he was gone, wherefore he went home to his inn more sad than he was before, wherefore his host gave him counsel to get him home and beware how he trusted any men in London.

This maltman, seeing none other comfort, went his way homeward. This poller, which lingered always there about the inn, heard tell that the maltman was going homeward afoot, and appareled him like a man's 'prentice, and got a little budget [3] stuffed full of stones on his back, and went before him to Charing Cross, and tarried till the maltman came, and asked whither he went—which said: "To Colbrook."

"Marry," quod the other, "I am glad thereof, for I must go to Brainford to my master to bear him money which I have in my budget, and I would be glad of company." This maltman, because of his own money, was glad of his company, and so they agreed and went together a while.

At the last, this poller went somewhat before to Knightbridge and sat upon the bridge and rested him with his budget on his

---

[3] *budget:* purse

back. And when he saw the maltman almost at him, he let his budget fall over the bridge into the water—and incontinent [4] started up and said to the maltman: "Alas, I have let my budget fall into the water, and there is forty shillings of money therein. If thou wilt wade into the water and go seek it and get it me again, I shall give thee twelve pence for thy labor."

This maltman, having pity of his loss and also glad to get the twelve pence, plucked off his hose, coat, and shirt and waded into the water to seek for the budget. And in the meanwhile, this poller got his clothes and coat whereto the purse of money was tied, and leaped over the hedge and went to Westminster.

This maltman within a while after, with great pain and deep wading, found that budget and came out of the water and saw not his fellow there—and saw that his clothes and money were not there as he left them. He suspected the matter and opened the budget and then found nothing therein but stones.

He cried out like a madman and ran all naked to London again, and said: "Alas, alas, help! or I shall be stolen! For my capons be stolen. My horse is stolen. My money and clothes be stolen. And I shall be stolen myself." And so he ran about the streets in London naked and mad, crying always: "I shall be stolen! I shall be stolen!"—and so continued mad during his life and so died like a wretch, to the utter destruction of himself and shame to all his kin.

By this, ye may see that many a covetous wretch that loved his goods better than God, and setteth his mind inordinately thereon, by the right judgement of God oftimes cometh to a miserable and shameful end.

92.

A welchman dwelling in England fortuned to steal an Englishman's cock and set it on the fire to seeth. This Englishman,

[4] *incontinent:* immediately

suspecting the welchman, came into his house and saw the cock seething on the fire and said to the welchman thus: "Sir, this is my cock." "Marry," quod the welchman, "and if it be thine thou shalt have thy part of it."

"Nay," quod the Englishman, "that is not enough."

"By Cott's blut and her nail," quod the welchman, "if her be not enough [1] now, her will be enough anon—for her hath a good fire under her."

93.

Certain of the vicars of Paul's disposed to be merry on a Sunday at high mass time, sent another mad fellow of their acquaintance unto a foolish drunken priest to give him a bottle—which man met with the priest upon the top of the stairs by the chancel door, and spake to him and said thus: "Sir, my master hath sent you a bottle to put your drink in because ye can keep none in your brains." This priest, therewith being very angry, all suddenly took the bottle and with his foot, flang it down into the body of the church upon the gentlemen's heads.

94.

A certain jury in the county of Middlesex was impaneled for the king to inquire of all indictments, murders, and felonies. The persons of this panel were foolish, covetous, and unlearned —for whosoever would give them a groat, they would assign and verify his bill whether it were true or false, without any other proof or evidence. Wherefore one that was a merry conceited fellow, perceiving their small consciences and great covetous-

[1] *enough:* the pun is on enough = done enough, cooked enough

ness, put in a bill entitled after this manner: "Inquiratur pro domino regi si Jesu Nazarenus furatus est unum asinum ad equitandum in Egiptum—"[1] and gave them a groat and desired it might be verified.

The said jury, which looked all on the groat and nothing on the bill, as was their use, wrote "billa vera"[2] on the back thereof. Which bill when it was presented into the court, when the judges looked thereon, they said openly before all the people: "Lo, sirs, here is the marveloust verdict that ever was presented by any inquest. For here they have indicted Jesus of Nazareth for stealing of an ass—" which when the people heard it, it made them both to laugh and to wonder at the foolishness and shameful privity[3] of them of the inquest.

By this, ye may see it is great peril to empanel any jurors upon any inquest which be foolish, and have but small conscience.

95.

In a certain parish a friar preached, and in his sermon he rebuked them that rode on the Sunday—ever looking upon one man that was booted and spurred, ready to ride. This man, perceiving that all the people noted him, suddenly half in anger answered the friar thus: "Why preachest ye so much against them that ride on the Sunday, for Christ himself did ride on Palm Sunday—as thou knowest well it is written in Holy Scripture."

To whom the friar suddenly answered and said thus: "But, I pray thee, what came thereof? Was he not hanged on the Friday after?" Which hearing, all the people in the church fell on laughing.

[1] *Inquiratur . . . Egiptum"*: i.e., "In the name of the king, let it be determined whether Jesus of Nazareth stole an ass for the purpose of riding over to Egypt.

[2] *"billa vera"*: true bill, i.e., there are grounds for prosecution

[3] *privity:* conspiracy

96.

There was a certain man that had two sons, unlike of conditions.[1] For the eldest was lusty and quick and used much to rise early and walk into the fields. Then was the younger slow and unlusty and used to lie in bed as long as he might. So, on a day, the elder—as he was wont—rose early and walked into the fields, and there by fortune he found a purse of money and brought it home to his father.

His father, when he had it, went straight to his other son, yet lying then in his bed, and said to him: "O, thou sluggard (quod he), seest thou not thine elder brother, how he by his early rising had found a purse with money whereby we shall be greatly helped all our life—while thou slugging in thy bed dost no good but sleep."

He then wist not what to say, but answered shortly and said: "Father (quod he), if he that hath lost the purse and money had lain in his bed that same time that he lost it, as I do now, my brother had found nor purse nor money today."

By this, ye may see that they that be accustomed in vice and sin will always find one excuse or another to cloak therewith their vice and unthriftiness.

97.

A certain wife there was which was somewhat fair, and—as all women be that be that fair—was somewhat proud of her beauty. And as she and her maid sat together, she—as one that was desirous to be praised—said to her thus: "I' faith, Joan, how thinketh thou? Am I not a fair wife?"

[1] *conditions:* habits

"Yes, by my troth, mistress," quod she. "Ye be the fairest that ever was except Our Lady."

"Why, by Christ," quod the mistress, "though Our Lady were good yet she was not so fair as men speak of."

By this, ye may see it is hard to find a beauteous woman without pride.

98.

A certain alderman of London there was, lately deceased, which now shall be nameless—which was very covetous as well before he was married as after. For when he was bachelor, ever when his hosen were broken so that he could wear them no longer for shame, then would he cut them off by the knee and put on a pair of leather buskins on his bare legs—which would last him a two or three years.

Furthermore, it was his manner when he was a bachelor every night where that he was to borrow a candle's end to bring him home—which he would always put in a chest that he had in his chamber. So that by that time he was married, he had a chest of candle ends that weighed two or three hundredweight.

Soon after that he was married to a rich widow and then folks thought he would be better than he was before, but so it happened that a gentleman gave him a pasty of an hart—which every day he caused to be set on the table for service—howbeit he would never for niggenship [1] let it be opened. So that it was a month or six weeks ere ever it was touched. At which time it fortuned a man of his acquaintance, being there often and seeing this pasty never to be opened, said: "Sir, by my troth, I will tame your pasty—" which opened the pasty, and incontinent [2] leaped out three or four mice upon other gentle-

---

[1] *niggenship:* niggardliness
[2] *incontinent:* immediately

men's trenchers [3]—which had creeped in at an hole underneath the bottom and had eaten up all the meat therein.

Also this alderman was of such condition that he would hear two or three masses every day. And when any poor folk came to beg of him, he would rebuke them and say that they did let him [4] in hearing of them, so that he would never give penny in alms.

And on a time, as he sat at Saint Thomas of Acres hearing mass, he saw a young beginner, a debtor of his that owed him 20 shillings—which as soon as he saw him, he commanded one of his servants to get a sergeant and to arrest him. Which young man immediately after was arrested, and when he was in the counter,[5] he desired divers of his friends to entreat with this alderman for days of payment.[6]

Which men, in the morning after, came to this alderman kneeling at mass and entreated him for this man, desiring him to take days of payment—which answered them thus: "I pray you trouble me not now, for I have heard one mass already and I will hear another ere I meddle with worldly matters. But if ye have the money here, I will take it now or else, I pray you, speak to me no more." And so these men could get no other answer.

And this alderman kept this young man still in prison till, at the last, he there died. And so he caused likewise divers others to die in prison and would never forgive them. Wherefore afterward this alderman died suddenly, divers and many were glad of his death.

[3] *trenchers:* dishes
[4] *let him:* prevent him, interrupt him
[5] *counter:* debtors prison
[6] *days of payment:* extension of time

99.

A northern man there was which went to seek him a service. So it happened that he came to a lord's place, which lord then had war with another lord. This lord then asked this northern man if that he durst fight. "Ye, by God's bones," quod that northern man, "that I dare, for I is all heart." Whereupon the lord retained him into his service.

So after, it happened that his lord should go fight with his enemies, with whom also went this northern man—which shortly was smitten in the heel with an arrow, wherefore he incontinently fell down almost dead. Wherefore one of his fellows said: "Art thou he that art all heart, and for so little a stroke in the heel now art almost dead?"

To whom he answered and said: "By God's sale,[1] I is heart—head, legs, body, heels, and all—therefore ought not one to fear when he is stricken in the heart?"

100.

In a certain town there was a wife somewhat aged that had buried her husband whose name was John, whom she loved so tenderly in his life that after his death she caused an image of timber to be made—in visage and person as like to him as could be—which image all day long lay under her bed. And every night she caused her maid to wrap it in a sheet and lay it in her bed, and called it Old John.

This wife also had a 'prentice whose name was John—which John would fain have wedded his mistress (not for no great pleasure, but only for her good,[1] because she was rich). Wherefore

[1] *sale:* soul
[1] *good:* property

he imagined how he might obtain his purpose, and spoke to the maid of the house and desired her to lay him in his mistress's bed for one night instead of the picture,[2] and promised her a reward for her labor. Which maid over night [3] wrapped the said young man in a sheet and laid him in his mistress's bed as she was wont to lay the picture.

This widow was wont every night before she slept, and divers times when she waked, to kiss the said picture of Old John. Wherefore that said night she kissed the said young man, believing that she had kissed the picture. And he suddenly started and took her in his arms and so well pleased her then that Old John from thenceforth was clean out of her mind and she was content that this young John should lie with her still all the night— and that the picture of Old John should lie still under the bed for a thing of nought.

After this, in the morning this widow intending to please this young John which had made her so good pastime all the night, bad her maid go dress some good meat for their breakfast—to feast therewith her young John. This maid, when she had long sought for wood to dress the said meat, told her mistress that she could find no wood that was dry, except only the picture of Old John that lieth under the bed. "Then," quod the wife again, "fetch him down and lay him on the fire, for I see well he will never do me good nor he will never do better service though I keep him never so long."

So the maid by her commandment fetched the picture of Old John from under the bed and therewith made good fire and dressed the breakfast. And so Old John was cast out for nought, and burnt, and from thenceforth Young John occupied his place.

By this tale ye may see it is no wisdom for a man to keep long or to cherish that thing that is able to do no pleasure nor service.

[2] *picture:* i.e., the wooden statue
[3] *over night:* when night came

Finis

Howleglas (?1528)

Howleglas, the English version of Til Eulenspiegel, descends from the mythical jester of King Solomon's court, Marcolfus, whose jests became popular in the twelfth century. Combined with proverbs, the jests of Solomon and Marcolf were printed in English about 1492 by G. Leeu in Antwerp. The text has been edited by E. Gordon Duff (London, 1892) and displays a woodcut on the title page identical with that on the title page of Howleglas. *Some of the witty answers of Marcolf to Solomon appear now in the mouth of Howleglas.*

Howleglas *appeared first in Antwerp, printed by J. van Doesborke about 1510. The British Museum has a fragment of this text, and also two more complete editions printed by William Copeland—one dating from about 1528 (STC 10564) and the other from about 1530 (STC 10565).*

Howleglas *was privately printed by Frederic Ouvry (London, 1867) and in a much bowdlerized version by K. R. H. Mackenzie (London, 1860), which forms the base for most of the currently numerous editions of "Til Eulenspiegel's Merry Pranks."*

The basis for the present text is the British Museum copy of the ?1528 edition, supplemented where faulty by the edition of ?1530. The text is complete except for editorial deletions indicated by ellipses.

Here beginnith a mir

rye Jest of a man that was called Howleglas, and
of many marueylous thinges and Jestes that
he dyd in his lyfe, in Eastlande and in many
other places.

HERE BEGINNETH THE TABLE

18. How Howleglas took upon him to be a painter.
19. How Howleglas had a great disputation with all the doctors of Pragem in Bremen.
20. How Howleglas became a pardoner.
21. How Howleglas did eat for money in the town of Banderbetch.
22. How Howleglas went to Rome to speak with the pope.
23. How Howleglas deceived three Jews with dirt.
24. How Howleglas had gotten the parson's horse by his confession.
25. How Howleglas was hired of a blacksmith.
26. How Howleglas was hired of a shoemaker.
27. How Howleglas sold turds for fat.
28. How Howleglas served a tailor.
29. How Howleglas through his subtle deceits deceived a wine drawer in Lubek.
30. How Howleglas became a maker of spectacles and how he could find no work in no land.
31. How Howleglas was hired of a merchant man to be his cook.
32. How Howleglas was desired to dinner.
33. How Howleglas won a piece of cloth of a man of the country.
34. How Howleglas gave 20 gildens to 12 poor men for Christ's love.
35. How Howleglas feared his host with a dead wolf.
36. How Howleglas flaid a hound and gave the skin for half his dinner.
37. How Howleglas served that same hostess another time and lay on a wheel.
38. How Howleglas set his hostess upon the hot ashes with her bare arse.
39. How Howleglas served a hollander with a roasted apple.
40. How Howleglas made a woman that sold earthen pots to smite them all in pieces.
41. How Howleglas broke the stairs that the monks should come down on to matins, and how they fell down into the yard.
42. How Howleglas bought cream of the women of the country that brought it for to sell.
43. How Howleglas came to a scholar to make verses with him to the use of reason.

Here beginneth a merry Jest of a man that was called Howleglas, and of many marvelous things and Jests that he did in his life in Eastland and in many other places.

For the great desiring and praying of my good friends—and I the first writer of this book might not deny them—thus have I compiled and gathered much knavishness and falseness of one Howleglas made and done within his life—which Howleglas died the year of our Lord God MCCCC and L.

Now I desire to be pardoned both before ghostly and worldly, afore high and low, afore noble and unnoble. And right lowly I require all those that shall read or hear this present jest my ignorance to excuse.

This fable is not but only to renew the minds of men or women of all degrees from the use of sadness, to pass the time with laughter or mirth. And for because that simple knowing persons should beware if folks can see, methinks it is better to pass the time with such a merry jest and laugh thereat and do no sin, than for to weep and do sin.

1. *How Howleglas as he was born was christened three times upon one day*

In the land of Sassen, in the village of Kuelnig, there dwelleth a man that was named Nicholas Howleglas that had a wife named Wipeke that lay a-childbed in the same village, and that child was borne to christening and named Til Howleglas.

And then the child was brought into a tavern where the father was with his gossips [1] and made good cheer. When the midwife had well drunk, she took the child to bear it home. And in the way was a little bridge over a muddy water.

And as the midwife would have gone over the little bridge, she fell into the mud with the child, for she had a little drunk too much wine. For had not help come quickly, they had both been drowned in the mud.

And when she came home with the child, she made a kettle of warm water to be made ready, and therein they washed the child clean of the mud. And thus was Howleglas three times in one day christened—once at the church, once in the mud, and once in the warm water.

2. *How that Howleglas when that he was a child answered a man that asked the way*

Upon a time went Howleglas' father and mother out and left Howleglas within the house. Then came there a man riding half into the door and asked: "Is there nobody within?" Then answered the child: "Yes, there is a man-and-a-half, and a horse head."

Then asked the man: "Where is thy father?" And the child answered and said: "My father is of ill making worse. And my mother is gone for scath [1] or shame."

And the man said to the child: "How understandest thou that?" And then the child said: "My father is making of ill worse, for he ploweth the field and maketh great holes that men should fall therein when they ride. And my mother is to borrow bread, and when she giveth it again and giveth less it is shame; and when she giveth it and giveth more that is scath."

Then said the man: "Which is the way to ride?" And the

---

[1] *gossips:* usually cousins, but here probably godparents
[1] *scath:* i.e., a hurtful shame

child answered and said: "There, where the geese go." And
then rode the man his way to the geese.

And when he came to the geese, they flew into the water. Then
wist [2] he not where to ride, but turned again to the child and
said: "The geese be flown into the water and thus wot [3] I not
what to do nor whither to ride."

Then answered the child: "Ye must ride where as the geese
go and not where they swim." Then departed the man and rode
his way and marveled of the answer of the child.

3. *How Howleglas sat upon his father's horse behind him*

Many great complaints came before the father of Howleglas,
how his son was a deceiver of folks and a great mocker. This
complaint was made on him when he could go.[1] And when he
lay in the cradle, he tumbled upon the cushions with his arse
upward. And when he came to the age of nine years old, he
let no ungraciousness 'scape from him, insomuch that all the
neighbors complained on him.

Then said his father to him: "How commeth this that the
people complaineth so to me? They say that ye be a mocker
and a deceiver." Then said Howleglas: "Good father, I do nobody harm, and that shall I show unto you. Take a horse and
go upon his back and I will ride behind you. Then you shall
see what the people will say to me."

And then 'lighted his father upon his horse and took his son
behind him. And when he was upon the horse, he showed the
people his arse. Then said the folk: "What ungracious knave
and beguiler is that?"

Then said Howleglas to his father: "Now may ye hear, I hold

[2] *wist:* knew
[3] *wot:* know
[1] *he could go:* he could crawl

my peace and speak never a word—and yet say they that I am a knave and a deceiver of folk."

And then his father took him and set him before him on the horse. And then began he to grin and put out his tongue upon the people, that his father saw not. And then the people said: "See what a cursed young knave is there!"

Then said his father to Howleglas: "Thou was born in an unhappy time. For now thou sittest before me and dost nobody harm, and yet for all that they do call thee a knave and a beguiler." And so departed Howleglas' father out of the land of Mayd and brought him to a village from thence where his wife was, and within short space died.

And then abided Howleglas' mother with him, and ate and drank together such as they might get, for she was but poor and Howleglas would go to no craft—but when he was sixteen years old, he began to dance upon a cord, and no otherwise.

4. *How Howleglas fell from the rope into the water, whereof the people had good sport*

Upon a time, Howleglas played upon the cord that was set over the water, where he made good sport. But at the last, there was one that cut the rope, so fell he into the water and was alto [1] wet. And he came out as well as he might. For that little spite he thought to quit [2] them again and said to them: "Come again tomorrow and I will do many more wonders upon the rope."

And the next day after came Howleglas and danced upon the cord. And then he said to the young folk: "Ye shall see what news [3] I can do. Give me everybody your right shoe upon the rope end." So they did, and the old men also. And when he had

---

[1] *alto:* thoroughly, totally
[2] *quit:* repay
[3] *news:* novelties, curious things

danced a while, he cast them their shoes upon a heap and bad them take their shoes each of them again.

Then ran they after their shoes and for haste one tumbled over the other. And then they began to lie together by the ears [4] and smite with their fists so hard that they fell both to the earth. One said, weeping: "This is my shoe." And the other laughed and cried: "That is my shoe!" And thus for their shoes lay they together by the ears.

Then began Howleglas to laugh, crying: "Seek your shoes! Yesterday ye bathed me!" And he leaped from the cord and went his way to his mother's and durst not come out again in the space of a month. And so he tarried with his mother, whereof his mother was glad, but she knew not the cause why he did with her, nor what he had done.

5. *How Howleglas' mother learned him and bad him go to a craft*

Wibek the mother of Howleglas was glad that her son Howleglas was so subtle and wise, and she said that he might not live so and get money therewith. And then she said to her son that he should learn a craft. And then answered Howleglas to his mother: "What thing is that, that a body should dispose himself to, that should abide by him all his life?"

And his mother answered clean contrary, and said: "That me also thinketh, for in three days I have had no bread in my house. Should I not abide and suffer all my life? I had lever [1] die."

Then said Howleglas: "This is not an answer to my question, but I will answer now to yours (and said): A poor man that hath nothing to eat, he must fast Saint Nicholas' day. And he that hath meat may eat on Saint Martins' even. And in likewise it is with you."

[4] *by the ears:* i.e., wrestling
[1] *lever:* rather

6. *How Howleglas got bread for his mother*

As Howleglas' mother was thus without bread then bethought Howleglas how he might best get bread for her. Then went he out of the village to a town thereby called Stafford, and went into a baker's house where he asked the baker if he would send his lord for three shillings bread—some white and some rye. And he named a lord that was of another land, but he at that time was lodged at an inn in the town, and bad the baker let one go with him and that he should have his money. And the baker was content.

And then Howleglas gave the baker a bag that had a hole in the bottom, and therein put he the bread, and so departed with the baker's lad. And when he was in another street, he let fall three white loaves at the hole into the dirt. And then bad Howleglas to the baker's servant: "Set down the bag and go fetch me other white bread for this, for I dare not bear it to my lord." And then went the baker's servant home to change the bread.

And in the meanwhile went Howleglas with the sack of bread home to his mother's. And when the baker's servant came again to the place and found not Howleglas, he returned home again and told his master how Howleglas had served him. And when the baker heard that Howleglas was gone his way with his bread, then ran the baker to the inn that Howleglas named him and asked the servants of the lord's for Howleglas. But they said there came none such, and then knew the baker that he was deceived and so returned home.

Then said Howleglas to his mother: "Eat and make merry now you have it, and when you have no more ye must fast."

7. *How Howleglas creeped into a bee hive and how he was stolen in the night*

Upon a time went Howleglas with his mother to the dedication of a church. And there he drank so much that he was drunken, and then went he into a garden thereby where stood many bee hives. And there he sought where he might have a place to sleep in. And at the last he found an empty bee hive wherein he put himself to sleep for that night.

Then came there in the dead of night two thieves for to steal away the hives. And they felt which of the hives was heaviest, for they thought therein was most honey. So at the last they felt the hive that Howleglas was in and then said the thief to his fellow: "Here is one that is very heavy. This will I have. Take thou another and let us go."

Then took they the bee hives on their necks [1] and departed. Then awoke Howleglas and heard all what they said. And it was so dark that the one knew not the other. Then put Howleglas his hand out of the hive and pulled the foremost by the hair—wherewith he was angry and said to his fellow behind him: "Why pullest ye me by the hair?"

And then he answered: "I pull thee by the hair! I have as much as I can do to bear my hive."

And within a while after, Howleglas pulled the hindermost by the hair—that was right angry and said: "I bear so heavy that I sweat, and for all that, thou pullest me by the hair." "Thou," answered the foremost, "thou liest. How should I pluck thee by the hair and I can scantly find my way?"

Thus went they chiding by the way, and as they were chiding, Howleglas put out his hand again and pulled the foremost by the hair—whereof he was angry and set down his hive and took his fellow by the head, and thus they tumbled together by the hive in the street. And at the last, when the one had well beaten

[1] *necks:* backs

the other, they ran their way and left the hives lying. And then slept Howleglas in the bee hive till in the morning.

And then he arose and went forth. And as he went, he came by a castle and went in. And the lord asked him if he would have a master, and he said yes. And then the lord hired him. And upon a time he rode with his master by the way where stood hemp. Then said his master to him: "When thou findest such seed, shite therein, for therewith men be hanged upon the gallows and upon the wheels, both thieves and murderers."

Then answered Howleglas that he would do it. And his master said so because that he was a thief, and in the night went a-robbing and a-stealing for he lived almost thereby.

On a time, as his master was at supper, the cook called Howleglas and bad him go into the cellar and fetch him the mustard out of the pot. And then went Howleglas, and he understood that the cook bad him go fetch a hempen rope. Then marveled he what he meant, for he never saw none afore. Then thought he, "Will he bind me therewith?"

Then went Howleglas into the cellar, and there he sought about, and at the last he found the pot with mustard. And then he remembered him and said: "My master bad me that where I found any such seed that I should shite therein." And then he put his arse over the pot and shite therein a great heap. And then he stirred it about together and brought it to the cook.

And then the cook dressed the mustard in saucers and sent them to the table, and the lord tasted and it savored ill. Then said he to the cook: "What have you ground in the mustard, for it savoreth like as there were a turd therein." And then began Howleglas to laugh. Then said his master: "Whereat laughest thou? Thinkest thou we can not taste? Then taste thou."

And then answered Howleglas: "I eat no mustard, for wote [2] you not what ye bad me do when that we rode over such seed— that when I found such seed, said you, that then I should shite in it for with such seed, you said, men were hanged. And so I have shitten in the seed."

[2] *wote:* i.e., don't you remember?

Then said his master: "A, thou unhappy knave, this seed is not like the seed of hemp. But I know this by very good reason that thou hast done it of cursedness and great falseness." And then he took a staff and would have smited Howleglas. And then Howleglas took his legs and ran away, and his master after him. But he could not overtake him. Then he returned home again, and Howleglas would no more come there.

8. *How Howleglas was hired of a priest*

As Howleglas ran out of the castle he came to a village that was called Buddest in the land of Brounswick. And there came a priest to Howleglas and hired him. But he knew him not, and the priest said to him that he should have good days and eat and drink the same meat that he himself and his woman did. And all that should be done with half the labor. And then said Howleglas that thereafter would he do his diligence.

Then dressed the priest's woman two chickens, and she bad Howleglas turn [1] and so he did. And he looked up and saw that she had but one eye. When the chickens were enough [2] then he broke one of the chickens from the spit and ate it without any bread.

And when it was dinner time came the woman into the kitchen where Howleglas turned and thought to take up the chickens. And when she was come she found no more there but one chicken. Then said she to Howleglas: "Where is the other chicken? There were two chickens!" Then answered he to her: "Lift up your eye [3] and then shall you see the other chicken."

Then was the woman therewith angry and knew well that Howleglas mocked her. And then she ran to the priest and told

[1] *turn:* turn the spit
[2] *enough:* sufficiently cooked
[3] *lift up your eye:* open your eye

him how she had dressed two chickens, and when she came to take them up she found but one. "And then he mocked me because I had but one eye."

Then went the priest to Howleglas and said: "Why mock ye my woman? There was two chickens?" Then answered Howleglas and said that was truth: "I have said to the woman that she should open her eyes and she should see well where that other chicken was become."

Then laughed the priest and said: "She cannot see. She hath but one eye." Then said Howleglas to the priest: "The one chicken have I eaten, for ye said that I should eat and drink as well as you and your woman—and the one I ate for you, and the other I ate for your woman, for I was afraid that you should have sinned for the promise that ye promised me. And therefore I made me sure."

Then said the priest: "I care not for the chickens, but I would have you please my woman and do after her." Then said Howleglas: "I do your commandment." And that, the woman bad him do, he did but half. For she bad him fetch a bucket of water, and he went and brought it but half full of water. And when he should bring two logs, he brought but one. And when he should give the beasts two botels [4] of hay, he gave them but one. And when he should fetch a pot full of beer, he brought it half full. And so did he of many other things more.

Then complained she to the priest of Howleglas. Again then said the priest: "I bad that you should do as she bad you." And Howleglas answered: "I have done as ye bad me, for ye said to me that I should do all things with half labor. And your woman would fain see with both eyes, but she seeth but with one eye and so do I half the labor."

And then the priest laughed. And then said the woman: "Will you have this ungracious knave any longer? Then will not I tarry no longer with you, but depart." Then gave the priest Howleglas leave to depart, for his woman's sake.

[4] *botels:* bales

But when the parish clerk was dead of the village, then sent the priest for Howleglas and helped him so much that he was made the parish clerk.

9. *How Howleglas was made clerk of Buddensted*

. . . And then in the mean season while Howleglas was parish clerk, at Easter they should play the resurrection of Our Lord. And for because then the men were not learned nor could not read, the priest took his leman and put her in the grave for an angel. And this seeing, Howleglas took to him two of the simplest persons that were in the town that played the three Mary's, and the parson played Christ with a banner in his hand.

Then said Howleglas to the simple persons: "When the angel asketh you whom you seek, you may say 'The parson's leman with one eye.'" Then it fortuned that the time was come that they must play, and the angel asked them whom they sought. And then said they as Howleglas had showed and learned them afore. And then answered they: "We seek the priest's leman with one eye." And then the priest might hear that he was mocked.

And when the priest's leman heard that, she arose out of the grave and would have smitten with her fist Howleglas upon the cheek, but she missed him and smote one of the simple persons that played one of the three Mary's. And he gave her another. And then took she him by the hair, and that seeing, his wife came running hastily to smite the priest's leman. And then the priest seeing this cast down his banner and went to help his woman, so that the one gave the other sore strokes and made great noise in the church. And then Howleglas, seeing them lying together by the ears in the body of the church, went his way out of the village and came no more there.

10. *How that Howleglas would fly from the town house of May-brough*

After that, came Howleglas to Maybrough where he did many marvelous things that his name was there well known. Then bad the principal of the town that he should do something that was never seen before. Then said he that he would go to the highest of the council house and fly from it. And anon that was known through all the town that Howleglas would fly from the top of the council house—insomuch that all the town was there assembled and gathered in the market place to see him.

Upon the top of the house stood Howleglas with his hands wavering as though he would have flown and then the people looked when he should have flied—whereat he laughed and said to the people: "I thought there had been no more fools but myself, but I see well that here is a whole town full. For had ye altogether said that ye would have flied, yet I would not have believed you. And now ye believe one fool that sayeth that he will fly, which thing is impossible for I have no wings. And no man can fly without wings."

And then went he his way from the top of the council house and left the folk there standing. And then departed the folk from thence—some blaming him and some laughing, saying: "He is a shrewd fool, for he telleth us the truth."

11. *How Howleglas made himself a physician, and how he beguiled a doctor of the Bishop of Mayborough*

The Bishop Erime of Mayborough, Earl of Quecforth, and all his nobles loved Howleglas, for that he did many proper conceits. And therefore the Bishop gave him meat and drink, clothes and wages. The Bishop had a right wise doctor with him and he in no wise might bear noise nor fools. So, upon a time as he saw Howleglas there, he said to the Bishop and the lord's men: "You should let come in lord's courts wise men and no fools. For the wise men will be conversant with wise men and give wise reasons. And fools will be conversant with fools and give foolish reasons."

And then answered they and said: "That reason is false, for he that foolishness will not hear nor see, he may well depart from them. There be also that think themselves wise that been oftentimes defiled of fools. It belongs to princes, lords, and barons to have in their courts fools. For oftentimes they drive away heavy thoughts and fantasies and melancholy. Where lords be, there will be also fools."

Then said Howleglas to the lords: "What argument have you had with the doctor for my sake? Forsooth, he shall be quit and you will help me [1] thereto." And they said all yes.

Then departed he out of the court by the space of three weeks, and then came again to Genckestaine, and then he came to the lodging there where the doctor [2] lay and was sick—for the which sickness he sought for help. Then said the lords that there was come a cunning man and a Master of Physic that had helped many people. The doctor knew not Howleglas, and then he took him by the arm and led him into his lodging where he spake to him and said: "And ye can help me, I shall content you well for your labor."

Then answered he: "I trust to help you, but first I must lie by you one night, that I may cover you well that you may sweat. And by the air of the sweat, I shall well know what sickness it is that you have." And then the priest, weening [3] that all had been true, granted to him. And then gave Howleglas to him a

[1] *and you will help me:* if you will help me
[2] *doctor:* a scholar rather than a medical doctor
[3] *weening:* imagining

strong purgation for to make him shite, but he said to the doctor that it was a medicine to make him to sweat, and the doctor believed him.

. . . And he took the pot and put it between the bed and the wall of the doctor, that the doctor knew it not. And the doctor went to bed, and then came Howleglas to bed. And the priest turned him to the wall where the pot stood. And then he felt such a stink of the dirt that stood in the pot, so that he turned his head again toward Howleglas.

. . . And then began the medicine to work so much that he beshit all the bed. Then said Howleglas: "How do ye, master doctor? Methink your sweat stinketh very sore." The doctor thought in his mind: "That know I well enough." But he might not speak because of the stink. . . .

Then began the day to appear, and so departed Howleglas his way. And then looked the doctor by the bedside, and there found the pot of dirt that stank so. And then took he it and cast it away. And then knew he well that he was mocked.

And within a while came the Bishop and his nobles to visit the doctor. And when they came to his chamber, they asked him how he fared and he answered and said: "Never worse, for I am almost dead." Then he told the Bishop how that Master of Physick had served him. And then began the Bishop to laugh and all his lords, and said: "This cometh to pass all after your words. For ye said that fools would have conversation with fools, and give foolish reasons; and wise men would have conversation with wise men and give wise reasons. But I see that many wisemen be made fools of fools, and so be you. For if that ye would have suffered Howleglas and said nothing, ye had not been mocked of him. For the physician that was with you was Howleglas, and that we all knew well enough. But in no wise we would show you for because ye were so wise that ye should be beguiled of a fool. For there is no man that is wise, but he must know fools—for where no fools be, how should men know wise folks?"

And then the doctor held his peace and spake no more, and then never after durst he complain more of fools, but let them do all that they would after their own minds.

12. *How Howleglas made a sick child shite that afore might not shite, and how he got great worship thereof and praise*

Men let alone and take no heed of cunning men that dwell by them, but proffer them a little or nought for their labor, nor be beloved. But rural persons and vagabonds have all their desire. As it is done to Howleglas that came into the land of Hildesh, in a lodging where the goodman was not at home, but Howleglas was welcome to the good wife of the house.

In the house there was a sick child lying by the fire, and then Howleglas seeing the sick child lie so, he asked his hostess what sickness that the child had. Then answered the woman to Howleglas and said: "If the child might go to the draught,[1] he should do well enough."

And then answered Howleglas thereto: "Know you no remedy?" Then answered the woman: "Can ye help the child? And ye can, I shall give you that ye shall be pleased therewith." Then answered Howleglas: "That is but a little thing to do, nor no cunning. For I will take no thing therefore." And so departed the wife into the garden.

And in the meanwhile did Howleglas shite a green turd, and then set he the shiting chair over the turd, and set the child thereon as though the child had done it. Then came the woman out of the garden and asked who had done that. And then answered Howleglas: "I have done it. Ye said that the child could not go to the draught, therefore I have set the child in the chair."

Then took the woman the child away and saw so much dirt underneath. Then said she to Howleglas: "This is it that hath

[1] *draught:* privy

hindered the child so long! For this great cure ye must have great thank [2] thereof." Then said Howleglas: "Such mastery can I do with less cost." Then said the woman: "I pray you learn me that cunning and I will give you therefore what you will have."

Then said Howleglas: "I must needs depart from hence, but when I come again I will learn you that science and learning." And then went he into the stable and saddled his horse and took his leave, and so departed from thence. But he taught not his hostess that science, but so departed.

13. *How Howleglas made hole all the sick folk that were in the hospital where the spear of our Lord is*

Upon a time Howleglas came to Northborough and he set upon the church doors and upon the guildhall and every place that all the people in the town might know, that he was a great Master of Physic, that all sick he could make hole.[1] And then the master of the spittle house,[2] where the spear of our Lord is, had many sick folks in his house. Then went the master of the hospital to Howleglas and asked him if he could help sick men or lame men and make them hole, and he would reward him after his own pleasure.

Then answered Howleglas to the master of the hospital: "Will ye give me 200 gold gildens and [3] I shall recover and make them hole of all their sickness and diseases, and will have no money till all the sick persons be delivered out of the hospital?" These words pleased the master of the hospital very well, and he gave him some money in his hand.

Upon the morrow after, came Howleglas to the hospital with two men after him. And then he asked the sick folk, one after

[2] *thank:* reward
[1] *hole:* cured
[2] *spittle house:* hospital
[3] *and:* if

the other, what disease they had. And when he had asked them all then he made them swear upon a book that they should keep his counsel whatsoever he said to them. They answered that they would. Then said Howleglas to them: "I have undertaken to make you all hole, which is impossible, for I must needs burn one of you all to powder. And then must I take that powder of him and give all the others to drink thereof, with other medicines that I shall minister thereto. And he that is the last when I shall call you out of the hospital, and he that can not go, shall be he that shall be burned.

"For on Wednesday next coming, then shall I come before the master of the hospital, and then shall I call—and he that sleepeth longest shall pay for all."

Then prepared every one of the sick folk their crutches and gear, that they would not be the last. And when Howleglas was come to the master of the hospital, then called he them. And then they ran out of the hospital, and some of them had not been out of their bed in ten years before.

Then when the sick folk were out of the hospital, then asked he his money. And then the master gave it him, and then he departed. And within three days after, came again the poor men to the hospital and complained of their sickness. And then the master of the hospital said to them: "How commeth this to pass? I gave the Master of Physic a great sum of money to make you hole."

Then answered the poor folk: "He hath deceived you and us both, for four days past, he came to every one of us and said to us that he should come on Wednesday next coming and heal us. But he said he must needs first burn one of us, and said that should be he that when he should call, should be the last out of his bed—" and the powder of him should they drink and be made hole therewith.

Then knew the master of the hospital that he was deceived and beguiled. And then took he the poor folk into the hospital and put every one in their bed as they were before. But he did all against his will.

14. *How that a baker hired Howleglas to be his servant*

Upon a time came Howleglas to a baker for to dwell, and the baker had need of a servant, and then he hired Howleglas. In the next morning after, must the baker bake. So the night before must Howleglas sift their meal without a candle. Then said he to his master: "Ye must give me a candle." Then answered the baker: "I never gave a candle to boult [1] with, but they did boult in the moonlight." Then answered Howleglas: "I am content."

Then went his master to bed to sleep three hours. And in the meanwhile let he the boulting bag out of the window in the moonshine and then began he to boult the flour upon the earth in the garden. Then arose his master and thought to have baked, and came to the boulting house. And then he saw that Howleglas had boulted the meal in the garden upon the bare ground.

Then said the baker to Howleglas: "What the devil dost thou think, the meal cost no more but strewing upon the earth?" Then answered Howleglas to his master: "I have done as ye bad me, for it is boulted in the moonshine."

Then answered the baker: "I bad thee that thou shouldest boult it by the moonshine!" And then answered Howleglas: "So I have done, for it is sifted in the moonshine and without the moonshine."

And then said Howleglas: "There is not much meal lost but that we may take it up again." And then answered the baker: "It is too late now for to bake, for our dough is not made." Then answered Howleglas to his master and said: "I shall help you well. Your neighbor hath dough ready made in the kneading trough, and I will go fetch that and put yours in the stead."

Then was the baker much angry and bad him to the gallows and fetch that was under it. And then said Howleglas he would. And then he departed to the gallows. And when he came there,

[1] *boult:* sift

he found nothing else but a few bones, and those he took up and brought home with him, and then said to his master: "I have brought that that I have found under the gallows. What will ye do with it?"

Then was the baker more angry and said: "I shall complain on thee. Thou hast stolen away the King's justice." Then went he out to the market and Howleglas followed. And then came the baker to the burgess of the town and began to complain. And then came Howleglas and stood by the baker. And therewith was the baker so angry that he wist [2] not what to say to the burgess, and said angrily to Howleglas: "What wilt thou have?" Then said Howleglas: "I must needs see the complaint that ye make on me."

Then answered the baker: "Go out of my sight, thou ungracious knave." Then answered Howleglas to the baker: "If I were in thy eyes, then must I needs pass through thy nostrils when ye shuttest thy eyes." Then departed the burgess and knew well that he mocked. And then showed Howleglas his arse to the baker, and asked him if he could bake such a loaf in his mouth—and then departed he and left the baker standing in the market place.

15. *How Howleglas was put in wages with the Foster of Anhalt for to watch upon a tower to see when his enemies came and then for to blow an horn to warn them thereof*

Upon a time the Earl of Anhalt hired for a true waiter [1] Howleglas, for he had many enemies and for that cause he must have many soldiers in wages that he must give meat to. But Howleglas that was in the top of the tower was not of the merriest, for he was forgot.

[2] *wist:* knew
[1] *waiter:* watchman

Upon a time came his enemies and fetched away a great flock of the Earl's beasts, and that saw Howleglas but he held his peace. And that was spied and showed to the Earl. And then the Earl asked him why he did lie so still and blew not. Then answered Howleglas: "I did dance for my meat." Then said the Earl: "Will ye not blow 'enemies'?" Then answered Howleglas: "I dare not. The field is so full of enemies. For if I should blow, they would come and slay you at your own gate." And then the Earl was content and departed.

And within a while after was Howleglas again forgotten. And when the Earl was at dinner and had great dainties before him, Howleglas blew "enemies." And by-and-by the Earl and all his soldiers rose from the table and dressed them in harness and ran to the gate. But they found no enemies. In the meanwhile took Howleglas as much meat as he would have from the Earl's table.

Then the soldiers and the Earl came in and called Howleglas to them, and the Earl asked him why he blew "enemies" and there were none. The Earl said it was a traitorous deed, and then he put him out of office. Then must he needs run with his footmen to fight with their enemies. Then said he: "That sore thinketh me, I would I were hence." But he could not.

Upon a time came enemies. Then went the soldiers out upon them, and Howleglas was last. And when they returned again, he was the first in at the gate. At the last, the Earl had knowledge and came to Howleglas and asked what was the cause that he was the last out and the first in. Then answered Howleglas to the Earl: "Worshipful Lord, if it please you, when your soldiers made good cheer I stood upon that tower fasting and therefore I am not so strong as your soldiers be. And that is cause that I am last out and the first in. And you will give me meat enough as ye do the others, then shall I be the first."

Then answered the Earl: "Thinkest thou that I will keep thee so long as I have kept ye, to do nothing but mock us in this manner as ye have done so often?" Then gave he Howleglas leave to depart, whereof he was very glad for he loved no fighting. And so departed he.

16. *How Howleglas won the king's fool of Casimir of Poland with a great point of foolishness*

The king of Casimir he had with him a certain fool, which fool could play upon the fiddle, wherefore the king loved him much and set great price by him. Also the king heard oftentimes tell of Howleglas, but he never could see him. And on a time it fortuned that Howleglas came into the king's palace for to ask dwelling, whereof when that the king wist [1] that Howleglas was come there to dwell, he was very glad thereof, and took him in, and made him goodly cheer.

So it fortuned that the king's fool and Howleglas could not agree, and that spied the king well and thought in his mind: "What shall I do?" And then he made them both to be brought before him in the hall, and then he said to them: "Which of you two can the most foolishness? And [2] one of you do that the other will not do, I shall give him new clothing and 20 ducats. And let it be done in my presence before me and all my lords in this hall."

And then they answered both to the king that they would prepare them, and within a while they came before the king and his lords. And then they began to do many proper conceits and merry touches of foolishness, one to the other, whereat the king and his lords had good laughter and good pastime thereat for to see how the one labored for to overcome the other and to win the new clothes and the 20 ducats.

Then thought Howleglas: "This is good for me." Then he thought in his mind how he might do a thing that the other fool would not do. And then came he before the king and his

[1] *wist:* knew
[2] *And:* if

lords, and before them all he did shite a great turd. And when he had done so, he took a spoon and divided it in the midst [3] with the spoon. And when he had done so, he came to the king's fool and said: "Do thou as I have done. Shite here in the midst, and when that ye have done, divide it in the midst, and take the spoon and take the one half of my turd and eat it, and I shall take the other half of thy turd and eat it."

Then answered the king's fool: "Yet had I lever [4] than I would eat half thy turd or yet mine own, I had lever all the days of my life go naked." Then gave the king and all the lords the mastery to Howleglas, and they gave to him the new clothes and the 20 ducats. Then took he his leave and thanked the king and so departed he from thence.

17. *How the Duke of Lunenborough banished Howleglas out of*
   his land

It befell on a time in the land of Lunenborough that Howleglas had done a great fault and an unhappy touch to the duke, wherefore the duke bad him that he should go out of his land and never after to come more therein, for if he were found there ever after that anymore he should lose his head.

And then departed Howleglas out of the duke's land for he durst no longer tarry there for the strait commandment that the duke had commanded him. And within a while after, it fortuned that Howleglas' way lay so that he must pass through the duke's land, of the which he was banished, to go to the place where him lust best.[1] And as he passed through the land, it fortuned that he spied the duke riding towards him so that he could no way pass but he must needs see him.

Then 'lighted Howleglas down from his horse that he rode

[3] *midst:* middle
[4] *lever:* rather
[1] *lust best:* i.e., where he wanted most to go

on and drew out his knife and cut the horse's throat. And then he turned up his horse's belly and ripped out all the bowels of his horse and cast them away. And then he set the horse with his belly upward and went and stood therein. And, within a while after, came the duke riding by, and as he passed by, one of the duke's servants spied him standing in the horse's belly. And he rode to the duke and showed to him where that Howleglas stood.

Then rode the duke to him, and when he came to him he said: "Who made thee so bold as to enter into my land!" Then Howleglas said: "Worshipful lord, I desire you the pardon of my life, for when I saw you not far from me, then put I myself in my horse's belly, for I have heard say that every man in his own ground is free, and now I stand in mine own ground and not in yours." Then laughed the duke and said: "I give thee pardon. Go out of the dead horse and do as ye were wont to do." And so departed the duke.

And then said Howleglas to his horse: "I thank thee for thou hast saved my life and caused the duke to give me pardon." And so departed Howleglas.

18. *How Howleglas took upon him to be a painter, etc.*

Then it fortuned that Howleglas might no longer tarry in the land of Sassen for his knavishness. Then departed he into the land of Hessen to Marchborough to the earl, and he asked Howleglas what occupation he was of. Then answered Howleglas: "Worshipful lord, I am a painter. My cunning doth excel all others, for in no land is naught so cunning as I."

Then answered the earl: "Have you here any example of your work?" Then answered Howleglas to the earl: "Yes, my lord." (Then had he been in Flanders and brought with him divers images that pleased the king wonderly well.) Then said the earl to Howleglas: "Master, what shall I give to you to take upon

you to paint upon the wall in my hall, all the lords and knights
of my progeny, from the first unto the last, in the goodliest and
fairest manner that ye can—with all earls of Hessen and their
ladies with them, and how our forefathers were married to ladies
of strange lands? And all this must you cast that it may be upon
the walls of my hall."

Then answered Howleglas to the earl: "Worshipful lord, if
it please you that ye will have all this that you have rehearsed
to me to be painted so costly and richly as you speak of, then
would it cost only the colors that should 'long thereto—above
three hundred gold gildens."

Then answered the earl Howleglas and said: "Make it well
and in the best manner that ye can and we twain shall agree
after the best manner. And also I shall do you a greater pleasure
than all that cometh to." And then took Howleglas the work
upon him. But he said to the lord that he must needs have an
hundred gildens in earnest, to buy the colors that belonged
thereto and for his mens' wages. And then bad the earl the rent-
master give to Howleglas an hundred gildens, and so he did.

Then went Howleglas and gat him three fellows. And then
he came again to the earl and asked him a boon before he began
to work, and the earl granted him. And then he did ask of the
earl that there should no person be so hardy to come into the
hall to trouble him and his workmen without they asked him
license. And the earl granted his desire.

And then went Howleglas into the hall with his servants, and
when he and they were in the hall, Howleglas set a pair of tables
before them and he bad them play. But he made them before to
swear that they should not bewray [1] him. And the fellows had
good pastime, wherewith they were well content and glad that
they might have meat, drink, and clothes, and do no other thing
but play and pass the time in that manner.

And Howleglas did no other thing, but hanged a white cloth
before the wall. That done, he came and played with his servants.

In the meantime, longed the earl greatly to see his work, if it

[1] *bewray:* disclose

were so goodly as the copy was, and to see if the colors were good. And so he departed and came to Howleglas and said: "Good master painter, I pray you let me go with you to see your work." Then said Howleglas to the lord: "Worshipful lord, before that you see my work, I must show to you one thing: He the which is not born in wedlock may not see my painting." Then said the earl that were a marvelous thing.

And then went he with Howleglas into the hall, and there had he hanged up a white cloth that he should have painted. And he had in his hand a white rod and he did away the cloth that hanged upon the wall, and pointed upon the wall with his white rod, and showed the earl that that was the first lord of the land and Earl of Hessen. "And this is an earl of Rome. He had a wife that they called Justine, the Duke's daughter of Beren. And after, he was made Emperor. And of the daughter of him came Adolphus, and of Adolphus came William the swarthy. And this William had one, Lewis, and so forth to your noble grace.

"And I know well, that there is no person living that can reprove my work, so curiously have I made, and with fair colors." But the lord saw no work but the plain wall. Then thought he in his mind: "Am I a bastard? Is my mother a whore? I see nothing but the white wall."

And for because that he would not be known for a bastard, he said to Howleglas: "Master, your work pleaseth me marvelously well. But my understanding is very small therein." And with that, he went out of the hall and came to his wife.

And she asked him how that work did please him. He said: "I have shrewd trust in him." Then said the earl: "I like it well. Shall it please you to look thereon?" And she granted.

And then she desired Howleglas that she might see his work, and he granted her. And then he said unto her secretly, as he had said before to the lord, and showed her the lords upon the wall, with the white rod in his hand, as he did to the lord. And there stood one foolish gentlewoman with the lady and she said that she saw no painting on the wall. And the others spake not one word.

And then thought Howleglas: "Will this fool tell truth? Then must I needs depart." Then hanged he up the white cloth and so departed the lady. And when she was come to her lord, he asked her how she liked the work. She said: "How that it liketh me, it liketh not my foolish gentlewoman." And she said that some of her gentlewomen said that it was but deceit. And so thought the lord.

Then said the lord to Howleglas that he should make ready his work, that he and his lords might see it tomorrow, that he might know which of them were born in wedlock and which were not—"for he that is not born in wedlock, all his land is forfeit to me." Then answered Howleglas: "I will do it with a good will."

Then went he to the rent master and received of him an hundred gold gildens. And when he had received the money, he said to his servants: "Now must we all depart." And he gave them money, of the which they were content, and so departed.

Then on the morrow came the earl with his lords into the hall, and they asked where the master painter was and his company, for he said he would see the work. Then turned he up the cloth and asked them and [2] they saw any work, and they said nay. Then said the earl: "We be deceived!" He said: "We have sore longed to see Howleglas, and now he hath beguiled us. But it maketh no great matter for the money. But let us banish him from our land for a beguiler of people," and so they did. And so departed the earl with his lords.

19. *How Howleglas had many and great disputations with all the noble doctors of Pragen in Bremen*

Then departed Howleglas from the land of Hessen and then came he to Pragen in Bremen where was a university of scholars and students, of doctors and bachelors. Then made Howleglas

[2] *and:* if

bills and set them up on every church door. And he wrote that he would answer to all manner of questions that were laid unto him, and give answer thereto.

And as he had set up the bills, then came the scholars of the university and read them. And when they had read them and found therein that he should give an answer to all that was asked him, then took they a bill and went to the rector and showed him that there was one come that had set up these letters upon the church doors: "And he sayeth therein that he will give answer to all manner of questions that were put to him."

Then the rector, hearing this, sent a scholar to the place where Howleglas was lodged, and charged the host of the house that he should tomorrow bring with him the man that had set up the bills, upon pain that should fall thereafter. And then the host answered he would. Then departed the scholar home.

Then on the morrow came Howleglas and his host to the university with two or three of his neighbors, and when they were come then was Howleglas taken by the arm and set in a chair. And then came the rector with many doctors, and shortly they were set about him.

Then asked he him how many gallons of water was in the sea. Then answered Howleglas: "Do stop all the rivers that run therein and then I shall mete [1] it, and then shall I show you how many there be." Then thought the rector that was impossible to do, but he was content with the answer.

Then asked he Howleglas the second answer: "How many days be past since Adam, to this time?" And then answered Howleglas to the rector: "It is eight days past and more. For when the week is done, then beginneth again the next week, seven other days, and so forth to the end of the world."

Then said the rector: "Tell me now the third answer." And Howleglas bad him say what he would. Then asked the rector him: "Where was the middle of all the world?" And then answered Howleglas to the rector: "That is here in the midst of this house. For and [2] you believe not me, then take a cord and mete

[1] *mete:* measure
[2] *and:* if

it, and if it lack a straw breadth, then will I be counted for an unlearned man."

And then the rector had lever ³ give him the mastery than he would mete it. But then he waxed angry and asked him: "How far is the earth from heaven?" Then answered Howleglas: "That is hereby, for let men sing never so softly here, but it is heard in heaven. And ye will not me believe, then take a ladder and go up into heaven, and I shall here speak softly—and if you hear it not, then will I lose the price." ⁴

Then the rector said to Howleglas: "How wide is all heaven, and how broad is it?" Then answered Howleglas to the rector and said: "It is twelve thousand miles broad and a thousand miles wide, and if ye will not me believe then must ye take the sun and the moon and all the stars of heaven, and then go mete them—and if you find it not as I say, then will I give the mastery to you and I will be overcome."

Then the rector and the doctors knew not what they should say more to Howleglas, but they said that he was too subtle for them. And then they gave to him the victory and praise. And then departed he out of the place, for he was afraid that they would have done to him some unhappiness.

20. *How Howleglas became a pardoner*

As Howleglas was known through all the country for his unhappy touches and beguilings that he had done to them—for that, he was welcome to no place that he came to, where he had been much made of before in all his youth. Then bethought Howleglas in what manner he might get money with little labor.

Then went Howleglas and gat him a priest's gown and dressed him like a scholar. Then went he into a certain churchyard where he found a dead man's head, and then he took the head up and made it clean. And when it was clean, he bare it to a

³ *lever:* rather
⁴ *price:* prize

certain goldsmith and bad him that he should band the head with silver bands, and he said that he would content him, and so he did.

And when it was done, he contented the goldsmith and then departed he to a village near thereby where it was the dedication day. And then came he to the parson of the church and saluted him, and then he told him that he had a relic and he prayed the curate that he would do so much for him: That he would show it unto his parish that they might offer to it. And he said to the parson that he should have the one half of the offering. And then the parson, moved with covetousness, granted to him—for he was glad to get money.

Then told he to the people of the parish: "This man that here standeth hath brought a precious relic. He that offereth thereto hath great pardon. He shall come into the pulpit and declare it unto you." Then went Howleglas into the pulpit and then he told the people of the relic that he had there. And he said that the head spake to him, and that it had bad him that he should build a church over him, and that the money that the church should be built with should be well gotten.

And when the men and the women should come offer, then said Howleglas to the women: All those that made their husbands cuckold should sit still and come not to offer. For the head bad him, "that I should not receive the offering." And then he came down out of the pulpit, and when he was come down, then came the poor men and their wives and offered to the head.

And there was not one woman but she offered because that he had said so, and he gave them the blessing with the head. And there were some that had no money, and they offered their rings. And some of them offered twice or thrice because they would be seen. And they that were guilty pressed first. And thus received he the offering both of the good and of the ill, so that he had gotten a great sum of money by that said practice.

And when they had all offered, and that there was no more that came, then he said to them: "All ye men and women that here hath come and offered to this head, be honest and good and moreover I charge you on pain of cursing that there be not one of you that the others slander or backbite. For if you had not been good and honest I should not have received your offering. And when the poor men of the country heard Howleglas speak in this manner, they believed him.

And when the mass was done, then came the parson to Howleglas and said to him that he should give to him half of the offering. And then divided Howleglas the offering and gave the parson a part thereof, that the parson was well content therewith. And then departed Howleglas from the parson and then the women thereabout were very glad of Howleglas and made much of him.

So abode he long with them and spent none of his money—in such manner could he cloak and hide his unhappiness and falseness.

21. *How Howleglas came to the town of Banberch and how he did eat for money*

Upon a time came Howleglas from Norenborough to Banberch where he entered into lodging where was a merry hostess. She bad Howleglas often times welcome, for she saw by his clothing that he was a merry guest. And, as dinner time came, the hostess asked him if that he would go to dinner. And she asked him also if it pleased him to be at the twelve penny table.

Then answered Howleglas and said to his hostess: "I am but a poor man. I pray you for God's sake to give me my dinner."

Then said the hostess: "The baker and the butcher will not be so paid, and therefore must I have money—for there is none in my house but they eat and drink all for money."

Then answered Howleglas: "For money do men eat and drink? In good faith, so will I."

Then answered the woman to him: "What table will you be at? For at the lords' table they give me no less than two shillings, and at the merchants' table sixteen pence, and at my household servants' table twelve pence."

Then answered Howleglas to his hostess: "Sith I must needs eat and pay money, then give me the best meat that you have." And then he set him down at the lords' table. And then his hostess brought to the table the best meat and drink that she had, and she bad him make good cheer.

She said oft: "Much good do it you, gentle sir." And Howleglas thanked his hostess many times. He ate and drank and made him well at ease. And he ate so much of that good meat that he sweat again.

When that he had made him well at ease and eaten and drunken all that he would, then bad he his hostess to avoid the table,[1] for he said he must depart from thence. And right shortly at his commandment the table was avoided. And so he arose and stood by the fire, and when he was thorough warm, he took his leave with his hostess and would have departed.

That seeing, the hostess took him by the sleeve and bad him to give her two shillings for his dinner. Then answered he: "God thank you, for you have remembered me. I must have two shillings of you. For you said to me that there came no manner of persons within your house but that they eat for money. And when you had told me that, I sat me down and said I would do the same. And I ate so much that I sweat again, and therefore you give me money."

Then said his hostess: "Must I give ye money to eat my meat and drink my drink? Such guests I may have great plenty! Pay me my money shortly, for the bakers and brewers will not be so answered."

Then answered Howleglas to his hostess: "Give me my money, for thinkest thou that I will eat so much and labor myself so sore as I did, not to be paid for my labor? Yet I had much lever [2] never to have seen ye nor thy house. For I have eaten so much for money that my belly is like to burst. Would you that I should

[1] *avoid the table:* clear the table
[2] *lever:* rather

have such great labor and not [be] paid therefore? I have other things to do than to stand chatting here with thee. And therefore come off lightly [3] and give me my money and let me be gone, for I have right well deserved it."

Then said his hostess to him: "Sir, you have eaten my meat and drunken my drink and by my fire you have had your ease, and all at your own desire—wherefore I pray you to give me money." And he answered right angrily: "Would you have me to pay money—and I did eat therefore, the which is to my great harm?"

Then she answered to Howleglas: "If your eating do you harm, I am not the cause thereof, but your eating is to my loss—not only that—I have lost more than that cometh to!" And then she said: "Depart thou from my house and never after this thou be so bold once to enter within my doors."

Then said Howleglas: "Will you on your conscience take my labor for nothing? Well, farewell." And then departed Howleglas, and he was glad that he had so 'scaped from her. And she was glad that she was so delivered of him.

22. *How Howleglas went to Rome to speak with the Pope*

Then when Howleglas had long occupied his falseness, then he remembered this old proverb: "I will to Rome my manners to amend, and home again my life for to end." And then departed he to Rome where he showed part of his ungraciousness.

And when he came to Rome, he lodged with a widow and this widow did oft behold him in the face. And because he was a fair young man she said oftentimes: "Sir, you be right welcome." "Good sir," she said, "from whence be you?"

"I am of Sasson, and my coming hither is for to speak with the pope."

Then answered she to Howleglas: "Good friend, you may see

[3] *come off lightly:* i.e., "come off it!" "cut it out!"

him but you shall not speak with him. For I that am born in Rome would have given an hundred ducats to speak to him, but I could never speak to him." Then said Howleglas: "Hostess, will you give me an hundred ducats and I shall bring you to the speech of the pope?" And she sware to him by her faith she would, for otherwise it would cost her more in gifts.

Then on a time should the pope sing mass in his own person at Saint John Lateran, for every four weeks he must sing mass there. And as the pope was at mass then Howleglas drew near to the altar. And when the pope was at the holy sacrament, then turned Howleglas his back to the altar. And that seeing, all the cardinals when mass was done then came to the pope. And they told to His Grace that there stood a fair young man: "all the while that ye were at mass, and heard it devoutly till the time of the elevation. And when that you lifted up the chalice above your head, then turned he his back toward the sacrament of the altar."

Then said the pope: "That is a thing to be looked on, for it is a great doubt whether that man believe well or not. And therefore it is needful for us to send for that man and to examine him what error it was that he held. The cardinals answered: "That were the best." Then the pope sent for Howleglas to his inn and the messenger brought him to the pope.

And when he came before the pope and the cardinals, they began straitly to examine him and they asked of him what was his belief. Then answered Howleglas to the pope: "I believe as a true Christian man ought for to believe. And I believe in Jesus Christ. And I believe in that, that our Holy Mother the Church doth teach me. And I believe as my good hostess doth believe"— and he named her before the pope and all that noble congregation. And then sent the pope a messenger to the inn where that Howleglas was lodged.

And when he was there, he came to the hostess and bad her that she should make her ready, for she must needs go with him to the pope—whereof she had great marvel, and made her ready, and so went with him to the pope. And when she was come before the pope, he asked her what her belief was. And she answered to the pope: "Reverend father, I believe as a true Christian woman should do. For I believe as the Holy Church believes, and also I believe in all that the Holy Church binds me to."

Then said Howleglas: "The same believe I." Then the pope asked him why he turned his back to the holy sacrament when he did minister it. Then said Howleglas to the pope: "Reverend father in God, I thought in my mind when that you lift up the blessed sacrament that I was not worthy it to behold, nor thereon to look, till the time that I was confessed and made clean of all my sins." And then was the pope with that answer marvellously well contented and pleased.

And after that, the pope bad him that he should confess him of his sins and to make him clean thereof. And that said, he gave his benediction to Howleglas and his hostess, and so they twain departed. And shortly after departed the pope with all his cardinals into the palace, and so Howleglas was quit thereof. And then said Howleglas to his hostess: "I must have my hundred ducats that I have earned." And then the woman gave him the hundred ducats, whereof he was glad. And he said to himself that he was the better for that Journey to Rome.

23. *How Howleglas deceived the Jews with dirt*

When Howleglas the great deceiver had been at Rome then came he to the town of Frankford, where a mart or a great market was kept. And as Howleglass went about the market, he spied a young man go with musk of Alexander to sell, that which was well sold and much set by. Then said Howleglas to himself: "I will go with some merchandise for to sell, as well as that young man doth." And he thought in his mind how he might find some practice to get money without labor.

Then thought he in his mind every night what was best to do, for the fleas did bite him and he could not sleep. And he would right gladly have taken them, but he could not. And when that the day began to spring, he arose and walked forth. And as he walked, then spied he by the way a fair fig tree, the which bare goodly fruit.

And then went he and gathered two or three of them and then he said to himself: "This is good for my merchandise—" and brought them with him into Frankford in Portingale,[1] to the place where he was lodged. And he dressed them after his mind. And when he had dressed them, he put them in his arse and tempered them with his dirt, and let them lie thereby him by the space of two or three days that they should not smell too much of dirt.

And in a morning, betimes he arose out of his bed and went to his hostess and hired a little table, and then he went into the market and bought two or three silken cloths. And there in a house he crushed these portingale figs, that had lain so long in his arse, with the silken cloths, like as they had been musk. Then took he his table and went into the market and set up his table. And when it was up, then showed he the portingale figs that he had made, like as they had been musk.

Then came there many merchants of divers lands to him, and they asked him what merchandise he had to sell. And he stood still and gave none of them no answer, whereof they marveled, and so departed. And at the last, there came to him two Jews and they asked him what merchandise he had there to sell. And then answered Howleglas to them and said: "This is a precious thing—for all those that do eat of it, or those that smell to it, they shall say the truth by-and-by."

Then went the Jews to counsel what was best to be done. Then said the oldest Jew of them all: "Me think it is best and most expedient for us to buy that merchandise, for then shall we know when that our Messiah shall come. Therefore I counsel you to buy it, for it shall be to us a great jewel and comfort." And continently[2] they were agreed all for to buy the merchandise of

---

[1] *Portingale:* Portugal
[2] *continently:* at once

Howleglas. And then they returned with right great haste unto Howleglas.

And when they were come, they asked the price of one of the Prophetus that was wrapped in the silk. Then answered Howleglas to the Jews: "Depart from hence and let my merchandise alone, for it is too costly for you to buy. For one of them shall cost you 500 gold gildens, and ye will have it." Then answered the Jews to Howleglas and said: "The price is all too great for us." Then said he: "That I told you before, and therefore if thou will not buy it then depart shortly from hence." And then the Jews, hearing Howleglas speak so sharply to them and made no more count unto them, then they believed him and continently they gave to him 500 gold gildens without speaking of any more words. For he spake so angrily that they were afraid to displease him.

And when they had bought it, they brought it to the principal Jew. And they caused him to aggregate all the Jews both old and young. When they were assembled, then was there one stood upon the scaffold that was called Akipna. And he said that by the might of God they had gotten a Prophetus. And he said he that should have it in his mouth should prophesy the truth. And then he said to the Jews: "By this Prophetus we shall know when our Messiah shall come!" And he commanded them to fast three days, and then should Isaac take it in his mouth and prophesy the truth.

And so he did. And as he had it in his mouth, one that hight [3] Moses and another Isaac, that were the servants of God, they asked him how it savored. And he answered: "I am inspired with the Holy Ghost to prophesy the truth! There must be another of God's servants to have it in his mouth." And so they did. [4]

When he had tasted thereof, he said: "I am inspired with the Holy Ghost! I shall tell you the truth! We are beguiled—for it is no other thing but a turd!" And they tasted . . . and then they knew well that they were deceived.

[3] *hight:* was named
[4] *they did:* they ordered

And forthwith departed Howleglas from thence. And he went toward his own country and made good cheer with good fellows homeward as long as the money would last.

24. *How Howleglas had gotten the parson's horse by his confession*

In Resenburg, in that village, was a parson that had a fair horse and a proper handmaiden which he loved one as the other. Then it fortuned that the Duke of Bronswick on a time saw the horse, and when that he had seen the horse, his mind ran so much on the horse that he must needs have him.

Then upon a time came the Duke and desired the horse oftentimes of the parson, and the parson said him nay. Then was the Duke sorry because he might not have the horse, and he durst not take by force, for he was one of the Council of Bronswick.

And when Howleglas heard that the Duke desired the horse, then said Howleglas to the Duke: "And [1] you will reward me, I shall get you the parson's horse." Then answered the Duke to Howleglas: "I shall give thee my gown of red chamlet,[2] the sleeves set with pearls." Then said Howleglas to the Duke: "I shall bring him, I have no doubt."

So departed Howleglas and he came to the inn where he was well known, and the host said he was welcome. And Howleglas rested there three days, and after that, he made himself sick. Then was he brought to bed sick, that the parson of the town and his maid were so heavy and knew not how to do nor him to help.

And then began he to wax sicker and sicker, and then said the parson to Howleglas: "I counsel you to be shriven and to take your rites of the Holy Church, as it belongeth to a true Christian man." And when Howleglas heard the parson speak to him, then

[1] *And:* if
[2] *chamlet:* a rich cloth of silk and camel hair

said Howleglas to the parson: "I desire you heartfully to be confesssed, for I know myself guilty and a great sinner."

Then the parson examined him under confession right busily. He bad him to remember that he had a soul for to keep, and he preached and teached to him the use of confession. And then showed Howleglas to him part of his mind. And at the last, when he spoke no more, then asked the parson of Howleglas if that he had no more sins in his mind that were great and abominable that he was ashamed to show.

Then answered Howleglas to the parson: "Yes, I have one more and that I dare not confess me of to you, and therefore you must fetch me another priest. For if I should show it unto you, then would ye be angry and out of patience."

Then answered the parson to Howleglas: "The way is far from this place and very foul. Moreover, if it fortuned you in the meanwhile to die, then were we both in great peril and danger. And therefore tell me that sin, and I shall absolve thee thereof—be it never so great and abominable. And if I were angry with you, yet you know I must keep your counsel. And if it be anything that 'longs to me, I forgive you freely—and therefore tell it me." Then longed he more than ever he did.

Then said Howleglas to the priest: "I know well that you will be angry, but I feel me so sore sick that I ween [3] that I shall die, and therefore I shall show it to you quickly." And then he said: "I have lain by your maid, your servant."

Then asked he: "How often have ye lain by her?" And then said Howleglas: "No more than five times." And then the priest thought in his mind: "Therefore the devil break thy neck—" and he gave him absolution shortly, and forthwith he departed from Howleglas and home to his house.

And when he came home, he called his maiden to him and asked her if she had lain by him, and the maid answered to him and said: "That did I never!" Then answered the priest: "Thou liest! For under confession he hath told me that he hath lain by thee more than five times." And then the maid said: "Nay!" And

[3] *ween:* imagine

the priest: "Yes!" And then the priest took a staff in his hand and he beat his maid therewith, that she was both black and blue.

And Howleglas lay in his bed and laughed and said to himself: "Now weeneth the priest to win his horns again of the maid." And in the morning waxed Howleglas hole,[4] and arose and said it was well amended with him. And he asked his hostess and the priest what he had spent in his sickness. And then reckoned the priest he knew not what, for he was so angry in his mind, and the maid also for she was beat for his sake.

And then said Howleglas: "Tell me what is my duty to pay." And the priest answered not a word. And then said Howleglas to him: "Remember you not, Master Parson, that you have disclosed my confession? I shall ride to Haverstadt to the bishop and I shall complain on you—that you descried my confession that I confessed me unto you."

When the priest heard Howleglas speak after that manner, then forgot he his anger and fell on his knees before him, for he thought that he was in more danger than ever he was before. And then he said to Howleglas: "If that you will keep your peace and make no more words hereof, I shall give to you twenty gold guildens, and I shall do as much for you as lies in me for to be done."

Then made Howleglas himself very angry with the parson and said unto him: "If that you would give me an hundred gold guildens, that I should not show, I will not take them for my gown." Then the priest prayed the maid with weeping tears that she would go to Howleglas to entreat him that he should not go to show the bishop—"and bid him ask what he will and he shall have it."

Then went the maid to Howleglas and she showed him what the priest said. And then came Howleglas to the priest and said: "Will you give to me your horse that you love so well, and then shall I keep your counsel? And I tell you plainly, I will have no other thing than that only." And then the priest was more sorrier than ever he was.

[4] *hole:* healed

And he said to Howleglas that he would give to him as much money as he would desire and not to ask his horse. Then said Howleglas: "I will have none other thing but only the horse." And then the parson had lever [5] lose his horse than he would have the bishop to know. Then gave he the horse to Howleglas with ill will.

And then when Howleglas had the horse, then he departed from the parson and was very glad. And then he came toward the Duke and when he was come there, the Duke spied Howleglas and the parson's horse. Then was he very glad. And then brought Howleglas the horse to him, whereof he was very glad. And then gave he the gown of red chamlet to Howleglas and he thanked him greatly for that gift and laughed.

And the priest was very angry for the loss of his horse and oftentimes he beat his maiden therefore, for he said she was the cause thereof. And he beat his maid so oft that at the last, she ran from him, and so he lost both his horse and the maid. And the priest lowered on Howleglas ever after, that loved him so well before.

25. *How Howleglas was hired of a blacksmith*

At Eastland in Rostick dwelleth a smith that hired Howleglas for his man, and when he was hired he put him to the bellows to blow. And when he blew not well, then took the smith the bellows in his hand and blew, and said: "Fellow, do thus: Bear the bellows upright." And then he gave the bellows to Howleglas again.

Then went the smith forthwith into the garden, and then took Howleglas the bellows on his neck [1] and followed after his master with them into the garden where his master was a-shiteing. And

---

[5] *lever:* rather
[1] *on his neck:* on his back

then said Howleglas to his master: "Where shall I leave this bellows, that I may go fetch the other unto you?"

Then answered his master and said: "Good man, what meanest thou? Art ye not well in thy mind? Go take the bellows and bare them where thou had them." He spake fair to Howleglas, and right loath he was to displease him. For every night by the space of eight days long, he called up every night his servants at midnight for to work. Whereof they marveled what he meant, for they were very angry therewith, and one said to the other: "I think our master is not well in his mind, that he rises every night at midnight to work. He was not wont so for to do in times past."

And as they were speaking of this rising together, then said Howleglas to his fellows and asked them if that they would be well content with him and if he asked of his master what was the cause that he did call them up every night at midnight to work. And then answered the servants: "We will not be displeased therewith, but right glad thereof, and well content therewith."

And then said Howleglas to the servants: "I will go to him." And forthwith spake Howleglas to his master and said to him: "Wherefore do ye wake us every night at midnight out of our sleep?" Then answered the smith and said: "That is my manner, that my men the first eight days suffer I not them to sleep but half the night."

Then held Howleglas his peace, and all his fellows, and said no more words. And the next night, the smith called his men at midnight to work. And Howleglas then took the bed and bare it on his back. And when the iron was hot, the master beat it so hard that the sparks flew on the head of Howleglas. Then said his master: "Will not that ungracious fellow arise?" Then came Howleglas with his bed on his back.

And when the master saw the bed on his back he said: "What wilt thou do with the bed? Bear it into the place where thou had it." Then answered Howleglas to his master: "Be ye not angry with me, for this is my manner ever. For when that I have slept the one half of the night, then bear I the bed on my back the other half of the night."

Then began the smith to wax angry and said: "Go bear the bed where thou had it and then go thou above out of my house!" Then answered Howleglas and said: "Master, with a good will." And then he bare the bed up into the place where it was before.

Then when he had borne the bed in his place, then took he a ladder and climbed up to the house top, and there he brake a great hole in the house top, and pulled away the thatching thereof. And he passed through and went over the houses and so went his way from thence, and never came there after.

And as the smith was busy working, he heard a great noise above in the chamber and a great knocking. Then asked he his servants who was above in the chamber that made such a noise. Then answered the men to their master and said: "We know not who is above." Then said the smith: "Then will I go look."

Then left the smith his work and went up into the chamber. And when he was above, he saw all the roof of the chamber was pulled down and alto² cast all about. Then was he angry and wist not what to do for he wist not who had done it. And at the last, he looked up and spied the ladder. Then knew he well that it was Howleglas' deed.

Then came he down and fetched a sword, and he would have run after him to have slain him. Then the servants, seeing the master taking the sword, they held him and asked him what he would do. Then answered he and told how Howleglas had done. Then answered the servants to their master: "Let him go, for he hath done as you bad him. For you bad him go upon the house, and so he hath done as ye may see." And so the smith was content, and then he caused his house to be thatched again.

² *alto:* altogether

26. *How Howleglas was hired of a Shoemaker*

Upon a time served Howleglas a shoemaker. And upon a time the shoemaker had business in the town, and then gave he to Howleglas a hide of leather and bad him that he should cut all the hide. And Howleglas asked him what fashion he should cut them. And the master said: "Little and great, as the swineherd did drive his beasts." And then said Howleglas: "With a good will."

And then departed the cordiner, and then took Howleglas the hide and began to cut the leather for oxen and sheeps' feet, and swine. Then came his master home and came to see what his servant had cut out and to look whether he had cut the leather as he bad him. And when that he had seen that he had cut out his leather all in beasts' claws, then was he angry and said to Howleglas: "Wherefore hast thou marred all my leather and cut it for beasts' feet?"

Then answered he to him and said: "I have done as ye bad me." The master said: "Thou liest, for I bad thee that thou should not mar my leather." Then answered Howleglas to his master and said: "I have done as ye bad me: Ye bad me that I should cut both great and small, as the swineherd driveth out his beasts, and that have I done."

Then answered the cordiner to Howleglas and said: "I meant not that. I meant that ye should have cut out of the hide both great shoes and little shoes." Then answered Howleglas to his master: "If that ye had told me it before, I would have done it with a good will. And I pray you, master, forgive me this and I shall now do it with a good will." And then did his master forgive him, for that time. And then promised Howleglas to his master that he would do that, that he bad him.

Then the next day after, cut Howleglas' master himself the shoes out, both little and great, and gave them to him and he bad him that he should sew the great with the small. And Howleglas said: "With a good will." And then took Howleglas the shoes and put the little shoes into the great shoes and sewed them both together—as his master bad him. And that spied his master and said: "Ye be a good servant! For ye do all things that I bid you!"

Then answered Howleglas and said: "They that do as they be bid, they be worthy to have thanks." Then said the master: "Ye do after my saying and not after my meaning. For I meant that first ye should have sewed a little pair, and after, a great pair." And the master was hasty and took him other leather and said: "Cut me all this leather upon one last." And the master thought no more of the falseness of Howleglas and so he departed to his chamber.

And when he was come home, then remembered he what he had said to Howleglas. Then went he as fast as he could toward the shop whereas Howleglas was. And ere he came there, Howleglas had cut all the leather upon the little last, all for the left foot. Then when his master saw all his leather cut for the left foot, then asked he Howleglas if there belonged not to the left foot a right foot? And he was very angry with him.

Then said Howleglas to his master: "If that ye had told to me before, I would have cut them. But, and it please you, I shall cut as many right shoes unto them." The master said: "I bad thee cut the one with the other." And then answered Howleglas: "Ye bad me cut all upon one last."

Then answered the shoemaker: "If that I should keep you long, you would make me so poor that I must needs go a-begging. But now give me money for my leather that thou hast marred me, and depart thou from hence." Then answered Howleglas to the shoemaker: "The hide of a bull will make two hides." [1] And with those words, he arose and said: "In this house have I been, but I will not come here again—" and so departed he from thence.

[1] *"The hide of a bull . . . hides":* the pun is on "bull" = to make a fool of, to mock.

27. How Howleglas sold turds for fat

And as Howleglas had destroyed much leather of the shoe-maker, whereof the shoemaker was very sorry, and that hearing, Howleglas returned again to the town and came to his master and told him that he had a last [1] of tallow. And he told his master that he should have it good cheap, for to restore him part of the harm that he had done to him before in his leather. And then said the shoemaker: "If it be good, I pray you let me have it before another." And then said Howleglas: "With a good will." And then departed they.

And then went Howleglas to the dung farmer's and made him fill twelve barrels with turds for a little money. And then took he a little tallow, and put it in the barrels four inches thick, as though it had been altogether grease, and closed it so close that it could not stink. (For it was in the winter when there was a great frost that the dirt was fast frozen to the barrel.) And the other six barrels he filled with other tallow or fat more thicker than the other six were—for they were the example of his merchandise.

And when that he had dressed all the barrels, he sent for his master the shoemaker and he asked him if that he would come to see the merchandise. And he said he would. Then within a while came the shoemaker to Howleglas.

And when he was come there, Howleglas made the heads of the best barrels to be broken up. When the cordiner saw the barrels they liked him [2] very well. And then Howleglas asked him how the barrels pleased him and he answered: "Very well." And then asked he the price. And then answered Howleglas: "Ye shall give me no more than four-and-twenty gildens—12 in hand and the other 12 at the year's end." And then was the shoemaker

[1] *last:* load
[2] *they liked him:* he liked them

content, and thought no deceit, and gave to him 12 gildens in hand. And Howleglas received the money and then departed he.

And the cordiner was glad of the bargain and thought that the foresaid harm that he had done him should be restored. And then he hired servants to melt the tallow, and they brought one barrel by the fire. And when the dirt began to wax hot it began to smell. Then said one to the other: "I ween some of us hath beshitten their breeches." And then came the master and bad them make clean their shoes—"For one of you hath trodden in a turd." And then they looked about, but they found nothing.

And then should [3] they have put one of the barrels in the cauldron, then saw they well that it was the barrel that stank, for it was full of turds. And then they left their work and went for to seek Howleglas, but he was gone. And so the shoemaker must suffer the last loss with the first.

28. *How Howleglas served a tailor*

On a time served Howleglas a tailor. And the tailor asked him if he could sew woolen cloth that no man might see the seam. And then said Howleglas yes. And then went Howleglas and sewed under a barrel. Then said his master: "What dost thou now? This is a marvelous sewing!" Then answered Howleglas: "I sew so close [1] that no man can see, as you bad me. Nor I myself see not." Then answered his master: "Good servant, I meant not so. I bad thee sew that every man might see."

And then the third night, the master had labored so sore that he must needs sleep. Then cast he to Howleglas a husbandman's gown and he bad him take a wolf and make it up. And then said Howleglas: "I shall do it." Then went he to bed. Then cut Howleglas the husbandman's gown, and made thereof a wolf

[3] *then should:* when they would
[1] *so close:* the pun is on "close" = secretly

with the head and feet. And when that he had sewed it together, then set he it upon the table with staves.

Then in the morning arose his master and came down, and when he saw the wolf standing upon the table, he was afraid and asked him what he had done. And he said: "Master, I have made a wolf as you bad me." Then said the master: "I meant that you should have made up the russet gown—for a husbandman's gown is called here a wolf."

Then answered Howleglas: "If that I had known that before I would have done so. For I had lever [2] have made a gown than a wolf." And, at the last, was the master content.

And within four days after, watched [3] the master so much that he must needs go to sleep. And there was a coat ready made, but it lacked the sleeves. Then the master took the coat and the sleeves and gave them to Howleglas. And he bad him that he should cast on the sleeves, and he said he would. Then went his master to bed.

And then took Howleglas the coat and hanged it on a balk [4] and set on every side a candle, and stood up, and cast the sleeves at the coat all the night long. And then arose the tailor and that spied Howleglas, and he cast the sleeves, more faster than ever he did before, at the coat.

And that espied well the tailor, and said: "What foolish touches be those that you do there?" And then answered Howleglas very angrily: "This is no foolish touch, for I have stood all the night casting the sleeves at the coat, and they will not abide thereon. And now I see it is but lost labor."

Then said the master to Howleglas: "It is my fault, for I weened that ye would have understood me better, for I meant you should have sewed on the sleeves on the coat." Then said Howleglas to his master: "The devil take you! For if ye had said so to me before, I might have sewed on the sleeves and have gone

---

[2] *lever:* rather
[3] *watched:* stayed awake
[4] *balk:* tie beam (ceiling)

to sleep. But now, master, go you and sew all the day long, and I will go sleep."

And then answered the tailor: "And have I hired you to sleep?" And thus began they to chide. And, as they were thus chiding, the tailor bad him pay for his candles that he had burned that night. And then Howleglas spake never a word more, but took all his clothes and went his way and came no more there.

29. *How Howleglas through his subtle deceits deceived a wine drawer in Lubeck*

On a time came Howleglas to Lubeck where is very strait Justice, and the while that Howleglas was there abiding, he heard tell of a wine drawer that was in a lord's cellar that was very proud and presumptuous. And it was said that there was no man that could deceive him, nor pass him in wisdom—and there was none of all the lords that loved him. Then thought Howleglas in his mind how he might deceive him.

Then upon a time took Howleglas two pots—one of water and the other empty—and he hid the empty pot that no man saw it. And he came to the cellar and gave the wine drawer the empty pot, and bad him fill the pot with wine, and so he did. And when it was full, he brought it up to Howleglas, and then he looked aside and, in the meanwhile, Howleglas set the pot of water in the place of wine, and hid the pot of wine.

And then asked he the wine drawer what he should pay. And the drawer said: "Ten miten." [1] Then said Howleglas: "The wine is too dear for me. I have but eight miten." Then was the drawer angry and said: "Will ye set another price on the wine than the lords have set?" Then said Howleglas: "I have no more

---

[1] *miten:* quarter-farthing

money, and I shall not have it, so then take your wine again for I knew it not before."

Then was the wine drawer very angry, and he took the pot with the water and bare it down into the cellar, and poured out the water into the vessel—he weened it had been the wine—and came and gave Howleglas the pot and said: "Make ye me sell wine and ye have no money to pay for it! I ween ye be a fool." And then said Howleglas: "Ye be beguiled of a fool." And with that word he went his way with the pots.

And then the drawer, mistrusting Howleglas for the words that he said, took a sergeant and overtook him and fetched him. And then they found that he had two pots under the mantle. Then took they Howleglas and 'peached him for a thief and brought him to the prison.

And then said some that he had deserved to be hanged. And some said that it was done for the nonce to deceive the wine drawer, and that was but well done, for he should have seen thereto before—for he said daily that no man should beguile him. But they that loved not Howleglas said that he was a thief and that he should be hanged. And then was Howleglas brought before the Judge, and he gave sentence that he should be hanged.

And on the morrow was he brought unto the gallows for to be hanged. For they that loved him not would fain have seen justice done on him. And there were gathered many of the town to see Howleglas suffer death. But the Lords of Lubeck were sorry for him—for some weened that he could do witchcraft, that he thereby might be delivered.

And as he was led toward the gallows, he lay all still as though he had been dead. And when he came under the gallows then desired he to speak with the Lords. And when the Lords were come, he fell upon his knees and he prayed them that they would grant him a boon. And the Lords said: "Thou wouldst desire thy pardon." Then said Howleglas: "That would I not ask, life nor money—nor it shall not cost you one penny."

Then all the Lords of Lubeck went to the other side of the gallows and there they laid their heads together, and there they rehearsed his words again. And they agreed to grant him his petition. That done, they came to him and they bad him ask what he would, save those words spoken of before to be except. And Howleglas thanked the Lords and said: "I pray you that every one of you give me your hands thereof." And they altogether gave him their hands, so that all the Lords had granted him both with word and hand.

Then said Howleglas to the Lords: "Because I know you be faithful of your words, I shall show to you my boon." And then he said: "This is my boon: That every Lord of Lubeck do come and kiss my arse when that I have hanged on the gallows by the space of three days long—with his mouth in the morning fasting—and the borough master first and all the Lords after in order."

Then answered the Lords to Howleglas and said that his desire was an unmannerly boon for to be asked. And then said Howleglas to the Lords of Lubeck: "I know the Council of Lubeck, so sure of their promise that they will hold that, that they have promised me both with hand and mouth."

Then went the Lords again to counsel. Then said they one to the other: "This thing that he asketh of us, it is unlawfully asked—for it were a great shame for us all that we that be the greatest lords of the town should come and kiss his arse. Better it were for to give him his pardon and let him go his way, for it is but a small fault that he hath done." Then agreed all the Lords and said that it was best for to do.

Then the Lords called the sergeants, and they bad them to unbind Howleglas and to let him go at large, for all they had granted him his pardon. And then they unloosed Howleglas. And when Howleglas was at large, he thanked the Lords. And then departed he from Lubeck and never came there after.

30. *How Howleglas became a maker of spectacles and how he could find no work in no land where he came*

On a time the senators of Rome had great discord among themselves which of all the lords should be Emperor. And at the last was the Earl of Supplembrough King of Romans and Emperor of Rome. But there were many other that looked for it. So when he was made, he lay six weeks long before the town of Frankford abiding there for all other lords to torment, where was a great company assembled.

And this hearing Howleglas, he thought in his mind to go thither, and so he did. And there he thought to get some gift, and [1] it were no more but the Emperor's silver harness. And as Howleglas passed by Frankford, he met with the Bishop of Taer. And because he was clothed adventure-like, he asked him what he was. Then answered Howleglas: "I am a spectacle maker come out of Braband, and I can find no work."

Then said the Bishop: "Methink your craft should be better daily, for the people the longer they live the less sight they have. Therefore your craft should be the better." And then said Howleglas to the Bishop: "My lord, you say truth. But there is one thing that destroyed our craft. And if you will take no displeasure, I shall show it to you." And then the Bishop bad him say what he would.

And then said he: "This destroyeth our craft: that such great lords as you be—kings, dukes, earls, lords, bishops, knights, lawyers, and governors of lands and towns—all these look through their fingers and not with spectacles. They were wont to study in the old time the right, and then behooved the men many spectacles. And also the priests were wont to study and read their service, but now they use no spectacles at all. And by this manner is our craft destroyed and nought set by. And by heads

[1] *and:* if

of the country, poor men of the country learn all to look through their hands, that they be almost as cunning as the heads of the country."

Then the Bishop understood the text but not the gloss, and he spake to Howleglas and said: "Come with me to Frankford and I shall give unto thee my harness or clothing." And then was Howleglas very glad, and he went with the Bishop to Frankford where the Emperor was chosen. And when their triumph was done, the Bishop gave him that, that he promised him. And then was he glad that he went with the Bishop, and so he returned again to Sassen.

31. *How Howleglas was hired of a merchant to be his cook*

At Heldersem dwelled a merchant that on a time went walking without the town, and as he walked he found Howleglas lying on a green hill. Then asked the merchant Howleglas what he was. Howleglas answered under his covered falseness: "I am a cook and without a master." Then said the merchant: "If you will be a good servant I will hire you and give unto you wages. I have a cook at home, but my wife complaineth on him always." Then promised Howleglas the merchant to be true to him.

Then asked the merchant his name. Then answered Howleglas: "My name is Bartholomeus." Then said the merchant: "That name is all too long. Your name shall be Dole." Then said Howleglas: "I hold me contented therewith." Then said the merchant: "Dole, my man, now let us go gather some herbs for young chickens, for tomorrow I must have guests to dinner—" and then went they home to his place together.

And when the merchant's wife saw Howleglas, she asked her husband: "What shall we do with this man. Ween you that our bread moulds?" Then said the merchant: "Be content, wife. This shall be your man, for he is a cook." Then called he his man and said: "Dole, take a basket and follow me to the flesh shambles." [1] And so he did.

And when they were there, the merchant bought meat for to roast. And when he came home, he called his man and said: "Dole, tomorrow lay the meat to the fire and roast it coldly that ye burn it not." And Howleglas said he would. And then he arose in the morning and brought the meat by the fire, and he took the meat that he should roast and put it on the spit, and bare it down into the cellar. And he laid it between two barrels of beer that it should lie cold enough and burn not.

And because the merchant should have guests, he came home before to see whether that his meat was well roasted or not. And when he came home he called Dole and asked him if that the meat was ready. And Howleglas answered: "Ye, master—all save the roasting." "Where hast thou done it?" "Beneath in the cellar, between two barrels, for in all the house could I not find so cold a place to lay it in for burning."

The merchant said: "Is it not roasted?" And Howleglas said: "Nay, for I did as ye bad me—I laid it cold enough, for I knew not the time that you would have it roasted." And as they were talking came in the guests, and the merchant told to his guests how that Howleglas had served him, and they laughed thereat. But his wife was not content therewith and right gladly she would have been rid of him, and very angry she was because of that touch.

Then said the merchant to his wife: "Be contented at this time, for tomorrow I must to Haller and he shall wait on me. And when I shall come home again, then shall I put him away from hence." And then went the merchant with his guests to dinner and made good cheer. And at night called the merchant his man and said: "Dole, make the wagon ready, for tomorrow I am in thought I and my priest to take our journey to Haller, and grease it that it may go trim."

And then went Howleglas and greased the wagon within and without. And in the morning went the merchant and the priest

[1] *flesh shambles:* meat market

to the wagon, and rode their way. And by the way, the priest laid his hand on the rails of the cart, and they made his hands all greasy. And then he looked better and both the merchant and the priest were all arrayed with grease.

Then they called Howleglas and they bad him see. And very angry they were with him. And in the meantime came there a man of the country with a load of straw, and then they bought part of his straw and dressed their wagon therewith for soiling [2] of their clothes. And then they went unto the wagon again. Then said the merchant all angrily: "Go, drive it under the gallows!"

And as he was a little further, he spied a gallows and thither drove he the wagon under the gallows. And when it was under the gallows, he made the wagon to stand still and he untied their horse. Then said the merchant: "What will you now do?" Then said Howleglas: "Tarry you here all night, for you bad me to drive you under the gallows."

And when they saw that they were under the gallows, the priest laughed. But the merchant was very angry and bad him to drive forthright, and never to stand still. Then said Howleglas he would. Then pulled he out a pin that was in the wagon that held it fast to the horse, and drove the horse forth, and he left them under the gallows.

Then the merchant seeing that, he leaped out of the wagon and the priest with him, and they ran after him. And at the last, they overtook him and then the merchant drew his sword and would have smitten him, but the priest would not suffer him. And then made he fast the horse again and so drove the journey to an end.

When the merchant was come home, his wife asked how he fared and how he liked his man. He answered: "Not of the best." Then he called Howleglas and he bad him tarry there that night and in the morning to depart from thence. For he said he was but a beguiler and a deceiver wheresoever he went. Then said Howleglas: "Good master, that shall I do."

And then arose Howleglas early in the morning. And as he was

[2] *for soiling:* to protect from soiling

up the merchant said: "Eat and drink your belly full, and rid the house of you, that I find you not here when that I come again, for I must to church. And when I return, if I find you here, stand to that, that shall befall." And Howleglas held his peace and spake never a word to him. And then the merchant went to church.

Then he began for to rid all the household stuff and bare it into the street. Then came word unto his master to the church that all his household stuff stood in the street. Then came the merchant home and saw that it was Howleglas that had borne out all his stuff. He asked his man why he did so, and Howleglas said: "I did as you bad me, for ye bad me that I should rid your house, and so I have of all your stuff that ye have."

Then said the merchant to Howleglas: "Depart from hence and come no more here. I give thee warning, for here is nobody that thanks thee for thy labor." And then departed Howleglas his way. And so was the merchant fain to carry in his gear again that Howleglas had borne out.

32. *How Howleglas was desired to dinner*

In Lunenborough dwelled a flute maker that knew vagabonds by sight. And on a time it fortuned him to spy Howleglas, to whom he said: "Tomorrow I desire you to dine with me." Then Howleglas thanked him and he said he would. And then departed the flute maker.

And on the morrow at noon, Howleglas went to the pipe-maker's house. And when he was there, the doors were shut. And he tarried till noon was past, and then he knew well that he was greatly deceived. And so he returned home again.

And on the morning, as he walked in the market, he spied the pipe-maker and then went he to him and thanked him for his dinner. And he said: "When ye bid a body to dinner, ye shut all your doors." And the pipe-maker said: "I bad you come to dinner." Then said Howleglas: "Your doors were shut." Then laughed the pipe-maker and said: "Go to my house before and I shall come after to dinner, for ye shall find both roast and sodden." [1]

And then departed Howleglas to the pipe-maker's house, and there he found all true as the pipe-maker had told him. And then said he to the pipe-maker's wife: that she should go as fast as she could to her husband, for he said that he had a great sturgeon given him. And he said that he would turn the spit till that she came again.

The woman said: "Good Howleglas, keep the house till that I come again, and let nobody in." Then departed the woman with her maid towards her husband as fast as she could, and met with him by the way. And when he saw her, he asked her whither she went so fast. And she said, to help him. For she said that Howleglas had told her that "ye had a sturgeon given you, and he said that ye bad that we should come and help you—for it was so great that you were not able to bear it."

Then was the man angry, and said: "Know ye not well that Howleglas is such a mocker and a deceiver?" Then went he home with his wife. And when he came home he knocked at the door and Howleglas said: "Let be your knocking! for the hostess hath charged me that I should let no guest in till dinner be done."

Then went the host to his neighbors and tarried there till Howleglas had dined. And when Howleglas had dined, then he opened the door, and the pipe-maker came with all his folks. And when he was within, he said to Howleglas that it was no honesty for a guest to shut his hostess out of doors. And in this manner he served the host and his hostess.

[1] *sodden:* boiled

33. *How Howleglas won a piece of cloth of a man of the country*

Howleglas would ever fare well and make good cheer, but he would not work. Then on a time came he to Ossem, to a goodly company of men of the country. And as he walked, he espied one man alone with a green cloth on his arm. Then imagined he in his mind how he might get the cloth.

So he came to him and he asked him where he was dwelling. And then the husband told him. And then departed Howleglas from him. And continently [1] he met with a shottish [2] priest and another knave, and he said to them: "I desire you to help me, and I shall give you for your labor." And they said they would.

Then said Howleglas: "When I call you to record to know what color yonder cloth is, ye shall say blue. I will go before and you come after." Then went he to the husbandman, and he asked him how he sold his blue cloth. Then said the husband-man that it was green and not blue.

"I hold [3] 20 gildens against thy cloth that it is blue."

Then said the husbandman: "I hold you." "It is done," said Howleglas, "and the first man that comes hereby shall be the judge thereto." "Agreed," said the husbandman.

And then made Howleglas a sign to the men that he had hired, and they came. Then said the husbandman: "We two strive [4] what color this cloth is. I pray you, break our strife." Then the fellow said: "It is fair blue cloth." Then said the husbandman: "Ye be too false for me to meddle with, for it is made betwixt you two to deceive me."

Then said Howleglas: "Cause that ye say we be agreed, let him go. Here cometh a priest. Will ye be contented what he sayeth?" And the man of the country said yes.

[1] *continently:* very soon
[2] *shottish:* good-for-nothing
[3] *hold:* bet
[4] *strive:* argue

Then came the priest by. Then said Howleglas: "I pray you to tell us what color this cloth is." The priest said: "Ye see well enough. What need you to ask me?" The husbandman said: "I know the color of the cloth well enough, but these two men say it is another color and therefore we strive."

Then said the priest: "What have I to do with your striving?" Then said the husbandman: "I pray you, sir, depart us of our striving." Then said the priest: "I can see no other but it is a fair blue."

And then said the husbandman: "And ye were not a priest, in faith, ye did lie. For ye be three false men. But sithen ye be a priest, I must believe you." And then gave he Howleglas the cloth and went his way. Then did Howleglas with his two fellows clothe them with the husbandman's cloth against the winter. But the good poor man prayed to God many a time and oft, that the devil might take them all three. For the poor man was the worse all the days of his life after that great loss.

34. *How Howleglas gave twenty gildens to twelve poor men for Christ's love*

On a time came Howleglas to Hanover, where he did many virtuous things. On a time rode Howleglas without the town, and as he rode he met with twelve blind men, to whom he said: "Whither will ye go?" The blind men, hearing that he was on horseback, they put off their caps for they weened that he had been a great gentleman, and said: "We have been at a dole [1] of a rich man that died yesterday in the town."

Then said Howleglas: "I take great thought for you, how you shall do this winter. For methink you shall freeze to death before the winter be done." And then he said: "Hold, here is 20 gildens, and return again all you to the place where that I was

---

[1] *at a dole:* living on charity

lodged—" and he named his host. And he bad them make good cheer till winter were done.

And then they thanked him, for they thought that he had given them money. But he did not. And then departed they to the place whither he sent them. And they thought that some of the company had the money. And when that they came to the inn, they said to the hostess that, by the way as they went, they met with a good man that gave them 20 gildens for God's sake—"and he bad us come hither, and make good cheer therefore, for he said that he had been lodged here. And for his sake we should have good cheer."

When the host heard that they had money, he took them in and made them good cheer. And when that their 20 gildens were spent, then said the host to them: "Now will ye reckon, good brethern? For now the 20 gildens be spent." The blind men said: "We be contented to pay you." And then spake one of the blind men and said: "He that hath 20 gildens pay our host."

And then said the one to the other: "I have not the 20 gildens." "Nor I have not the 20 gildens." And then some sat and clawed their heads, and some clawed their arms. And then they knew that they were deceived.

Then thought the host in his mind: "What shall I do with them? Shall I let them go, that they spend me no more money? Nay, not so." Then shut he the blind men in the stable, and brought to them hay and straw.

And when that Howleglas thought that all the money was spent, then came he riding into the same inn where the blind men were. And he had changed his clothing that they should not know him, and so entered into the inn where the blind men were. And he led his horse into the stable where the poor men were. After he had set up his horse, he came to his host and asked his host wherefore that he had kept the blind men in the stable so fast shut in. And he asked him what harm they had done to him.

Then said the host: "I would that they were together in the water so that I had my costs paid me." And then he told him all the matter. And then said Howleglas: "And [2] you had a bor-row [3] would you let them go?" And the host said: "Yes, with a good will." Then said Howleglas: "I will go see if I can find any borrow for them."

Then went he to the curate of the church and said: "Master Parson, I have an host that this night was taken with the fiend. I desire you for to help him." The curate said: "With a good will. But you must tarry two or three days, for it may not be done in haste." "Well," said Howleglas, "that is well said, but I will go fetch his wife that she may hear what you say." And the priest said: "I shall tell to her the same that I told to you without fail."

And then went Howleglas home to his host and he told them that he had found a borrow and that it was the parson of the church—"and let your wife go with me and she shall hear him speak the same that he hath said to me." And then was his host glad, and he sent his wife with Howleglas to the curate.

And when they were come to the curate, Howleglas said to him: "Master Parson, here is the wife of the man that I spake of to you. Now tell her the same that you have said to me." And the curate said: "With a good will." Then said he to the woman: "Tarry a day or two, and I shall help your husband well." And then was the woman glad and returned home again with Howle-glas.

And when she came home, she told her husband what the curate said, whereof the host was glad. And he went unto the stable and let the blind men loose, and they went their way. And then Howleglas reckoned with his host, and so departed from thence.

And when the third day came, then went the woman to the priest and she asked him twenty gildens that the blind men had spent. The curate asked her: "Hath your husband that [which] ye told to me?" And the woman said: "No." Then said the curate: "That is the false devil that would have the money."

---

[2] *And:* if
[3] *borrow:* a pledge or bondsman

Then said she: "What false devil meanest thou? Give me my money for my costs."

Then said the curate to the woman: "It was told me that your husband was taken with the false devil. Bring him hither and I shall help him thereof, by the grace of God." Then said the woman to the priest: "Such beguilers find I many. Now you should pay me for my costs—you bring to me a back reckoning and you say my husband is taken with the devil—and that you shall know shortly." And then she ran to her husband and told him how the priest said to her.

And when the host heard those words he was angry and took the spit with the roast that lay at the fire, and ran to the priest's chamber. And when the curate spied him he was afraid and called the neighbors to help him. And he made a sign of the holy cross before him and he cried for help to take that man that was so beset with the devil.

Then said the host: "Thou priest, pay me my money!" And the priest gave him no answer. Then would the host have run through him with the hot spit, but the neighbors went between them and departed them, and they held the host still with great pain from Master Parson.

But as long as the host lived, he asked his money of the priest for the costs of the blind men. But the priest answered to him that he owed him nought, and nought he would pay him—but said: "And you be taken with a devil, I shall help you thereof." But never after, loved one the other.

35. *How Howleglas feared his host with a dead wolf*

In Eastleven dwelled an inn-holder that was very spiteful and mocking. And he praised greatly his boldness. Upon a time it befell in the winter season when there had been a great snow, Howleglas came riding with others, three merchants, from Sasson to Eastleven. And it was very late ere they came there. And when they were come they entered into the inn that the man kept.

Then said their host angrily: "Where have you been so late! It is no time now to take your inn." Then they answered: "Be ye not angry, for we have been hunted with a wolf in the snow. We could not escape till now." Then the host mocked them because they four were hunting of one wolf, and said: "If there came ten wolves to me in the field, I would have slain them every one—" and mocked the merchants till they went to bed. And Howleglas sat by the fire and heard all together.

Then should they go to bed, and it fortuned that Howleglas and the merchants should lie in one chamber. And when they were in the chamber together they took counsel together how they might stop their host of his mocking. Then said Howleglas: "Our host is full of mocking. Let me alone, I shall pay him well enough that he shall not mock us no more." Then promised the merchants to Howleglas to pay all his costs and give him more money for his labor. Then said Howleglas: "Do your journey and business of your merchandise and when ye have it, come again and lodge at this inn, and ye shall find me here. And then we shall make our host that he shall mock no more."

And then arose the merchants in the morning and called the host and paid him for their costs and Howleglas' also. Then they took their horses and departed from thence. And when they were passed a little, he cried to the merchants: "Take heed that the wolf bite you not—" in mockage. They thanked their host because he gave them warning before.

And as they rode, Howleglas found a wolf that was frozen to the death and that he took up and put in a bag and hid it before him. And then they returned again to Eastleven, to that inn where they were lodged before. And he kept the wolf so close [1] that no man knew thereof.

And when the night was come and that they sat all at supper, then the host began to laugh at them, and he reasoned against

[1] *close:* secretly

their hardiness and against the wolf. Then said they: "So it fortuned at that time you said that you would slay ten wolves, but first I would see you kill one." And then said the host: "That should I do alone." And thus they jested till they went to bed.

And Howleglas held his peace till that he and the merchants went above all together in the chamber. And then said Howleglas to the merchants: "Friends, let me now begin to work, and wake you a little while." And then went the host and all his folk asleep. Then went he privily into the chamber and he fetched the dead wolf that was stiff frozen, and dressed him with sticks and put two children shoes in his mouth, and made him stand as though he had been alive. And then left he the wolf standing in the hall and he came again into the chamber to the merchants.

And when he was above, he and the merchants called their host. And their host asked them what they would have. Then answered they to him that they would have some drink for they had so great thirst that they must needs drink. "Let your maid or man bring us some and we will pay for it tomorrow."

Then waxed the host angry and said: "This is the Sasson's manner, for to drink both day and night." And then he called his maid and bad her that she should give the merchants to drink. And then the maid rose, and as she went to light a candle, she saw the wolf with two shoes in his mouth. Then she was afraid and ran to the garden for she thought that he had eaten both the children.

Then called they again. Then called the host his man and bad him arise and bear the Sassons drink. Then arose he and lighted a candle, for he weened that the maid had slept still. Then looked he aside and saw the wolf stand. He was afraid and he thought that the wolf had eaten the maid, and let fall the candle and ran into the cellar.

Then called Howleglas and the merchants the third time and prayed that he himself would bring them some drink, for they said there came nobody—or else give them a candle and they would draw it themselves. Then arose the host himself, for he weened that his man and his maid were fallen asleep again. And then lighted he a candle, and when that he had done, he looked aside and spied the wolf. And he was so afraid that he fell unto the ground and then arose he and cried to the merchants—and he prayed them for to come help him, for there was a wolf that had eaten both his man and his maid.

And this heard the maid in the garden and the man in the cellar, and come to help their master—and the merchants also. And Howleglas laughed at this hardy man that would have slain ten wolves, and he was made afraid of one dead wolf. And when the host saw that it was done in mockage then was he ashamed, and he wist not what for to say. And then left he his boasting and jesting, and went to bed again.

And on the morrow it was known through the town, whereof the host was sore ashamed. And then in the morning arose the merchants and paid their costs and Howleglas' also, and rode their way. And then never after praised the host his manhood.

36. *How Howleglas flayed a hound and gave the skin for half his dinner*

On a time came Howleglas very late into an inn where the host was not at home, but only the hostess. This hostess had a bloodhound the which she loved very well. And as she had nothing to do, she took the hound on her lap and played with him, and Howleglas sat by the fire drinking a pot of beer.

And the hostess had taught her hound to drink beer in a dish, and as Howleglas was drinking of his beer, the hound fawned on him and wagged his tail on Howleglas. And then said the hostess: "Give the hound some drink in his dish, for that is the meaning." And Howleglas said: "With a good will." And then gave he the hound often to drink, and he gave him also part of all thing that was on the table, that the hound was as full as he might be, and then went he and laid him down, stretching him by the fire.

And within a while Howleglas had eaten enough, and then asked the hostess if she would reckon and she said yes. Then asked he his hostess if she had had a guest that had eaten her meat and drinketh her drink should pay nothing, "Would ye be content therewith?" Then weened the hostess that he had meant himself and thought not of her hound. Then said she to him: "Good friend, here is no man that eateth here but he payeth money or a pledge."

Howleglas said: "I am content therewith to pay my part, and the other must pay his part." And then went the hostess into her chamber for to do her business. And then took Howleglas the hound under his gown and went unto the stable and flayed off his skin. And then came he again to his hostess that sat by the fire, and he had the hound's skin under his gown. And then called Howleglas for a reckoning.

When she had reckoned, he gave her half thereof. Then asked she him who should give to her that other half. Then said Howleglas: "Chose you.[1] Here is my part. Ye had another guest that went away and paid nothing, and he ate and drank as well as I did. Let him pay the other half of the money." Then said the hostess: "What guest was that? And what pledge had he to give?"

Then said Howleglas: "The best coat that he had on." Then drew he out the dog's skin and said to his hostess: "Here is the best coat that the guest hath." And when she saw her dog's skin, then spake she very angrily and cursedly: "Wherefore have ye flayed my hound?" Then said Howleglas: "Let alone your banning and your cursing in this manner, for it is your fault—for ye bad to me that I should give to your hound meat and drink, and I told to you that the guest had no money. And ye said that ye would not trust him but that ye would have a pledge or money to pay for his costs. So have I brought to you the best coat that he hath for a pledge."

Then was the hostess more angry and said: "Go out of my

[1] *Chose you:* i.e., suit yourself; whoever you please

house shortly, and never come here more within my doors." Then said Howleglas: "Shall I go out of your doors? Nay, but I shall ride out of your doors." Then took he his saddle and saddled his horse, and 'lighted on him, and ere he parted from thence he said to his hostess: "Keep well your pledge that ye may have your money. And within a while I shall come unto you unbidden, and if I drink not of your drink then need I not to pay nothing." And then departed he from thence and rode his way.

37. *How Howleglas served the same hostess another time and how he lay on a wheel*

Within a while after came Howleglas to Stafford in the same inn where he had been lodged before, and he had done [1] other clothes on because that his hostess should not know him. And when he was come into the inn, he spied a wheel lie thereby and then he alighted and came and laid him thereon, and bad his hostess good morrow. And he asked her if she heard any news of Howleglas. And she said: "Nay, what should I hear of him? I can not suffer him to be named."

Howleglas said: "What harm hath he done to you that ye may not hear speak of him? He is a knave indeed. I never heard tell yet that he came in any place but ere he departed he did some shrewd touch."

Then said the hostess: "That is truth. For it is but eight days agone that (for the great cheer that I made to him) like a traitor he flayed my hound and he gave me the skin for my meat and drink."

Then said Howleglas: "That was a knavish touch." And the woman said: "Therefore shall he come to evil end." Then said Howleglas: "Is this all his reward? It is not three hours agone sithen [2] I saw him lie upon a wheel."

---

[1] *done:* put
[2] *sithen:* since

Then said the hostess: "If I had known that, I should have beat him with a staff that I should have broken some of his ribs, for that he hath done to me." And then arose Howleglas and said: "Let be your anger, for when I spake to you he lay upon the wheel. And now, adew, I come not here again."

38. *How Howleglas set his hostess upon the hot ashes with her bare arse*

As Howleglas was come from Rome, he came to an inn where his host was not at home. And when he was within, he asked his hostess if that she knew not Howleglas, and the hostess said: "Nay, but I hear say that he is a false deceiver and beguiler." Then said Howleglas: "Wherefore say ye so? Ye know him not." Then said the hostess: "That is truth. But I have heard speak much of his unhappiness."

Then said Howleglas: "Good woman, he hath done to you never no harm. Wherefore slander ye him for the words of other people?" The hostess said: "I say no other of him than the people do. For I have heard him be spoken of, of many of my guests that have lodged here." Then held Howleglas his peace, and spake no more till in the morning.

And then spied he abroad the hot ashes on the hearth, and then took he the hostess out of her sleep and set her thereon on her bare arse. And so was his hostess well burned. Then said he to her: "Now may ye say boldly that ye have seen the false deceiver and beguiler Howleglas."

Then cried the hostess for help and lowered upon him. Then went he out of her doors and said to her: "Should not men correct and reprove slanderers and backbiters that say it of men and never saw them—nor never had done harm to them? Yes, it is a charitable thing to do." And then took he his horse and departed from thence.

39. *How Howleglas served a hollander with a roasted apple*

Upon a time came Howleglas to Antwerp to an inn where was many hollanders merry. And he brought with him two eggs which he roasted for to eat, for he was sick and could eat no flesh. And this seeing, a hollander said: "Ye, Thom of the country, will not your hostess meat serve you but ye must bring meat with you? Ween ye that ye should have no meat here?" And with those words, he took the eggs and supped them up.

And when he had done, he gave to Howleglas the shells and said to him: "Hold, here is their box. The relics be gone." And then laughed all the guests at that touch. And Howleglas also.

And in the evening fetched Howleglas a fair apple and cut out all the core thereof and put therein a strong purgation, and roasted the apple in the fire. And then took Howleglas the apple and cut it in pieces upon his trencher,[1] and strewed thereon powder of ginger, and set it upon the table, and went from the table as though he would have gone and fetched more.

And as soon as Howleglas had turned his back, the hollander took the apple and ate it in a great haste. And by-and-by he fell to parbraking[2] and cast up all that was within him, and he was very sick thereof—that the host and all the guests weened that he should have died of the apple.

And then said Howleglas to the guests: "Be not afraid of him, for it is a little purgation that I have given him. He was too hasty to eat the apple so soon. I should have warned him thereof, for the roasted apple could not suffer the raw eggs in his maw, but that they must needs come out again."

And then the guests made good cheer and laughed. And when the purgation had wrought all that it would, and that the hollander was amended, he said to Howleglas: "Roast and eat whatsoever ye will, for I will never eat with you more."

[1] *trencher:* dish
[2] *parbraking:* vomiting

40. *How Howleglas made a woman that sold earthen pots to smite them all in pieces*

Upon a time took Howleglas his journey to Bremen, to the Bishop that loved him well, for at all times he did some mad touch whereat he made the Bishop to laugh. Then on a time as the Bishop and Howleglas were a-walking, the Bishop desired of him that he would do some merry jest. But Howleglas went talking to himself as though he had said his paternoster, and answered not the Bishop.

But at the last he said to him: "I pray thee to say some news." [1] And he said he would, but he prayed the Bishop to tarry a while and he gave him silence. And in the meanwhile went Howleglas to a woman that hath earthen pots to sell in the market, the which pots he bought on a condition that when he made a sign to her then she should smite all the pots in pieces. And she granted to him, and then he paid her and returned to the Bishop.

And when he was come, the Bishop asked him where he had been. And Howleglas said: "I was at church." He said: "My lord, go with me unto the market." And so he did. And when they were there Howleglas said to the Bishop: "See you the woman with the earthen pots? I shall stand here still by you and speak never a word, and yet shall I make her to smite her pots all in pieces."

Then said the Bishop: "I hold thee [2] thirty gildens that thou shalt not do it." And Howleglas did hold the thirty gildens with the Bishop. And then went they into the town house and there they tarried. And then cried he and called the woman, and at the last made he the sign to her that was made between them. And then took she a staff and smited upon the pots so long till

---

[1] *news:* novelties, jokes
[2] *I hold thee:* I bet you

that she had broken them every one, so that the Bishop and all they that were in the market place did laugh thereat.

And as the Bishop was come home, then called he Howleglas aside unto him and said: "Tell me shortly what thing ye did to the woman that ye made her take a staff and smite all the pots to pieces, and then shall I give unto you the thirty gildens." Then said Howleglas to the Bishop: "My lord, I did it not with sorcery nor witchcraft, but I had paid the woman before for her pots and we were both agreed."

And then laughed the Bishop thereat and gave unto Howleglas thirty gildens. And he made him to swear on a book that he should not show nobody that thing and he said he would give him a fat oxe. Then said Howleglas: "That thing shall I do with a good will and speak never a word." And then departed Howleglas from thence and he let the Bishop do what he would.

[Then went the Bishop to the nobles and told them that he would show them the thing Howleglas did to the woman that made her take a staff and smite all the pots to pieces, if that they would each give him a fat oxe.[3]]

And then went every man home and fetched a fat oxe and brought it unto the Bishop. And when that they were all come in, they stood talking with the Bishop and then came Howleglas riding by them. And he saw all the oxen standing there. Then he said unto the Bishop: "These gains is half mine." Then said he to Howleglas: "Will you not hold that thing that ye have promised me?" And then said Howleglas: "Yes, for another fat oxe."

Then gave the Bishop unto Howleglas a fat oxe, and he bad him that he should depart, and so he did and left the Bishop with all his lords talking. Then called the Bishop all the nobles together. And when that they were come, he said to them: "Now shall I show unto you all this great cunning of the breaking of the pots openly."

Then said he to them: "This is it—Howleglas had been before with that woman that sold the earthen pots in the market,

---

[3] [*Then . . . oxe*]: This is a reconstruction of a corrupt passage.

and he had paid her for all the pots. And he bad her then, when he should make a sign to her, then should she smite the earthen pots in pieces, and this was the cunning that Howleglas did."

Then were the nobles ashamed and angry in their mind with the Bishop, but they durst not speak one word, but clawed their heads, when they saw their fat oxen before their face that they had given to the Bishop for that foolish deed. But after, they comforted themselves again and said: "He is our lord and master, and if that he had asked the oxen for nought, we would have given them to him."

And Howleglas had for his part one of the fat oxen, whereof he was glad and the other was, for that gift amounted to twenty fat oxen.

41. *How Howleglas brake the stairs that the monks should come down on to matins, and how they fell down into the yard*

Howleglas, as he waxed old and feeble and had been in many countries, then began he to take a little repentance on him, and thought to go to be a religious person. Then took he his way to Mariendall, and when he came there he went into the Abbey to the Abbott.

And when he came to him, he desired of the Abbott that he might be a brother in the place and to have a place. And he promised the Abbott that he would leave in the Abbey all the money that he had. Then said the Abbott to him, and jested with him, for he was a merry jester, that he should have a place but he must have an office therewith for to do some labor—"For ye see well that all my brethren do that thing that I command them, and take the office that is given unto them, and be content therewith."

Then said Howleglas to the Abbott: "Whatsoever it please you to bid me do, I shall do it with a good will." Then said the Abbott: "The labor is not great that I shall give unto you. For ye shall be porter, so that ye may have conversation with the people daily, and no other thing than for to open the gate and for to shut it again."

Then said Howleglas to the Abbott: "God thank you, my lord, that ye have ordained for me, a poor old man, so light an office. And therefore shall I do all that ye bid me, and leave all that ye forbid me." Then said the Abbott to him: "Take, here is the keys. Ye must not let in everybody, nor scarce let in but the third or fourth—for there be so many vagabonds and land-runners, for if that ye should let them all in that comes, they would eat and drink so much, that at the year's end they would bring the place to a low ebb."

Then said Howleglas to the Abbott: "That shall I do with a good will." And then kept he the gate and when that the servants and the monks should have come in, then would he let in no more but the third or the fourth. And then they complained to the Abbott of Howleglas and told him that Howleglas was a deceiver and a beguiler of folk, for he would not let them in that belonged unto the place.

Then called the Abbott Howleglas to him and asked him why that he did not let in the servants of the place. And Howleglas answered: "I have done as ye bad me. For ye bad me that I should let in but the third or the fourth and no more, and so I did. And therefore have I not broken your commandment." Then said the Abbott: "Ye have done like a false knave, and therefore shall I put ye out of thy office, for ye will not leave your false touches." And then gave he that office to another monk.

And then said he to Howleglas: "This shall be your office—you shall tell [1] every night how many monks come to matins. And ye miss one, ye shall out of the Abbey." Then said Howleglas to the Abbott: "My lord, that were I loath for to do, for to go out of the Abbey. Well I will do after your commandment."

But the Abbott gave to him that office because that he should

[1] *tell:* count

have him out of the Abbey, and so for to be rid of him. And Howleglas thought in his mind not for to tarry long. And then went Howleglas and pulled away two or three steps of the stairs that the monks should come down on to matins.

And at midnight came the prior first that was a good old man and was wont to be the first. And when he thought to have gone down, he fell and brake his leg. And then he cried piteously so that the other monks heard him, and came running hastily for to see what that he ailed and lacked—and then fell they each after other down the stairs.

Then in the morning complained the monks to the Abbott, and showed him how that Howleglas had served them. Then was the Abbott more angry and said to Howleglas: "What have ye done?" Howleglas said: "As ye bad me, for ye bad me that I should tell the monks when they came to matins, and so I have done. Look, here is the tally." Then said the Abbott: "Go out of the Abbey, for ye have tolled them like a false knave!" And then departed Howleglas from that Abbey and went to Mollen.

42. *How Howleglas bought cream of the women of the country that brought it for to sell to Mariandra*

Within a while after, ere he would enter into the Abbey of Mariandra to be a monk, he went a-walking on the market day to Bremen, where he saw many women standing there to sell cream. And then went Howleglas to the house where he was lodged and borrowed a tub of his hostess and went again into the market.

And when he was there, he set down his tub and came to a woman of the country and he asked the price of her cream. And when they were both agreed, he made her for to put the cream into his tub. And then went he to another and agreed with her

also, and made her to put her cream into his tub. And so went
he from the one to the other till that he had made all the women
that had there cream to put it into his tub. And when he had
so done, then asked the poor women their money of Howleglas,
for they would depart home.

Then said Howleglas to the women: "Ye must do so much
for me, as to trust me these eight days. For I have no money
at this time." Then were the women of the country angry, and
they ran to the tub for to take every one of them their cream
again, for they would not trust him.

And as they would have taken their cream again, then began
they to fall together by the ears and said: "Thou takest more
than thou should have!" And the others stood all weeping and
said to them: "Shall I lose my cream?" And other twain were
tumbling by the hair in the midst of the channel.[1] And thus
they pulled and hauled on the other that at the last, the tub
fell down and arrayed them very foul, so that they were all dis-
figured and wist not of whom they should be avenged of.

And then arose they and asked: "Where is this false knave
that hath bought our milk and hath deceived us so? For had
we him here among us, we should christen him here in the cream
that is in the channel, and paint him therewith as well as we
be. For he is a false beguiler and deceiver." But he was gone
from thence, for he cast [2] before that such a thing should follow.

And when the burgess of the town and many other folk of the
town saw that the channel ran with cream, then went they to
the market place for to see. And when they were there they
asked how the cream was spilt, and then it was told them. And
when that they knew it, then they returned home laughing and
praised greatly that falseness and subtlety of Howleglas.

[1] *channel:* open sewer in the street
[2] *east:* decided, forecast

43. *How Howleglas came to a scholar to make verses with him to that use of reason and how that Howleglas began as after shall follow*

Howleglas

Mars with scepter, a king coronate
Furious in affliction, and taketh no regard
By terrible fighting, he is our primate
And god of battle, and person right froward;
Of wars the tutor, the lock, and the ward,
His power his might who can them resist?
Not all this world if that himself list.

The Scholar

Not all this world? Who told thee so?
Where is that written? Right fain would I see.
Ye came like a fool and so shall ye go.
By one person only, deceived ye may be;
And by all astronomy, I tell it unto thee:
If that will not help, some shift shall I find
By craft, or cunning, Mars for to blind.

Howleglas

Venus a god of love most decorate,
The flower of women and lady most pure,
Lovers to concord she doth aye aggregate
With parfit love, as marble to 'dure;
The knot of love she knits on them sure
With friendly amity, and never to discord
By deeds, thought, cogitation, nor word.

The Scholar

Not to discord? Yct did I never see,
Know, nor hear tell of lovers such twain,
But some fault there was, learn this of me;
Other in thought or yet in words plain
Your reasons be nought, your tongue goeth in vain;
By natural persons such love is not found
In France, Flanders, nor yet in English ground.

Howleglas

The god of wine, that Bacchus hath to name,
The sender of fruits that maketh wines all
May slake, or make, or put them in frame
All at his pleasure and use diurnal;
He may thee exalt, in likewise to fall
Their lord and master and chief governor,
He may them destroy and make in an hour.

The Scholar

All to destroy? It is not by his might
Nor yet for to make, of that be thou sure;
(Omnia per ipsum, Saint Johan says full right,
That we call Christ, our God and our treasure;)
Presume not so high—you fail of your measure;
Rcad, hear and see, and bear well away
Unknown, unsaid and for grace thou pray.
    Vale

44. How Howleglas at Mollen was sick and how he did shite in the 'pothecary's boxes and how he was borne in the Holy Ghost

As Howleglas was come from Meriendass then he fell sick, and when he was sick he went to Mollen where he was lodged in a 'pothecary's house for to make medicines therefore. Then should the 'pothecary give to him a medicine for his sickness, and then he gave to Howleglas a strong purgation. And in the morning, the purgation began to work. And then arose Howleglas for to have gone to the draught,[1] but he could not find none, and so he beshit all the chamber. And then he took the twelve boxes that the medicines were in and he shite in every one of them, and he said: "Here come out the medicines again. It were great pity to lose them, for I have no money to give him for them."

When the 'pothecary heard these words, then was he angry and he would have him no longer in his house, but took and bear him into an hospital of the Holy Ghost. And when he was within, then he said: "I have prayed God long that the Holy Ghost might come unto me, but my prayer is clean contrary, for I am come into the Holy Ghost, and He abideth without me and I in Him." Then laughed the people and said: "As men live, so is their end."

Then heard his mother say that he was sick. Then she came to him and she had thought for to have had some money of him, for she was old and poor. And when she saw him, she wept and said: "Where be ye so sick?" And Howleglas said: "Here between the bed and the wall."

Then said his mother: "Speak to me one sweet word." Then said Howleglas: "Honey, honey. Is not that a sweet word?" Then said his mother: "Tell me something that may do me ease." Then said Howleglas to his mother: "When that you first turn

[1] *draught:* privy

your arse with the wind, and then you shall feel no stink." Then said his mother: "Give me some of your good." [2] Then said Howleglas to his mother: "He that hath none shall give none. For my good is so secret that no man can find it. And you can find any, take it."

And then Howleglas waxed sicker and sicker, so that the folk asked him whether that he would be shriven, for they saw well that he should not recover. Then said an old sister that was a good friend of his, she counseled him to be confessed and take repentance for his sins, and so to be the servant of God. And Howleglas said: "I will not confess me secretly, for all that I have done I have done it openly to many men in divers lands, and that is well known. For they that I have done good to, they will say good of me. And they that I have done harm to, they will say harm of me. But I am very sorry of two things that which I could never bring to pass in my life."

Then said the sister: "Be sorry of thy sins and be glad that you did not those two things if they were ill. And if they were good, be sorry because they were not done." Then said Howleglas: "It is as men will take it. For I was sorry in my mind when I saw a rich man prick his teeth with his knife, that I had not shitten on the end of it. The other is that I am sorry for that I did not drive a wooden wedge in all women's arses that were above 50 years, for they be neither cleanly nor profitable. I desire it for no other cause but this: that is, that they should not shite on the ground, the which bringeth fruits."

Then said the sister to Howleglas: "God save all women of that age, and all those that been more. For I bear [3] well, and you [4] were strong and that you had your might as you have had before this time, you would ere you departed wedge mine arse with a wooden wedge, for I am a woman of 60 years and more." Then he answered to the sister: "I am right sorry and heavy because it is not done." Then answered the sister: "It

[2] *good:* property
[3] *I bear well:* I well imagine
[4] *and you:* if you

were much better that the devil had thee." Then answered
Howleglas: "That is truth, for a woman is no sooner angry
but she is worse than the devil." And then the sister departed
and let him lie.

45. *How Howleglas deceived his ghostly father*

And as Howleglas was thus sick then they brought to him a
priest. And when the priest was come there he thought in his
mind: "This hath been a great [adventurer wherewith he hath
gotten much goods." Then said the priest unto him: "Take heed
for yourself, for ye have done many sins, and must you remember
that you have gotten much money by falsehood, and now bestow
that money to the weak and] [1] poor priests as I am. And that
I counsel you for to do. And I shall order it well and remember
you hereafter, and do many masses for you."

Then said Howleglas: "Good father, if it please you to come
at noon again, then shall I make ready some money for you."
Then was the priest glad and then departed.

Then took Howleglas an earthen pot and filled it half full of
turds, and he strewed thereon a little money so that the dirt
was covered. And when it was noon, the priest came and he
said to Howleglas: "Friend, shall I have that that you promised me? And Howleglas said: "Ye." Then he set the pot before
him and said: "Take now yourself, but be not too hasty nor
put not your hand too deep." Then said the priest: "I shall do
as you bid me."

And Howleglas did open the pot, and he bad the priest to
grip softly, for it was almost full. Then was the priest hasty, and
put his hand into the pot and he gripped a great handfull. And
when he felt it soft, he pulled out his hand and it was allto [2]

[1] [*adventurer . . . and*]: Brackets here and elsewhere indicate that text is
reconstructed because of damaged page in the original.
[2] *allto:* altogether

beshitten. Then the priest said: "Ye may well be called a deceiver and beguiler, that have deceived his ghostly father, and when ye be at the point of death."

Then said Howleglas to the priest: "Good sir, did I not show unto you before that you should not grip too deep? And if that ye were covetous it was not my fault." Then said the priest: ["That is the worst ungraciousness of all others, and great pity that ye do it when thou shouldest have been sick and dying."] And then the priest departed from thence, and Howleglas called the priest again and said to him: "Master Parson, come again and take your money with you." But he went his way and made it as he heard it not.

46. *How Howleglas made his testament*

In the meantime waxed Howleglas sicker and sicker. Then he called for the lords to make his testament. And when they were come, he gave his goods [1] in three parts: One part to his kinfolk, another to the lords of Mollen, and the other to the parson of Mollen, whensoever he died. And he asked to be buried in Christian man's burial and to sing for his soul Placebo and Dirige [2] with masses and other good services after the custom and usage.

And then he showed to them a great chest that was well barred with iron, and four keys thereto belonging. And he told unto them that in that chest was all his goods. And then he gave the chest to them to keep—that were right heavy for him —and then within a month after his death then the four should take the keys thereof and open the chest and deal all the money for his soul.

And within a while after, he departed. And when he was dead, they wound him in a winding sheet, and after in a coffin, and

---

[1] *goods:* property
[2] *Placebo and Dirige:* funeral services

after on a bier. Then came the priests and fetched him to church and sang for him Placebo and Dirige. And, in the meantime, came in a sow with her pigs and went under the bier—for she had found the taste of dead flesh—and with her snout she cast down the bier, whereof the priests and clerks were afraid. And they saw that it was down, then they ran so fast that each fell on the others' necks, for they thought that he had been risen again, and so they left him there.

And then the sisters of a nunnery took the corpse and brought it to grave and buried it. And when a month was past, then came the three parties for to unlock the chest, and for to deal the money for his soul. And when that they had opened the chest, they found no other but stones therein.

Then they wondered thereof, and the one looked on the other, and the parson had weened that the lords had had the money because they had the chest in keeping. And the lords weened that his friends had opened the chest and taken out the treasure, and put in stones the while that he was sick, and so to have shut the chest again. And his friends weened that the curate had conveyed the treasure when that he confessed him.

And then in a great anger they departed from thence, for at the last they knew that it was he that had done it for to mock them. And after that, the lords and the curate agreed together again to bury him under the gallows. And so they did. And as they were delving of his grave, he stank so sore that they could not abide the air thereof, and so they covered him with earth again and let him lie still—and so they departed.

47. *How Howleglas was buried*

Thus as Howleglas was dead then they brought him to be buried. And as they would have put the coffin into the pit with two cords, the cord at the feet brake, so that the foot of the coffin fell into the bottom of the pit and the coffin stood bolt upright in the midst of the grave. Then desired the people that stood about the grave that time, to let the coffin to stand bolt upright. "For in his lifetime, he was a very miraculous man and he did many wonderful things, and shall be buried as marvelously." And in this manner they left Howleglas stand bolt upright in his grave, and they covered him with earth. And then they laid a stone, and on the stone was graven an owl holding a glass with her claws. And thereon was graven this scripture:

Presume no man away this stone
to take. For under this stone
was Howleglas bu-
ried late.
In the year of our Lord
God M C C C &
fifty.

Thus endeth the life of Howleglas.
Imprinted at London in Thames Street at the
Vintre on the three Craned wharf
by William Copland.

Tales and Quick Answers
(?1535)

Two different texts of Tales and Quick Answers *remain. The first, dating from about 1535, was printed by Thomas Berthelet and contained 113 jests (although numbered as though 114). The second, dated 1567, was printed by Henry Wykes and added twenty-six new jests.*

Berthelet was the Royal Printer, responsible for printing all Parliamentary acts, proclamations, and other official documents. He printed such English classics as Elyot's Boke of the Governor, *while Wykes is perhaps best known for printing* The Golden Ass of Apuleius.

S. W. Singer printed the Berthelet text in 1814 and then the Wykes text in 1831 and 1845. W. C. Hazlitt and H. Oesterley printed the Wykes text in 1864 and 1866 respectively and it is available in the many editions of Hazlitt's Shakespeare's Jestbooks *(London, 1864).*

The basis for the present text is the Berthelet copy (STC 23665) now in the Huntington Library.

¶ Tales, and quicke
answeres, very mery,
and pleasant to
rede.

THE TABLE

81. Of him that feigned himself dead to prove what his wife would do.
82. Of the poor man into the whose house thieves brake by night.
83. Of him that should have been hanged for his scoffing and jesting.
84. Of him that had his goose stolen.
85. Of the beggar that said he was of kin to King Philip of Macedon.
86. Of Dante's answer to the jester.
87. Of him that had sore eyes.
88. Of the old woman that had sore eyes.
89. Of him that had the custody of a ward.
90. Of the excellent painter that had foul children.
91. Of the scoffer that made one a soothsayer.
92. Of the merchant of Florence, Charles.
93. Of the Cheshire man called Evlyn.
94. Of him that desired to be set upon the pillory.
95. Of the widow's daughter that was sent to the abbot with a couple of capons.
96. Of the two men that drank a pint of white wine together.
97. Of the doctor that desired to go with a fowler to catch birds.
98. Of him that undertook to teach an ass to spell and read.
99. Of the friar that confessed the fair woman.
100. Of the chaplain of Louven called Sir Antony that deceived an usurer.
101. Of the same chaplain and his spiter.
102. Of the old man that put himself in his son's hands.
103. Of him that had a fly painted in his shield.
104. Of the Emperor Augustus and the old men.
105. Of Phocion's oration to the Athenians.
106. Of Demosthenes and Phocion.
107. Of the answer of Phocion to them that brought him a great gift from Alexander.
108. Of Denise the tyrant and his son.
109. Of Pomponius the Roman that was taken and brought before Mithridates.
110. Of Titus and the scoffer.

Thus endeth the Table

1. *Of him that rode out of London and had his servant following on foot*

There was a man on a time that rode five mile out of London and had his servant following after him on foot, the which came so near that the horse struck him a great stroke upon the thigh. The servant, thinking to be revenged, took and threw a great stone at the horse and hit his master on the rains [1] of the back, who thought it had been his horse.

He within a while looked back and chided his servant because he came halting so far behind. The servant answered: "Sir, your horse hath given me such a stroke upon my thigh that I can go no faster."

"Truly," said the master, "the horse is a great kicker, for likewise with his heel right now he gave me a great stroke upon the rains of my back."

2. *Of him that preached on Saint Christopher's day*

A friar that preached upon a Saint Christopher's day, greatly lauding Saint Christopher, said: "What a prerogative had he here on earth in his arms to bear our Savior! Was there ever any like him in grace?"

A homely, blunt fellow, hearing him ask twice or thrice that

[1] *rains:* small

question so earnestly, answered: "Yes, marry, the ass that bore both Him and his mother."

3. *Of the Frenchman that strove with the Janway for his arms*

There was one among the Janways,[1] that the French king had hired to make war against the Englishmen, which bare an ox head painted in his shield—the which shield a nobleman of France challenged. And so long they strove [2] that they must needs fight for it. So, at a day and place appointed, the French gallant came into the field richly armed at all pieces.[3] The Janway all unarmed came also into the field and said to the Frenchman: "Wherefore shall we this day fight?"

"Marry," said the Frenchman, "I will make good with my body that these arms were mine ancestors' before thine."

"What were your ancestors' arms?" quod the Janway.

"An ox head," said the Frenchman.

Then said the Janway: "Here needeth no battle, for this that I bear is a cow's head."

By this tale ye perceive how nicely the vain bragging of the Frenchman was derided.

4. *Of the curate that said our Lord fed five hundred persons*

A certain curate, preaching on a time to his parishioners, said that our Lord with five loaves fed five hundred persons. The clerk, hearing him fail,[1] said softly in his ear: "Sir, ye err. The gospel is 'five thousand.' "

[1] *Janways:* Genoese
[2] *strove:* argued
[3] *pieces:* i.e., head-to-toe
[1] *fail:* err

"Hold thy peace, fool," said the curate. "They will scantly believe that they were five hundred."

5. *Of him that proffered his daughter in marriage*

There was a man upon a time which proffered his daughter to a young man in marriage, the which young man refused her, saying that she was too young to be married.

"I wis," quod her foolish father, "she is more able than ye ween. For she hath borne three children by our parish clerk."

Lo, by this tale ye see that fools can not tell what and when to speak; therefore it were best for them to keep always silence.

6. *Of them that came to London to buy a crucifix*

There were certain men upon a time sent out of a village to London to buy a crucifix of wood. The carver that they came to, seeing and hearing by their words that they were but foolish, blunt fellows, asked them whether they would have the image alive or else dead—which question so abashed them that they went aside to devise whether was best.

So when they had spoken privily together, they came to the carver again and said they would have the image alive, for if their neighbors at home were not so content they might lightly [1] kill him.

[1] *lightly:* easily

7. *Of him that followed his wife to burying*

A man that, weeping, followed his wife to burying, rebuked his little son that went with him because he sang, saying that he was peevish and mad to sing at his mother's burying, but he should rather be sorry and weep. The child answered: "Father, seeing ye give to these priests money to sing at my mother's burying, why be ye angry with me that ask you nothing for my singing?" His father answered: "The priest's office and thine is not all one."

By this tale ye may perceive that all things beseem not everybody.

8. *Of him that fell into the fire*

A fellow that was forward to his wife used to be out drinking many times very late. So on a night he tarried so long out that his wife went to bed and bad her maid make a good fire and tarry up for him. About 12 of the clock, home he came, and as he stood warming him by the fire his head was so totty that he fell into the fire. The maid, seeing him fall, ran up crying to her mistress and said: "Alas! my maister is fallen and lieth long straught [1] in the fire!"

"No force, maid," said her mistress. "Let him lie and take his pleasure in his own house wheresoever him listeth." [2]

[1] *straught:* stretched out
[2] *listeth:* pleases

9. *Of him that used to call his servant the king of fools*

There was a man that had a dull, lumpish fellow to his servant, wherefore he used commonly to call him the king of fools.
The fellow at last waxed angry in his mind to be always so called
and said to his master: "I would that I were the king of fools,
for then no man could compare with me in largeness of kingdom,
and also you should be my subject."

By this one may perceive that too much of one thing is not
good. Many one calleth another fool and is more fool himself.

10. *Of the young woman that sorrowed so greatly her husband's
    death*

There was a young woman the which for her husband that lay
a-dying sorrowed out of all measure, wherefore her father came
often to her and said: "Daughter, leave your mourning, for I
have provided for you another husband, a far more goodly [1]
man."

But she did not only continue in her sorrow but also was
greatly displeased that her father made any motion to her of
another husband. As soon as she had buried her husband and
the soul mass was sung, and that they were at dinner—between
sobbing and weeping, she rowned [2] her father in the ear and
said: "Father, where is the same young man that ye said should
be mine husband?"

Lo, thus may ye see that women sorrow right long after their
husbands be departed to God.

[1] *goodly:* wealthy
[2] *rowned:* whispered

11. *Of him that kissed the maid with the long nose*

A babbling gentleman the which on a time would have bussed a fair maid that had not the least nose [1] said: "How should I kiss you? Your nose will not suffer our lips to meet."

The maiden, waxing shamefast and angry in her mind (for with his scoff he a little touched her), answered on this wise: "Sir, if ye can not kiss my mouth for my nose, ye may kiss me there as I have nary a nose."

Ye may by this tale learn that it is folly so to scoff that yourself thereby should be laughed to scorn again. One that is over-covetous ought not to a-twit another of prodigality. "Thou art her brother (said Alcmeon to Adrastus) that slew her husband." But he blamed not Alcmeon for another's fault, but objected against him his own: "Thou hast with thy hand (said he) slain thine own mother."

It is not enough to have rebukes ready and to speak evil words against others, for he that so should do, ought to be without any vice. For of all men, saith Plutarchus, he ought to be innocent and have the life unculpable that would reprehend the faults of others. The little moral book [2] saith:

> It is a foul thyng, worthy rebuke and blame
> A vice to reprehend and do the same.

[1] *least nose:* i.e., not the smallest nose in the world
[2] *book: Parvus et magnus Cato,* a poetical paraphrase of some Distichs by Cato, which Caxton translated from the French about 1477.

12. *The uplandish man's answer concerning the steeple and pulpit*

In a certain place on a time the parishioners had pulled down their steeple and had builded it up new again, and had put out their bells to be new-founded. And because they rang not at the bishop's entering into the village, as they were wont and accustomed to do, he asked a good, homely man whether they had no bells in their steeple. He answered no.

"Then," said the bishop, "ye may sell away your steeple."

"Why so, and please your lordship?" said the man.

"Because it standeth vacant," said the bishop.

"Then," said the man, "we may well sell away another thing that we have in our church."

"What is that?" said the bishop.

"That is a pulpit," quod he. "For this seven years there was no sermon made therein."

13. *Of the beggar's answer to M. Skelton the poet*

A poor beggar that was foul, black, and loathly to behold came upon a time unto Master Skelton the poet and asked him his alms. To whom Master Skelton said: "I pray thee, get thee away from me, for thou lookest as though thou camest out of hell."

The poor man, perceiving he would give him nothing, answered: "Forsooth, sir, ye say truth. I came out of hell."

"Why didst thou not tarry still there?" quod Master Skelton.

"Marry, sir," quod the beggar, "there is no room for such poor beggars as I am—all is kept for such gentlemen as ye be."

14. *Of the chaplain that said Our Lady matins abed*

A certain lord's chaplain boasted on a time, sitting at his lord's table, that he said Our Lady matins every morning besides all his other service and orisons. The lord, to prove whether his chaplain did as he said, arose early on a morning and went to his chaplain's chamber and called him, saying: "Where be ye, Sir William?"

"Here, and please your lordship (quod he), in my bed."

"Why," said the lord, "I thought ye had been up and saying of Our Lady matins."

"I am now saying it," quod the chaplain.

"What! lying in your bed?" quod the lord.

"Why, sir," said the chaplain, "where should women be served but abed?"

15. *Of him that lost his purse in London*

A certain man of the country, the which for business came up to London, lost his purse as he went late in the evening. And because the sum therein was great, he set up bills in divers places—that if any man of the city had found the purse and would bring it again to him, he should have well for his labor.

A gentleman of the Temple wrote under one of the bills how the man should come to his chamber and told where. So when he was come, the gentleman asked him first what was in the purse; secondly, what countryman he was; and, thirdly, what was his name.

"Sir," quod he, "twenty nobles was in the purse; I am half a welshman; and my name is John up Janken."

"John up Jankin (said the gentleman), I am glad I know thy name. For, so long as I live, thou nor none of thine name shall have my purse to keep. And now farewell, gentle John up Janken."

Thus he was mocked to scorn and went his way.

Hereby ye may perceive that a man can not have a shrewd turn but otherwhile a mock withal.[1]

16. *Of the merchant that lost his budget between Ware and London*

A certain merchant between Ware and London lost his budget [1] and a hundred pounds therein, wherefore he caused to proclaim in divers market towns, who soever that found the said budget and would bring it again should have twenty pounds for his labor.

An honest husbandman, that chanced to find the said budget, brought it to the baillie [2] of Ware, according to the cry, and required his twenty pounds for his labor, as it was proclaimed.

The covetous merchant when he understood this, and that he must needs pay twenty pounds for the finding, he said that there was an hundred-and-twenty pounds in his budget, and so would have had his own money and twenty pounds over. So long they strove, that the matter was brought before Master Vavasour the good judge.

When he understood by the baillie that the cry was made for a budget with an hundred pounds therein, he demanded where it was. "Here," quod the baillie, and took it unto him.

"Is it just an hundred pounds?" said the Judge.

"Ye, truly," quod the baillie.

"Hold," said the Judge (to him that found the budget), "take

---

[1] *a man . . . withal:* i.e., insult will be added to injury
[1] *budget:* wallet
[2] *baillie:* chief magistrate

thou this money unto thine own use, and if thou hap to find a budget with a hundred-and-twenty pounds therein, bring it to this honest merchant man."

"It is mine. I lost no more but an hundred pounds," quod the merchant.

"Ye speak now too late," quod the Judge.

By this tale ye may understand that they that go about to deceive others be often times deceived themselves. And some time one falleth in the ditch that he himself made.

17. *Of him that was called cuckold*

A certain man, which upon a time in company between earnest and game was called cuckold, went angrily home to his wife and said: "Wife, I was this day in company called cuckold. Whether am I one or not?"

"Sir, truly," said she, "ye be none."

"By my faith (said he), thou shall swear so upon this book," and held to her a book. She denied it [1] long, but when she saw there was no remedy she said: "Well, sith [2] I must needs swear, I promise you by my faith I will swear truly."

"Yea, do so," quod he.

So she took the book in her hand and said: "By this book, sir, ye be a cuckold."

"By the mass, whore," said he, "thou liest! Thou sayest it for none other cause but to anger me."

By this tale ye may perceive that it is not best at all times for a man to believe his wife, though she swear upon a book.

[1] *denied it:* refused
[2] *sith:* since

18. *Of the jealous man*

A man that was right jealous on his wife dreamed on a night as he lay abed with her and slept, that the devil appeared unto him and said: "Wouldst thou not be glad that I should put thee in surety of thy wife?"

"Yes," said he.

"Hold," said the devil, "as long as thou hast this ring upon thy finger no man shall make thee cuckold."

The man was glad thereof, and when he awaked he found his finger in his wife's arse.

19. *Of the fat woman that sold fruit*

As a great fat woman sat and sold fruit in a Lent, there came a young man by and beheld her fruit earnestly. And specially he cast his eyes on her figs. She asked him, as was her guise: "Sir, will ye have any figs? They be fair and good." And when she saw he was content, she said: "How many? Will ye have five pounds?" He was content, so she weighed him out five pounds into his lap.

And while she laid aside her balance, he went his way fair and softly.[1] When she turned her to have taken money and saw her chapman [2] go his way, she made after apace, but faster with her voice than with her foot. He, dissembling the matter, went still forth on.

She made such a crying and folks gathered so fast that he stood still. So, in the press,[3] he showed to the people all the matter

---

[1] *softly:* slowly
[2] *chapman:* customer
[3] *press:* crowd

and said: "I bought nothing of her. But that that she unbidden gave me I took. And if she will, I am content to go before the Justice."

20. *Of a poller that beguiled a priest*

Upon a time in Antwerp, a false polling fellow [1] came unto a certain priest that had his purse hanging at his girdle (strouting [2] out full of money that he a little before had received) and genteelly greeting him said: "Good Master, our parish priest bad me buy him a palle (which is the uppermost vestment that a priest singeth mass in). If it would please you to go with me, I were much bound to you, for our curate and you be of one stature." The priest was content.

When they came there where he would buy it, the palle was brought forth, and the priest did [3] it on. The poller looketh and toteth [4] thereon, and praiseth it, but he laid a wyte [5] that it was too short before. "Nay," quod the seller, "the fault is not in the vestment. It is in the strouting purse underneath that beareth it up."

Shortly to speak, the priest did off his purse and laid it by, and then the vestment they beheld again. When the poller saw the priest was turned, he snatched up the purse and took to his legs to go. The priest ran after, with the vestment on his back, and the vestment-maker after the priest. The priest bad: "Stop the thief!" The seller bad: "Stop the priest!" The poller bad: "Hold the mad priest!" And every man weened he had been mad indeed because he had the vestment on his back. And so, while one letted [6] another, the false poller went his way.

[1] *polling fellow:* confidence man
[2] *strouting:* bulging
[3] *did:* put
[4] *toteth:* looks it all over
[5] *laid a wyte:* found fault with
[6] *letted:* stopped

21. *Of Papyrius pretextatus*

Aulus Gellius [1] rehearseth how the Senators of Rome on a time held a great council. Before which time the senators' children, called of their garments—Pueri pretextati—used to come into the parliament house with their fathers. So at this time a child called Papyrius came in with his father and heard the great counsel, the which was straitly commanded to be kept secret til it was decreed.

When this child came home, his mother asked him what the counsel was. The child answered: "It ought not to be told." Now was his mother more desirous to know it than she was before; wherefore she enquired more straitly and more violently.

The child, being sore constrained of his mother, shortly devised a proper merry leasing. [2] "It is reasoned in the parliament (quod he), whether of both should be more profitable for the commonwealth—a man to have two wives or else a woman two husbands." When she heard him say so, her mind was pacified, and forthwith she went and told it to the other matrons.

On the morrow, a great company of the most notable wives of Rome came to the parliament house weeping and humbly praying that rather one woman should be married unto two men than two women to one man. The senators entering into the court, what with the sudden assembling of the wives and of their request, were right sore astonished.

Then the child Papyrius stood forth and informed the senators how his mother would have compelled him to utter the secret counsel, and how he, to content her mind, feigned that leasing. For which deed the senators right highly commended the child's fidelity and wit. And forthwith they made a law that no child after that (save only Papyrius) should come into the parliament house with his father. And for his great prudence in

[1] *Gellius: Noctes Atticae*, tr. Belne, II, 86 (Hazlitt)
[2] *leasing:* little white lie

that tender age, he had given to him—to his great honor—this surname Pretextatus.

Whereby ye may see that the high treasure of man, and greatest grace, resteth in well ordering of the tongue. That most prudent poet Hesiodus sayeth: "The tongue should not run at large, but be hid as a precious treasure." For, of all the members of men, the tongue ill-ordered is the worst. The tongue blasphemeth God. The tongue slandereth thy neighbor. The tongue breaketh peace and stirreth up cruel war, of all things to mankind most mischiefull. The tongue is a broker of bawdry. The tongue setteth friends at debate. The tongue, with flattering, detraction and wanton tales, infecteth pure and clean minds. The tongue without sword or venom strangleth thy brother and friend. And, briefly to speak, the tongue teacheth cursed heresies, and of good Christians maketh Antichrists.

22. *Of the corrupt man of law*

There was a man of law which on a time should be judge between a poor man and a rich. The poor man came and gave him a glass of oil (which was as much as his power would stretch to) and desired that he would be good in this matter.

"Yes (quod he), the matter shall pass with thee."

The rich man, perceiving that, sent to the same judge a fat hog and prayed him to be favorable on his side. Wherefore he gave judgement against the poor man.

When the poor man saw that he was condemned, piteously complaining he said to the judge: "Sir, I gave you a glass of oil and ye promised by your faith the matter should pass with me."

To whom the judge said: "For a truth, there came a hog into my house which found the glass of oil and overthrew and brake it. And so through spilling of the oil I clean forgot thee."

> Whereby ye may see that evermore among,
> The rich hath his will, the poor taketh wrong.

23. *Of King Louis of France and the husbandman*

What time King Louis of France (the eleventh of that name) because of the trouble that was in the realm kept himself in Burgoyne, he chanced by occasion of hunting to come acquainted with one Conon, a homely husbandman and a plain-meaning fellow, in which manner of men the high princes greatly delight them. To this man's house the king oft resorted from hunting, and with great pleasure he would eat radishes roots with him.

Within a while after, when Louis was restored home and had the government of France in his hand, this husbandman was counseled by his wife to take a goodly sort of radish roots and to go and give them to the king, and put him in mind of the good cheer that he had made him at his house. Conon would not assent thereto. "What, foolish woman! (quod he) the great princes remember not such small pleasures."

But for all that she would not rest til Conon chose out a great sight of the fairest roots and took his journey toward the court. But as he went by the way, he ate up all the radishes save one of the greatest.

Conon peaked [1] into the court and stood where the king should pass by. By and by, the king knew him and called him to him. Conon stepped to the king and presented his root with a glad cheer.[2] And the king took it more gladly, and bad one that was nearest to him to lay it up among those jewels that he best loved, and then commanded Conon to dine with him. When dinner was done, he thanked Conon. And when the king saw that he would depart home, he commanded to give him a thousand crowns of gold for his radish root.

When this was known in the king's house, one of the court gave the king a proper minion [3] horse. The king, perceiving that

[1] *peaked:* sneaked
[2] *cheer:* countenance
[3] *minion:* dainty

he did it because of the liberality showed unto Conon, with very glad cheer took the gift and counseled with his lords how and with what gift he might recompense the horse that was so goodly and fair. This meanwhile, the pickthank [4] had a marvelous great hope, and thought in his mind thus: "If he so well recompensed the radish root that was given of a rustical man, how much more largely will he recompense such an horse that is given of me that am of the court?"

When every man had said his mind, as though the king had counseled about a great weighty matter, and that they had long fed the pickthank with vain hope, at last the king said: "I remember now what we shall give him." And so he called one of his lords and bad him in his ear go fetch him that that he found in his chamber (and told him the place where) neatly folded up in silk.

Anon, he came and brought the radish root, and even as it was folded up. The king with his own hand gave it to the courtier, saying: "We suppose your horse is well recompensed with this jewel, for it hath cost us a thousand crowns." The courtier went his way never so glad, and when he had unfolded it, he found none other treasure but the radish root almost withered.

24. *Of another pickthank and the same king*

Upon a time, a servant of the forenamed king's, seeing a louse creep upon the king's robe, kneeled down and put up his hand as though he would do somewhat. And as the king bowed himself a little, the man took the louse and conveyed her away privily. The king asked him what it was, but he was ashamed to show. So much the king instanted him, that at last he confessed it was a louse. "Oh! (quod the king), it is good luck, for this declareth me to be a man. For that kind of vermin prin-

[4] *pickthank:* sycophant

cipally grieveth mankind, specially in youth." And so the king commanded to give him fifty crowns for his labor.

Not long after, another, seeing that the king gave so good a reward for so small a pleasure, came and kneeled down and put up his hand and made as though he took and conveyed somewhat privily away. And when the king constrained him to tell what it was, with much dissembling shamefastness he said it was a flea. The king, perceiving his dissimulation, said to him: "What! wouldst thou make me a dog?" And so, for his fifty crowns that he prowled for, the king commanded to give him fifty stripes.

Whereby ye may note that there is great difference between one that doth a thing of good will and mind, and him that doth a thing by craft and dissimulation—which thing this noble and most prudent prince well understood. And one ought to be well 'ware how he hath to do with high princes and their business. And if *Ecclesiastes* forbid that one shall mind none ill to a king, how should any dare speak ill?

25. *Of Thales the astronomer that fell in a ditch*

Laertius writeth that Thales Milesius went out of his house upon a time to behold the stars for a certain cause, and so long he went backward that he fell plump into a ditch over the ears. Wherefore, an old woman that he kept in his house laughed and said to him in derision: "O Thales, how shouldest thou have knowledge in heavenly things above, and knowest not what is here beneath under thy feet?"

26. *Of the astronomer that thieves robbed*

As an astronomer sat upon a time in the market place of a certain town and took upon him to divine and to show what their fortunes and chances should be that came to him, there came a fellow and told him (as it was indeed) that thieves had broken into his house and had borne away all that he had. These tidings grieved him so sore that all heavy and sorrowfully he rose up and went his way. When the fellow saw him do so, he said: "Oh, thou foolish and mad man, goest thou about to divine other men's matters and art ignorant in thine own?"

This tale (besides the blind error of such fools) toucheth them that handle their own matters lewdly, and will intermeddle in other men's. And Cicero sayeth: "That wise man that can not profit himself hath but little wisdom."

27. *Of the plowman that said his Pater noster*

A rude uplandish plowman, which on a time reproving a good holy father, said that he could say all his prayers with a holy mind and steadfast intention without thinking on any other thing. To whom the good holy man said: "Go to. Say one *Pater noster* to the end, and think on none other thing, and I will give thee mine horse."

"That shall I do," quod the plowman, and so began to say: "Pater noster qui es in celis . . ." til he came to "Santificetur nomen tuum," and then his thought moved him to ask this question: "Yea, but shall I have the saddle and bridle withal?" And so he lost his bargain.

28. *Of him that dreamed he found gold*

There was a man that said in company upon a time how he dreamed on a night that the devil led him into a field to dig for gold. When he had found the gold, the devil said: "Thou canst not carry it away now, but mark the place that thou mayst fetch it another time."

"What mark shall I make?" quod the man.

"Shite over it," quod the devil, "for that shall cause every man to shun the place, and for thee it shall be a special knowledge." The man was content and did so.

So when he awaked out of his sleep he perceived that he had fouly defiled his bed. Thus between stink and dirt up he rose and made him ready to go forth, and last of all he put on his bonnet—wherein also the same night the cat had shit. For great stink whereof he threw away his cover knave [1] and was fain to wash his bush.[2] Thus his golden dream turned all to dirt.

Tibullus sayeth: "Dreams in the night beguile and cause fearful minds to dread things that never shall be." But yet Claudian sayeth: "Dreams, in sundry wise figured, giveth warning of unlucky things." And Valerius Maximus writeth that as Hamilcar besieged the city of Syracuse, he dreamed that he heard a voice say that he the next day should sup within the city. Wherefore he was joyful as though the victory from heaven had been to him promised, and so apparelled his host to assault the town— in which assault he chanced to be taken in his lodging by them of the city, and so, bound like a prisoner, they led him into their city. Thus he, more deceived by hope than by his dream, supped that night within the city as a prisoner and not as a conqueror as he presumed in his mind. Alcibiades also had a certain vision in the night of his miserable end.

This tale showeth that dreams sometime come to pass by one means or other. And he that desireth to know more of dreams written in our English tongue, let him read the tale of the nun's priest that G. Chaucer wrote; and for the skills how dreams and swevens [3] are caused, the beginning of the Book of Fame the which the said Chaucer compiled with many another matter full of wisdom.

---

[1] *cover knave:* hat
[2] *bush:* hair
[3] *swevens:* perhaps a distinction between day dreams and night dreams

29. *Of the craking young gentleman that would overthrow his
enemies a mile off*

A young gentleman in a city that was besieged, rebuked the
others and called them cowherds because they would not issue
out and fight with their enemy. So he, armed at all pieces,[1] leapt
on horseback and galloped out at the gates. When he, thus
craking,[2] had pricked on about a mile, he encountered with
many that returned home from the skirmish sore wounded;
wherefore he began to ride a softer pace. But when he heard
the hideous noise and saw a mile from him how fiercely they of
the city and their enemies assailed each other, he stood even
still. Then one, that heard his craking before, asked him why
he rode no nearer to fight with their enemies. He answered and
said: "Truly, I find not myself so able and strong in arms that
my heart will serve me to ride any nearer to them."

Whereby may be noted that not only the force of the mind
but also of the body should be well considered. Nor one should
not brag and boast to do more than he may well achieve. There
be many which with their words slay their enemies a great way
off, but when they see their enemy they put on a sure breast
plate and a gorget [3] of a mile in length. Plutarch writeth that
when Memnon made war for Darius against Alexander, he heard
one of his soldier crake and speak many ill words against Alexander; wherefore he rapped him on the pate with a javelin, saying: "I hired thee to fight against Alexander and not to crake and
prate."

Otherwhile sayeth Quintus Curtius: The covetousness of glory
and insatiable desire of fame causeth that we think nothing overmuch or overhard. But Sallust saith: Before a man enterprise

[1] *pieces:* points
[2] *craking:* boasting
[3] *gorget:* collar, armor

any feat, he ought first to counsel, and after to go ahead neither heedling [4] nor slowly.

30. *Of him that fell off a tree and broke his rib*

There was a husbandman which, on a time, as he climbed a tree to get down the fruit, fell and broke a rib in his side. To comfort him there came a very merry man which, as they talked together, said he would teach him such a rule that if he would follow it, he should never fall from tree more.

"Marry," said the hurt man, "I would ye had taught me that rule before I fell. Nevertheless, because it may hap to profit me in time to come, let me hear what it is."

Then the other said: "Take heed that thou go never down faster than thou wentest up, but descend as softly [1] as thou climbest up, and so thou shalt never fall."

By this tale ye may note that abiding and slowness otherwhile are good and commendable specially in those things wherein speed and hastiness cause great hurt and damage. Seneca sayeth: A sudden thing is nought.

31. *Of the friar that brayed in his sermon*

A friar that preached to the people on a time would otherwhile cry out aloud (as the manner of some fools is)—which braying did so move a woman that stood hearing his sermon that she wept. He, perceiving that, thought in his mind her conscience being pricked with his words had caused her to weep. Wherefore, when his sermon was done, he called the woman to

[4] *heedling:* headlong
[1] *softly:* slowly

him and asked what was the cause of her weeping, and whether his words moved her to weep or not.

"Forsooth, master (said she), I am a poor widow, and when my husband died he left me but one ass, which got part of my living, the which ass the wolves have slain. And now, when I heard your high [1] voice, I remembered my silly [2] ass, for so he was wont to bray both night and day. And this, good master, caused me to weep."

Thus the lewd brayer (rather than preacher) confuted with his foolishness went his way—which, thinking for his braying like an ass to be reputed for the best preacher, deserved well to hear himself compared to an ass.

> For truly, one to suppose himself wise
> Is unto foolishness the very first grise.[3]

32. *The oration of the ambassador sent to Pope Urban*

Out of the town of Parusyn were sent upon a time three ambassadors unto our holy father Pope Urban, whom they found sick in his bed, before whose holiness one of the said ambassadors had a long and tedious oration that he had devised by the way. The which, ere it was ended, right sore annoyed the Pope's holiness. When he had all said, the Pope asked: "Is there anything else?"

Another of the three, perceiving how greatly the ambagious [1] tale grieved the Pope's holiness to hear it out, said: "Most holy father, this is all the effect,[2] and if your holiness speed us not forthwith, my fellow shall tell his tale again." At which saying, the Pope laughed and caused the ambassadors to be sped incontinently.[3]

[1] *high:* loud
[2] *silly:* poor, innocent
[3] *grise:* step
[1] *ambagious:* long-winded
[2] *effect:* office
[3] *incontinently:* at once

By this tale one may learn that superfluous words ought diligently to be avoided, especially where a matter is treated before an high prince.

33. *Of the ambassador sent to the prince Agis*

Not much unlike the foresaid tale, Plutarch reciteth that when the ambassador of the Abderties had at last ended a long tale to the prince Agis, he asked what answer he should make to them that sent him. "Say unto them (quod the prince), when thou comest home, that all the long time that thou didst spend in telling thy tale I sat still and heard thee patiently."

34. *The answer of Cleomenes to the Samiens ambassador*

Plutarch rehearseth also that, what time an ambassador that was sent from the Samiens had made a long oration unto Cleomines to persuade him to make war to Polycrates, he answered the ambassador in this manner of wise: "I remember not what thou saidest in the beginning of thy tale and therefore I understand not the midst, and thy conclusion pleaseth me not."

Whereby we may perceive that the noble wise men love few words. And as the rhetoricians say: among the vices of an orator, there is none more hurtful than the superfluous heap of words.

35. *Of the wise man Piso and his servant*

A certain wise man called Piso, to avoid grievous jangling, commanded that his servants should say nothing, but answer to that they were demanded and no more. Upon a day, the said Piso made a dinner and sent a servant to desire Claudius the Consul to come and dine with him. About the hour of dinner, all the guests came save Claudius—for whom they tarried till it was almost night and ever sent to look if he came. At last Piso said to his servant: "Didst thou bid the Consul come to dinner?"

"Yes, truly," said he.

"Why cometh he not, then?" quod Piso.

"Marry," quod the servant, "he said he would not."

"Wherefore toldest me not so incontinent?" [1] quod Piso.

"Because," quod the servant, "ye did not ask me."

By this tale, servants may learn to keep their master's bidding, but yet I advise masters thereby to take heed how they make an injunction.

36. *Of the merchant that made a wager with his lord*

A certain merchant, before his lord that he was subject unto, among other things praised his wife and said that he never heard her let a fart. Whereat the lord marveled and said it was impossible, and so laid and ventured a supper with the merchant that before three months were ended, he should hear her let a fart or twain. On the morrow, the lord came to the merchant and borrowed fifty crowns, the which he promised truly to repay again within eight days after. The merchant right sore against his will lent it, and thoughtfully abode till the day of payment was come, and then he went to his lord and required his money.

The lord, making as though he had more need than before, desired the merchant to lend him another fifty crowns, and promised to pay all within a month. And although the good man denied it long, yet for fear lest he should lose the first sum, with much grutching [1] he lent him the other fifty crowns, and so went

[1] *incontinent:* immediately
[1] *grutching:* grudging

home to his house right heavy and sorrowful in his mind. Thus thinking and dreading divers things, he passed many nights away without sleep. And as he lay waking, he heard his wife now and then rap out farts.

At the month's end, the lord sent for the merchant and asked him if he never since heard his wife let a fart. The merchant acknowledging his folly, answered thus: "Forsooth, sir, if I should for every fart pay a supper, all my goods and lands would not suffice thereto." After which answer, the lord paid the merchant his money and the merchant paid the supper.

Hereby ye may see that many things pass by them that sleep, and it is an old saying: "He that sleepeth, biteth nobody." By this tale ye may note also that they, the which fortune sweetly embraceth, take their rest and sleep soundly; and, contrariwise, they that been oppressed with adversity watch sorrowfully when they should sleep. This man, which for a very foolish thing praised his wife, afterward when a little care began to creep about his stomach, he perceived that fault in her right great. The moral book, called *Cato*,[2] counseleth us to watch for the more part, for much slumber and sleep is the nourishing of vice.

37. *Of the friar that gave scrolls against the pestilence*

Among the limitours[1] in the city of Tiburtine was a certain friar, which used to preach about in the villages to men of the country, and forasmuch as they greatly suspected that a plague of pestilence should come among them, he promised each of them a little scroll which he said was of such a virtue that whosoever bore it hanging about his neck 15 days should not die of the pestilence.

The foolish people trusting hereupon, every one after his power gave him money for a scroll, and with a thread of a

[2] *Cato:* printed by Caxton *ca.* 1477.
[1] *limitours:* friars licensed to beg within certain territory

maiden's spinning they hanged it about their necks. But he charged them that they should not open it till the 15 days end, for if they did, he said, it had no virtue. So when the friar had gathered much money, he went his way.

Soon after (as the desire of folks is to know news) the said scrolls were read, in which was written in Italian speech: "Donna, si fili et cadeti lo fuso, quando ta fieti, tieni lo culo chiuso—" which is to say in English: "Woman, if thou spin and thy spindle fall away, when thou stoopest to reach for him, hold thine arse close." He said that this passed all the precepts and medicines of the physicians.

By which tale one may learn that all is not gospel that such wanderers-about say, nor every word to be believed, for often-times—Gelidus jacet anguis in herba.[2]

38. *Of the physician that used to write bills over eve*

A certain physician of Italy used overnight to write for sundry diseases divers bills, called receipts, and to put them in a bag all together. In the morning when the urines (as the custom is) were brought to him, and he desired to show some remedy, he would put his hand into the bag and at all adventures [1] take out a bill. And in taking out the bill he would say to him that came to seek remedy in their language: "Prega dio te la mandi bona—" that is to say, "Pray God to send thee a good one."

By this tale ye may see that miserable is their state which fortune must help and not reason. Such a physician on a time said to Pausanius: "Thou ailest nothing." "No (said he), I have not had to do with thy physick."

And another time a friend of his said: "Sir, ye ought not to blame that physician, for his physick did you never hurt."

[2] *Gelidus . . . herba:* loosely translated = "There's a snake in the grass"
[1] *at all adventures:* by chance

"Thou sayest truth," quod he, "for if I had 'proved [2] his physick, I should not now have been alive."

And again, to another that said: "Sir, ye be an old man," he answered: "Yea, thou were not my physician."

Such manner checks are too little for the lewd [3] fools that will practise physick before they know what longeth to their name.

39. *Of him that would confess himself by writing*

There was a young man on a time which wrote a long libel [1] of his sins. Whether he did it for hypocrisy, foolishness, or oblivion, I can not say. And when he should confess himself, he gave it to the confessor to read. Which confessor, being well learned and expert in that business, perceived it would require a long time to read over. Wherefore, after a few words, he said: "I absolve thee from all the sins contained in this libel."

"Yea, but what shall my penance be?" quod the young man.

"Nothing else," said the confessor, "but that thou shalt the space of a month read this libel over every day seven times." And although he said it was impossible for him to do, yet the confessor would not change his sentence. By which merry subtle answer he confuted the brebble-brabble of the foolish fellow.

By this tale ye may perceive that he that occupieth this office, that is to say, a confessor, ought to be discreet, prudent, and well learned. This confessor knew well the ordinance of the holy church which willeth confession to be made with the mouth and not by writing.

[2] *'proved:* approved, taken
[3] *lewd:* stupid
[1] *libel:* list

40. *Of the hermit of Padowe*

An hermit of Padowe, that was reputed for a holy man, under the semblance of confession enticed many of the notablest wives of the town unto folly and lewdness. So at last when his offence was divulged and known (for hypocrisy can not long be hid) he was taken by the provost and brought before the prince of Padowe, Duke Francis the seventh of that name, which for his disport sent for his secretary to write the women's names that the hermit had lain by.

When the hermit had rehearsed many of the Duke's servants' wives and the secretary, merrily laughing, had written them, he seemed as he had all said. "Be there any more?" said the Duke.

"No, forsooth," said the hermit.

"Tell us truth," quod the secretary, "who be more, or else thou shalt be sharply punished."

Then the hermit sighing said: "Go to, write in thine own wife among the number of the others." Which saying so sore grieved the secretary that the pen fell out of his hand and the Duke laughed right heartily and said it was well done—that he that with so great pleasure heard the faults of other men's wives should come in the same number.

By this jest we may learn that one ought not to rejoice at another's grief or hurt. For little woteth [1] a man what hangeth over his own head.

---

[1] *woteth:* knows

41. *Of the uplandish man that saw the king*

An uplandish man, nourished [1] in the woods, came on a time to the city when all the streets were full of people and the common voice among them was: "The king cometh!" This rural man, moved with novelty of that voice, had great desire to see what that multitude hoved [2] to behold. Suddenly the king, with many nobles and 'states before him, came riding royally. Then the people all about steadfastly beheld the king and cried aloud: "God save the king! God save the king!"

This villein [3] hearing them cry so, said: "O, where is the king? Where is the king?"

Then one, showing him the king, said: "Yonder is he that rideth upon the goodly white horse."

"Is that the king?" quod the villein. "What, thou mockest me," quod he. "Methink that is a man in a painted garment."

By this tale ye may perceive (as Lycurgus proved by experience) that nourishing, good bringing up and exercise been more apt to lead folk to humanity and the doing of honest things than Nature herself. They for the most part are noble, free and virtuous which in their youth been well nourished up and virtuously endoctrined.

42. *Of the courtier that bad the boy hold his horse*

A courtier on a time that alighted of his horse at an inn gate said to a boy that stood thereby: "Ho! sir boy, hold my horse."

[1] *nourished:* reared
[2] *hoved:* hovered
[3] *villein:* bumpkin

The boy, as he had been afraid, answered: "O master, this a fierce horse—is one able to hold him?"

"Yes," quod the courtier, "one may hold him well enough."

"Well," quod the boy, "if one be able enough then I pray you hold him your own self."

43. *Of the deceitful scrivener*

A certain scrivener, which had but a bare living by his craft, imagined how he might get money. So he came to a young man and asked him if he were paid 10 pounds which a certain man that was dead borrowed and ought to have paid his father in time past. The young man said there was no such duty [1] owing in his father's name that he knew of. "It is of truth," quod the scrivener, "for here is the obligation [2] thereof which I made myself."

He provoked the young man so much that he gave him money for the obligation, and before the mayor he required the duty. The son of the man that was named to be debtor said plainly that his father never borrowed money; for if he had, it would appear by his books, after merchants' manner. And forthwith he went to the scrivener and said to him that he was a false man to write a thing that never was done.

"Son," said the scrivener, "thou wottest [3] not what was done that time. When thy father borrowed that sum of money, thou were not born. But he paid it again within three months after. I made the quittance thereof myself, whereby thy father is discharged."

So the young man was fain to give him money for the quittance. And when he had showed the quittance, he was dis-

---

[1] *duty:* debt
[2] *obligation:* contract
[3] *wottest:* know

charged of that grievance. Thus by his fair fraud the scrivener scraped money from them both.

By this tale ye may see that the children in this our time be very prudent to get money.

44. *Of him that said he believed his wife better than others, that she was chaste*

A certain man, whose wife (as the voice went) was not very chaste of her body, was warned of his friends to look better to the matter. The man went home and sharply rebuked his wife and told her between them both what his friends had said. She, knowing that perjury was no greater offense than avoutry,[1] with weeping and swearing defended her honesty, and bore her husband on hand [2] that they feigned those tales for envy that they had to see them live so quietly. With those words her husband was content and pleased.

So yet another time, again his friends warned him of his wife and bad him rebuke and chastise her. To whom he said: "I pray you trouble me no more with such words. Tell me, whether knoweth better my wife's faults, you or she?"

They said: "She."

"And she (quod he), whom I believe better than you all, saith plainly that ye lie."

This was well and wisely done. For one ought not to give light credence to those things wherein resteth perpetual grief of mind.

[1] *avoutry:* adultery
[2] *bore her husband on hand:* i.e., pulled the wool over his eyes

45. *Of him that paid his debt with crying "Bea"*

There was a man on a time which took as much ware of a merchant as drew to fifty pound, and riotously played and spent the same away within short space. So when the day of payment came he had neither money nor ware to pay, wherefore he was arrested and must come before the Justice.

When he saw there was none other remedy but that he should be constrained either to pay the debt or else to go to prison— wherefore he went to a subtle man of law and showed to him his case and desired him of counsel and help. "What wilt thou give me (quod the man of law), if I rid thee of this debt?"

"By my faith," said the debtor, "five marks—and lo, here it is ready. As soon as I am quit, ye shall have it."

"Good enough," quod the man of law, "but thou must be ruled by my counsel, and thus do: When thou comest before the Justice, whatsomever be said unto thee, look that thou answer to nothing, but cry 'bea' still, and let me alone with the rest."

"Content," quod he.

So, when they were come before the Justice, he said to the debtor: "Dost thou owe this merchant this sum of money or no?"

"Bea!" quod he.

"What! beast," quod the Justice, "answer to thy plaint or else thou wilt be condemned."

"Bea!" quod he again.

Then his man of law stood forth and said: "Sir, this man is but an idiot. Who would believe that this merchant, which is both wise and subtle, would trust this idiot, that can speak never a ready word, with 40 pennyworth of ware?" And so with such reasons he persuaded the Justice to cast the merchant in his own action.[1]

[1] *cast . . . action:* decide against the merchant

So when the sentence was given, the man of law drew the debtor aside and said: "Lo, how sayest thou now? Have not I done well for thee? Thou art clear quit of the debt that was demanded of thee. Wherefore, give me my money and God be with thee."

"Bea!" quod he.

"What!" quod the man of law, "thou needest not to cry 'bea' no longer. Thy matter [2] is dispatched. All is at a point [3]—there resteth nothing but to give me my wages that thou promised."

"Bea!" quod he again.

"I say," quod the man of law, "cry 'bea' no longer now, but give me my money."

"Bea!" quod he.

Thus the man of law, neither for fair nor foul, could get any other thing of his client but "Bea!" Wherefore, all angrily he departed and went his way.

By this tale ye may perceive that they which be the inventors and devisers of fraud and deceit been oftentimes thereby deceived themselves. And he that hath hid a snare to attrap others with, hath himself been taken therein.

46. *Of the woman that appealed from King Philip to King Philip*

A woman which, guiltless, on a time was condemned by King Philip of Macedon when he was not sober, said: "I appeal."

"Whither?" quod the king.

"To King Philip," quod she, "but that is when he is more sober and better advised—" which saying caused the king to look better on the matter and to do her right.

This writeth Val. Maximus. But Plutarch sayeth it was a man, and King Philip was half asleep when he gave sentence.

[2] *Thy matter:* thy case
[3] *All is at a point:* everything is decided

47. *Of the old woman that prayed for the welfare of the tyrant Denise*

What time Denise the tyrant reigned, for his cruelty and intolerable dealing he was hated of all the city of Syracuse, and everybody wished his death save one old woman, the which every morning prayed God to save him in good life and health.

When he understood that she so did, he marveled greatly at her undeserved benevolence—wherefore, he sent for her and asked why and how he had deserved that she prayed for him.

She answered and said: "I do it not without a cause. For when I was a maid we had a tyrant reigning over us whose death I greatly desired. When he was slain, there succeeded yet another yet more cruel than he—out of whose governance to be also delivered I thought it a high benefit. The third is thyself, that hast begun to reign over us more importunately than either of the other two. Thus, fearing lest when thou art gone a worse should succeed and reign over us, I pray God daily to preserve thee in health."

48. *Of the physician Eumonus*

A physician called Eumonus told a sick man that lay in great pain that he could not escape but he must needs die of that disease. This sick man within a while after, not by the physician's help but by the will of God, guerished [1] and was hole [2] of his disease. Howbeit, he was very low and bare brought. [3] And as he walked forth on a day, he met the same physician which,

[1] *guerished:* flourished
[2] *hole:* healed
[3] *bare brought:* very weak, barely brought through

doubting whether it were the same sick man or not, said: "Art not thou Gaius?"

"Yes, truly," quod he.

"Art thou alive or dead?" said the physician.

"I am dead," quod he.

"What dost thou here then?" said the physician.

"Because," quod he, "that I have experience of many things, God hath commanded me that I should come and take up all the physicians that I can get to him." Which saying made Eumonus as pale as ashes for fear.

Then Gaius said to him: "Dread thou not, Eumonus, though I said all physicians. For there is no man that hath wit that will take thee for one."

49. *Of Socrates and his scolding wife*

Laertius writeth that the wise man Socrates had a cursed scolding wife called Xantippe, the which on a day after she had alto [1] chided him, poured a piss pot on his head. He, taking all patiently, said: "Did not I tell you that when I heard Xantippe thunder so fast, that it would rain anon after?"

Whereby ye may see that the wiser a man is, the more patience he taketh. The wise poet Virgil saith: "All fortune by suffrance must be overcome."

50. *Of the physician that bare his patient on hand, he had eaten an ass*

A physician which had but small learning used, when he came to visit his patients, to touch the pulse; and if any appeared,[1]

---

[1] *Alto:* altogether, thoroughly
[1] *appeared:* grew worse

he would lay the blame on the patient and bear him on hand [2] that he did eat figs, apples, or some other thing that he forbad. And because the patients otherwhile confessed the same, they thought he had been a very cunning man.

His servant had great marvel how he perceived that, and desired his master to tell him whether he knew it by touching of the pulse or else by some other higher knowledge. Then said his master: "For the good service that thou hast done me I will open to thee this secret point. When I come into the patient's chamber, I look all about. And if I spy in the floor—shells, paring of cheese, of apples, or of pears, or any other scraps, anon I conject [3] that the patient hath eaten thereof. And so to th'end I would be blameless, I lay the fault on their misdieting."

Not long after, the same servant took on him to practice physick, which in like manner blamed his patients and said that they kept not the diet he gave them. And he bare them on hand that they ate somewhat, whereof he saw scraps on the floor. On a time, he came to a poor man of the country and promised to make him hole,[4] if he would be governed after him, and so gave him to drink (I wote not what) and went his way till on the morrow.

When he came again, he found the man sicker than ever he was. The rude [5] fool, not knowing the cause, beheld here and there about, and when he could see no scraps nor parings, he was sore troubled in his mind. So at the last he espied a saddle under the bed. Then said he all aloud that he had at length perceived how the sick man impaired: "He hath so excessively passed diet (quod he), that I wonder he is not dead!"

"How so?" quod they.

"Marry," quod he, "ye have made him to eat an whole ass! Lo, where the saddle lieth yet under the bed." For he thought the saddle had been left of the ass, as bones are of flesh. For which foolishness he was well laughed to scorn and mocked.

[2] *bear . . . on hand:* chastise
[3] *conject:* conjecture
[4] *hole:* well
[5] *rude:* unlearned

Thus as a good faithful physician is worthy of great honor
—for truly of him dependeth the greatest part of man's health
—so likewise a foolish and an unlearned that thinketh to cure
with words what he ought to do with herbs is not only worthy
to be derided and mocked but also punished, for nothing is more
perilous.

51. *Of the innholder's wife and her two lovers*

Near unto Florence dwelled an innholder whose wife was not
very dangerous [1] of her tail. Upon a night, as she was abed with
one of her lovers, there came another to have lain with her.
When she heard him come up the ladder, she met him and bad
him go hence, for she had no time then to fulfill his pleasure.
But for all her words, he would not go away, but still pressed
to come in.

So long they stood chiding that the good man came upon them
and asked them why they brawled so. The woman, not unpro-
vided of a deceitful answer, said: "Sir, this man would come
in perforce to slay or mischief another that is fled into our house
for succour, and hitherto I have kept him back."

When he that was within heard her say so, he began to pluck
up his heart and say he would be a-wreaked [2] on him without.
And he that was without made a face as he would kill him that
was within. The foolish man, her husband, inquired the cause
of their debate and took upon him to set them at one. [3] And
so the good silly man spake and made the peace between them
both. Yea, and farther, he gave them a gallon of wine, adding
to his wife's advoutry [4] the loss of his wine.

[1] *dangerous:* careful
[2] *a-wreaked:* avenged, wreak vengeance
[3] *set them at one:* reconcile them
[4] *advoutry:* adultery

52. *Of him that healed frantic men*

There dwelled a man in Italy which used to heal men that were frantic in this manner: He had within his house a gutter, or a ditch, full of water wherein he would put them—some to the middle leg, some to the knee, and some deeper, as they were mad.[1]

So one that was well amended and went about the house to do one thing and other for his meat, as he strode on a time at the gate looking into the street, he saw a gentleman ride by with a great sort of hawks and hounds. The which called to him and said: "You, gentleman, whither go ye?"

"On hunting," said the gentleman.

"What do you with all those kites and dogs?" quod he.

"They be hawks and hounds," quod the gentleman.

"Wherefore keep you them?" quod the other.

"For my pleasure," quod the gentleman.

"What costeth it you a year to keep them?" quod the other.

"Forty ducats," quod the gentleman.

"And what do they profit you?" quod he.

"Four ducats," quod the gentleman.

"Get thee lightly[2] hence," quod the madman, "for if my master come and find thee here, he will put thee into the gutter up to the throat!"

This tale toucheth such young gentlemen that dispend overmuch good[3] on hawks, hounds, and other trifles.

[1] *as they were mad:* according to the degree of their madness
[2] *lightly:* swiftly
[3] *good:* money

53. *Of him that said he was not worthy to open the gate to the king*

As a king of England hunted on a time in the county of Kent, he happed to come riding to a great gate whereby stood a husbandman of the country, to whom the king said: "Good fellow, put open the gate." The man, perceiving it was the king, said: "No, and please your grace, I am not worthy. But I will go fetch Master Cooper that dwelleth not past two miles hence, and he shall open to you the gate."

54. *Of Master Vavasour and Turpin his man*

Master Vavasour, sometime a judge of England, had a servant with him called Turpin which had done him service many years, wherefore he came unto his master on a time and said to him on this wise: "Sir, I have done you service long, wherefore I pray you give me somewhat to help me in mine old age."

"Turpin," quod he, "thou sayest truth, and hereon I have thought many a time. I will tell thee what thou shalt do. Now shortly I must ride up to London and if thou wilt bear my costs thither I will surely give thee such a thing that shall be worth to thee an hundred pounds."

"I am content," quod Turpin. So all the way as he rode, Turpin paid his costs till they came to their last lodging, and there after supper he came to his master and said: "Sir, I have borne your costs hitherto, as ye bad me. Now I pray you let me see what thing it is that should be worth an hundred pounds to me."

"Did I promise thee such a thing?" quod his master.

"Yea, forsooth," quod Turpin.

"Show me thy writing," quod Master Vavasour.

"I have none," said Turpin.

"Then thou art like to have nothing," said his master. "And learn this at me—whensoever thou makest a bargain with a man, look that thou take sure writing, and be well 'ware how thou makest a writing to any man. This point hath 'vailed me an hundred pounds in my days, and so it may thee." When Turpin saw there was none other remedy, he held himself content.

On the morrow, Turpin tarried a little behind his master to reckon with the hostess where they lay, and of her he borrowed so much money on his master's scarlet cloak as drew to [1] all the costs that they spent by the way.

Master Vavasour had not ridden past two miles but that it began to rain, wherefore he called for his cloak. His other serv-ant said Turpin was behind and had it with him. So they hovered under a tree till Turpin overtook them. When he was come, Master Vavasour all angrily said: "Thou knave, why comest thou not away with my cloak?"

"Sir, and please you," quod Turpin, "I have laid it to gage [2] for your costs all the way."

"Why, knave," quod his master, "didst thou not promise to bear my charges to London?"

"Did I?" quod Turpin.

"Yea," quod his master, "that thou didst."

"Let see, show me your writing thereof," quod Turpin, whereto his master, I think, answered but little.

55. *Of him that sought his wife against the stream*

A man the whose wife, as she came over a bridge, fell into the river and was drowned; wherefore he went and sought for

---

[1] *drew to:* covered
[2] *laid it to gage:* pawned it

her upward against the stream. Whereat his neighbors that went with him marveled and said he did nought—he should go seek her downward with the stream. "Nay," quod he. "I am sure I shall never find her that way, for she was so wayward and so contrary to everything while she lived, that I know very well now she is dead she will go against the stream."

56. *Of him that at a skirmish defended himself with his feet*

A lusty young gentleman of France that on a time was at a skirmish and defended himself valiantly with his feet, came into the court, into a chamber among ladies, with a goodly ring upon his finger—to whom a fair lady said: "Sir, why wear ye that ring upon your finger?"

"Wherefore ask you, madame?" quod he.

"Because (said she), your feet did you better service than your hands at the last skirmish that ye were at."

By this tale young men may learn to bear them well and valiantly for dread of reproach. Better it is with worship to die than with shame to live, albeit that Demosthenes said: "He that fleeth cometh again to battle."

57. *Of him that would give a song for his dinner*

There came a fellow on a time into a tavern and called for meat. So, when he had well dined, the taverner came to reckon and to have his money, to whom the fellow said he had no money —"but I will (quod he), content you with songs."

"Nay," quod the taverner, "I need no songs. I must have money."

"Why," quod the fellow, "if I sing a song to your pleasure will ye not then be content?"

"Yes," quod the taverner.

So he began and sang three or four ballads, and asked if he were pleased. "No," said the taverner.

Then he opened his purse and began to sing thus:

> When you have dined make no delay
> But pay your 'ost and go your way.

"Doth this song please you?" quod he.

"Yes, marry," said the taverner, "this pleaseth me well."

"Then, as covenant was (quod the fellow), ye be paid for your vitaile." [1] And so he departed and went his way.

This tale showeth that a man may be too hasty in making of a bargain and covenanting, and therefore a man ought to take good heed what he sayeth—for one word may bind a man to great inconvenience if the matter be weighty.

58. Of the fool that thought himself dead

There was a fellow dwelling at Florence called Nigniaca which was not very wise nor all a fool, but merry and jocund. A sort [1] of young men, for to laugh and pastime, appointed together to make him believe that he was sick. So, when they were agreed how they would do, one of them met him in the morning as he came out of his house and bad him good morrow, and then asked him if he were not ill at ease. "No," quod the fool, "I ail nothing, I thank God."

"By my faith, ye have a sickly pale color," quod the other, and went his way.

Anon after, another of them met him and asked him if he had not an ague—"for your face and color (quod he), showeth

---

[1] *vitaile:* food
[1] *sort:* pack

that ye be very sick." Then the fool began a little to doubt whether he were sick or no, for he half believed that they said truth.

When he had gone a little farther, the third man met him and said: "Jesu! man, what do you out of your bed? Ye look as ye would not live an hour to an end." Now he doubted greatly and thought verily in his mind that he had had some sharp ague —wherefore he stood still and would go no further.

And as he stood, the fourth man came and said: "Jesu! man, what dost thou here and art so sick? Get thee home to thy bed, for I perceive thou canst not live an hour to an end." Then the fool's heart began to faint and he prayed this last man that came to him, to help him home. "Yes," quod he, "I will do as much for thee as for mine own brother."

So home he brought him and laid him in his bed. And then he fared with himself as though he would give up the ghost. Forthwith came the other fellows and said he had well done to lay him in his bed. Anon after, came one which took on him to be a physician, which, touching the pulse, said the malady was so vehement that he could not live an hour.

So they, standing about the bed, said one to another: "Now he goeth his way, for his speech and sight fail him. By and by he will yield up the ghost. Therefore let us close his eyes and lay his hands across, and carry him forth to be buried." And then they said, lamenting one to another: "O! what a loss have we of this good fellow, our friend!"

The fool lay still, as one that were dead—yea, and thought in his mind that he was dead indeed. So they laid him on a bier and carried him through the city. And when anybody asked them what they carried, they said the corpse of Nigniaca to his grave.

And ever as they went, people drew about them. Among the press, there was a taverner's boy, the which when he heard that it was the corpse of Nigniaca, he said to them: "O! what a vile beastly knave, and what a strong thief is dead! By the mass, he was well worthy to have been hanged long ago."

When the fool heard those words, he put out his head and

said: "I wis, whoreson, if I were alive now as I am dead I would prove thee a false liar to thy face." They that carried him began to laugh so heartily that they set down the bier and went their way.

By this tale ye may see what the persuasion of many doth. Certainly he is very wise that is not inclined to folly, if he be steered thereunto by a multitude. Yet sapience is found in few persons, and they be lightly [2] old sober men.

59. *Of the old man and his son that brought his ass to the town to sell*

An old man on a time and a little boy, his son, drove a little ass before them which he purposed to sell at the market town that they went to. And because he so did, the folks that wrought by the wayside blamed him—wherefore, he set up his son and went himself on foot. Others, that saw that, called him fool because he let the young boy ride and he, being so aged, to go afoot.

Then he took down the boy and leapt up and rode himself. When he had ridden a little way, he heard others that blamed him because he made the little young boy run after as a servant, and he his father to ride. Then he set up the boy behind him and so rode forth.

Anon he met with others that asked him if the ass were his own, by which words he conjectured that he did not well so to overcharge the little silly [1] ass, that unethe [2] was able to bear one.

Thus he, troubled with their divers and manifold opinions—which neither with his ass vacant, nor he alone, nor his son alone, nor both together riding at once on the ass—could pass forth without detraction and blame. Wherefore, at last he bound the ass's feet together and put through a staff; and so he and his

[2] *lightly:* usually
[1] *silly:* poor, pathetic
[2] *unethe:* hardly

son began to bear the ass between them on their shoulders to the town. The novelty of which sight caused everybody to laugh and blame the foolishness of them both.

The silly old man was so sore aggrieved that, as he sat and rested him on a river's side, he threw his ass into the water. And so when he had drowned his ass he turned home again. Thus the good man, desiring to please everybody, contenting none at all, lost his ass.

By this tale appeareth plainly that they which commit themselves to the opinion of the common people been oppressed with great misery and servage [3]—for how is it possible to please all, when every man hath a divers opinion and diversly judgeth? And that was well known to the poet when he said:

> Scinditur incertum studia in contraria vulgus.[4]

And as Cicero, Persius, and Flaccus say: "As many men, so many minds; as many heads, so many wits." "That, that pleaseth one, displeaseth another." "Few allow that, that they love not; and that, that a man alloweth, he thinketh good." Therefore the best is that every man live well, as a good Christian man should, and care not for the vain words and jangling of the people. For babbling (as Plutarch sayeth) is a grievous disease, and hard to be remedied. For that, that should heal it (which is words of wisdom) cureth them that hearkeneth thereto; but prattlers will hear none but themselves.

60. Of him that sought his ass and rode on his back

There was in the country of Florence an husbandman that used to carry corn to the market upon many little asses. On a time, as he came homeward, because he was somewhat weary, to

---

[3] *servage:* servitude
[4] *Scinditur . . . vulgus:* "The wavering crowd is split into opposing parties" (*Aeneid,* II, 39).

ease himself he rode on one of the strongest of them. And as he rode, driving his asses before him, he counted them and forgot the ass that he rode on—wherefore he thought still that he lacked one.

Thus sore troubled in his mind, he bad his wife set up his asses and hastily rode again back to the town seven miles off to seek the ass that he rode on. He asked of everybody that he met if they saw an ass stray alone. When he heard everybody say they saw none such, making great sorrow he returned home again.

At last, when he was alighted, his wife perceived and showed him plainly that the ass that he rode on was the same that he sought and made such sorrow for.

This jest may be well applied unto such as note the defaults that they lightly [1] spy in others, and take none heed nor cannot see what ills they have or been spotted with themselves.

61. *The answer of Fabius to Livius*

When Hannibal, the captain of Carthage, had conquered Tarent (a town pertaining to the Romans)—all save the castle, and had left a garrison to keep it, the worthy Roman Fabius had knowledge thereof. He privily conducted an army thither and got the town again and pillaged it. Then M. Livius that kept the castle with a garrison said, boasting himself, that Fabius had gotten the town through him and his help. "You say truth," quod Fabius, "for if you had not lost the town, I should never have gotten it."

[1] *lightly:* readily

62. *The answer of Poltis, the king of Thrace, to the Trojan ambassadors*

Plutarch likewise rehearseth that during the war of Troy the Greeks and also the Trojans sent ambassadors to a king of Thrace called Poltis. Which king answered the ambassadors and bade that Alexander should deliver again Helen (for she was the cause of the war) and he would give him two fair wives for her.

63. *The wise answer of Hannibal to King Antiochus, concerning his rich army*

When King Antiochus had prepared to make war to the Romans, he caused his army to muster before Hannibal. So they showed and mustered, both horsemen and foot men, of whose rich and sumptuous armor and apparel all the field glistened and shone. "How say you?" quod the King to Hannibal. "Is not this army sufficient enough for the Romans?"

"Yes," quod Hannibal, "and though [1] they were the most covetous of all the world." The King meant one thing, and he answered another.

64. *The words of Popilius the Roman ambassador to Antiochus the king*

One C. Popilius was sent upon a time by the Senators of Rome with letters to Antiochus the king of Syria, wherein the King was

[1] *and though:* even if

commanded to call his army back again out of Egypt, and that he should suffer the children of Ptolemy and their realm in peace. As the ambassador came by the King's tents and pavilions, Antiochus a good way off saluted him, but he did not salute the king again, but delivered to him his letters.

When the King had read the letters, he said that he must take counsel before he made him an answer. Popilius, with a rod that he had in his hand, made a compass [1] about the King, and said: "Even here standing, take counsel and make me an answer."

Every man had marvel at the gravity and stout stomache of the man, and when Antiochus was content to do as the Romans would have him, then Popilius both saluted and embraced him.

65. *Of him that loved the merchant's wife*

There was a young lusty gentleman upon a time that was right amorous and loved a certain merchant's wife out of all measure—insomuch that he followed her to the church and other places—but he durst never speak. At the last, he, with two or three of his fellows, followed her to a friar's where he had time and place convenient to speak three or four words to her that he before had devised. So one of his fellows said: "Go now. Speak to her." But he stood still, all astonished.

They egged and provoked him so much that at last he went unto her and, clean forgetting those words that he had thought to have spoken, he said to her in this wise: "Mistress, I am your own little servant."

Whereat she smiled and said: "Sir, I need not your service, for I have servants enough at home that can brush, sponge, wash and do all my other business." The which answer and foolish bashment of the gentleman caused his fellows to laugh heartily.

This manner of folly was well known to the poet when he said:

[1] *compass:* circle

Incipit affari, mediaque in voce resistit.[1]

> Foolish love maketh folks astonied [2]
> And eke to rave without remembrance
> When they should speak, they bene abashed
> And of their words can make none utterance
> Nor be so hardy themselves to advance
> What time they see of her the swete face
> Of whom the love their hearts doth embrace.

66. *Of the woman that covered her head and showed her tail*

As a woman that for a certain impediment had shaved her head sat in her house bareheaded, one of her neighbors called her forth hastily into the street, and for haste she forgot to put on her kerchief. When her neighbor saw her so, she blamed her for coming abroad bareheaded. Wherefore she whipped up her clothes over her head, and so to cover her head she showed her arse. They that stood by began to laugh at her foolishness, which to hide a little fault showed a greater.

This tale toucheth them that would cover a small offense with a greater wickedness, and as the proverb sayeth: "Stumble at a straw and leap over a block."

67. *How Alexander was 'monished to slay the first that he met*

When great Alexander would enter into Persia land with his army, he counseled with Apollo of his good speed. And by lot he was warned that he should command to slay the first that he met when he issued out at a gate. Perchance, the first that he met

---

[1] *Incipit . . . resistit:* She begins to speak and stops short in mid-word (*Aeneid*, IV, 76).
[2] *astonied:* paralyzed, numb

was a man driving an ass before him. Incontinent the King commanded to take and put him to death.

When the poor man saw that they would slay him, he said: "What have I done? Shall I that am an innocent be put to death?" Alexander, to excuse his deed, said that he was warned by divine monition to command to slay the first that he met coming out at that gate.

"If it be so, mighty King (quod the man), then the lot divine hath ordained another to suffer this death and not me, for the little ass that I drove before me met you first." Which subtle saying greatly pleased Alexander, for else he had done amiss; and so he caused the beast to be slain.

By this tale one may note that it is better sometimes to be last than first.

68. *How the city of Lamsac was saved from destruction*

As great Alexander on a time was fully purposed to have utterly destroyed a great city called Lamsac, he saw his master Anaximenes come toward him without the walls. And because the King perceived manifestly that he came to entreat him for the city, he swore a great oath that he would not do that that he came to desire him for. Then Anaximenes said: "Sir, I desire your grace that this same city Lamsac may be utterly destroyed." Through which sage and subtle saying the noble ancient city was saved from ruin and destruction.

69. *How Demosthenes defended a maid*

There were two men on a time the which left a great sum of money in keeping with a maiden on this condition: that she should not deliver it again except they came both together for it. Not long after, one of them came to her mourningly arrayed and said that his fellow was dead, and so required the money, and she delivered it to him.

Shortly after, came the other man and required to have the money that was left with her in keeping. The maiden was then so sorrowful—both for lack of the money and for one to defend her cause—that she thought to hang herself. But Demosthenes, that excellent orator, spake for her and said: "Sir, this maiden is ready to 'quit her fidelity [1] and to deliver again the money that was left with her in keeping, so that [2] thou wilt bring thy fellow with thee to receive it." But that he could not do.

70. *Of him that desired to be made a gentleman*

There was a rude clubbish [1] fellow that long had served the Duke of Orleans, wherefore he came on a time to the Duke and desired to be made a gentleman. To whom the Duke answered: "In good faith, I may well make thee rich, but as for gentleman I can never make thee."

By which words appeareth that goods and riches do not make a gentleman, but noble and virtuous conditions [2] do.

71. *Of the gentleman and his shrewd wife*

There was a certain gentleman that had a cursed chiding wife that went every day and complained on him to a religious man, the which religious man took upon him by way of confession to

[1] *'quit her fidelity:* acquit her trust
[2] *so that:* provided that
[1] *clubbish:* uncouth
[2] *conditions:* manners

reconcile and accord them together. And the gentleman was very well content that he so should do, and came to him therefore.

When the gentleman was come, the religious man bad him show his offenses and trespasses. "No," quod the gentleman, "that needeth not, for I know very well my wife hath showed unto you all the offenses that ever I did and much more."

72. *Of the two young men that rode to Walsingham*

One John Roynolds rode out of London upon a time toward Walsingham in company of a young man of the same city that had not much been accustomed to ride. So they came to an inn where a great company was lodged. And in the morning when every man made him ready to ride, and some were on horseback setting forward, John Roynolds found his companion sitting in a brown study at the inn gate, to whom he said: "For shame, man. How sittest thou? Why dost thou not make thee ready to horseback, that we might set forward with company?"

"I tarry (quod he), for a good cause."

"For what cause?" quod Roynolds.

"Marry (quod he), here be so many horses that I can not tell which is mine own among the others, and I know well—when every man is ridden and gone, the horse that remaineth behind must needs be mine."

73. *Of the young man of Bruges and his spouse*

A young man of Bruges that was betrothed to a fair maiden came on a time when her mother was out of the way and had to do with her. When her mother was come in, anon she perceived by her daughter's cheer [1] what she had done. Wherefore she was so sore displeased that she sued a divorce, and would in no wise suffer that the young man should marry her daughter.

Not long after, the same young man was married to another maiden of the same parish, and as he and his wife sat talking on a time of the foresaid damsel, to whom he was betrothed, he fell in a nice [2] laughing. "Whereat laugh ye?" quod his wife.

"It chanced on a time (quod he), that she and I did such a thing together and she told it to her mother."

"Therein (quod his wife), she played the fool. A servant of my father's played that game with me an hundred times, and yet I never told my mother."

When he heard her say so, he left his nice laughing.

74. *Of him that made as he had been a chaste liver*

A fellow that took upon him as he had been the most chaste and best disposed man living was by one of his fellows on a time taken in advoutry [1] and sharply rebuked for it, because he prated so much of chastity and yet was taken in the same fault. To whom he answered again: "O fool, dost think that I did it for bodily pleasure? No! No! I did it but only to subdue my flesh and to purge my reins." [2]

Whereby ye may perceive that of all other, dissembling hypocrites are the worst.

[1] *cheer:* countenance
[2] *nice:* foolish
[1] *advoutry:* adultery
[2] *reins:* kidneys

75. *Of him that the old rood fell on*

As a man kneeled upon a time praying before an old rood,[1] the rood fell down on him and broke his head; wherefore he would come no more in the church half-a-year after. At length, by the provocation of his neighbors, he came to the church again. And because he saw his neighbors kneel before the same rood, he kneeled down likewise and said thus: "Well, I may cap[2] and kneel to thee, but thou shalt never have mine heart again as long as I live."

By which tale appeareth that by gentle and courteous entreating, men's minds been obtained. For though the people cap and kneel to one in high authority, yet little woteth[3] he what they think.

76. *Of the widow that would not wed for bodily pleasure*

There was a rich widow which desired a gossip[1] of hers that she would get her an husband: "Not for the nice play," quod she, "but to th'intent he may keep my goods[2] together, which is a hard thing for me to do, being a lone woman." Her gossip, which understood her conceit, promised her so to do.

About three or four days after, she came to her again and said: "Gossip, I have found an husband for you that is a prudent, a wary, and a worldly wise man. But he lacketh his privy members whereof ye force[3] not."

[1] *rood:* wooden cross
[2] *cap:* take off my cap
[3] *woteth:* imagines
[1] *gossip:* cousin
[2] *goods:* property
[3] *force:* care

"Go to the devil with that husband (quod the widow), for though that I desire not the nice play, yet I will that mine husband shall have that wherewith we may be reconciled if we fall at variance."

77. *Of the covetous ambassador that would hear no music*

When a covetous man on a time was come unto a certain city whither he was sent as ambassador for his country, anon the minstrels of the city came to him to fill his ears with sweet din, to th'intent he should fill their purses with money. But he, perceiving that, bad one of his servants go and tell them that he could not then attend to hear their music but he must demean great sorrow, for his mother was dead. So the minstrels, disappointed of their purpose, all sadly went their way.

And when a worshipful man of the city that was his friend heard tell of his mourning, he came to visit and comfort him. And so in talking together he asked how long ago was it that his mother deceased. "Truly (quod he), it is 40 years ago." Then his friend, understanding his subtlety, began to laugh heartily.

This tale is applied to the covetous men which by all craft and means study to keep and increase their money and substance, against which vice many things been written. "As far (sayeth one), is that from a covetous man that he hath, as that he hath not." [1] And Diogenes calleth covetousness the head of all evils, and Saint Hieronyme calleth covetousness the root of all evils. And for an example, the tale following shall be of covetousness.

[1] *As far . . . he hath not:* i.e., the more he has, the more he wants.

78. *How Denise the tyrant served a covetous man*

It was showed to Denise the tyrant that a covetous man of the city had hid a great sum of money in the ground and lived most wretchedly. Wherefore, he sent for the man and commanded him to go dig up the money, and so to deliver it unto him. The man obeyed, and delivered unto the tyrant all the gold and treasure that he had, save a small sum that he privily kept aside—wherewith he went into another city and forsook Syracuse, and there bought a little land whereupon he lived.

When the tyrant understood that he had so done, he sent for him again. And when he was come, the tyrant said to him: "Sith[1] thou hast learned now to use well thy goods, and not to keep them unprofitably, I will restore them all to thee again." And so he did.

79. *Of the old man that conjured the boy out of the apple tree with stones*

As an old man walked on a time in his orchard he looked up and saw a boy sit in a tree stealing his apples, whom he entreated with fair words to come down and let his apples alone. And when the old man saw that the boy cared nought for him because of his age and set nought by his words, he said: "I have heard say that not only in words but also in herbs should be great virtue." Wherefore he plucked up herbs and began to throw them at the boy. Whereat the boy laughed heartily and thought that the old man had been mad to think to drive him out of the tree with casting of herbs.

[1] *Sith:* since

Then the old man said: "Well, seeing that neither words nor herbs have no virtue against the stealer of my goods, I will prove [1] what stones will do, in which, I have heard men say, is great virtue." And so he gathered his lap full of stones and threw them at the boy and compelled him to come down and run away.

This tale showeth that they that been wise prove many ways before they arm themselves.

80. *Of the rich man that would not have a glister*

There was a certain rich man on a time which fell sick, to the whose curing came many physicians (for flies by heaps flee to honey). Among them all there was one that said that he must needs take a glister [1] if he would be hole.[2] When the sick man, that was not enured with [3] that medicine, heard him say so, he said in a great fury: "Out-a-doors with those physicians! They be mad. For whereas my pain is in my head, they would heal me in mine arse."

This fable showeth that wholesome things to them that lack knowledge and experience seem hurtful.

81. *Of him that feigned himself dead to prove what his wife would do*

A young married man on a time to prove, to hear and to see what his wife would do if he were dead, came into his house

[1] *prove:* try
[1] *glister:* enema
[2] *hole:* healed
[3] *enured with:* used to

while his wife was forth washing of clothes and laid him down on the floor as he had been dead. When his wife came in and saw him lie so, she thought he had been dead indeed, wherefore she stood even still and devised with herself whether was better to bewail his death forthwith or else to dine first, for she had eat no meat of all the day.

All other things considered, she determined to dine first. So she cut a collop [1] of bacon and broiled it on the coals and began to eat thereon apace. She was so hungry that she took no heed of drink. At last the saltiness of the meat made her to thirst so sore that she must needs drink. So as she took the pot in her hand and was going down into her cellar to draw drink, suddenly came one of her neighbors for a coal afire. Wherefore she stepped back quickly. And though she was right thirsty, yet she set the pot aside, and as her husband had then fallen down dead, she began to weep—and with many lamentable words to bewail his death—which weeping and wailing and sudden death of her husband caused all the neighbors to come thither.

The man lay still on the floor and so held his breath and closed his eyes that he seemed for certain to be dead. At last, when he thought he had made pastime enough, and hearing his wife say thus: "Alas! dear husband, what shall I do now?"—he looked up and said: "Full ill, my sweet wife, except ye go quickly and drink." Wherewith they all from weeping turned to laughing, especially when they understood the matter and the cause of her thirst.

Whereby ye may see that not without a good skill the poet said:

Ut flerent ocules erudiere suos.[2]

---

[1] *collop:* slice
[2] *Ut flerent . . . suos: i.e.,* "Women train their eyes to weep" (Ovid, *Remedia Amoris,* l. 690).

82. *Of the poor man into whose house thieves broke by night*

There was a poor man on a time the which unto thieves that broke into his house on night, he said in this wise: "Sirs, I marvel that ye think to find anything here by night, for I ensure you I can find nothing when it is broad day."

> By this tale appeareth plainly
> That poverty is a wealthy misery.

83. *Of him that should have been hanged for his scoffing*

There was a merry fellow in high Almayn the which with his scoffing and jesting had so much displeased a great lord of the country that he threatened to hang him if ever he could take him in his country. Not long after, this lord's servants took him, and hanged he should be.

When he saw there was no remedy but that he should die, he said: "My lord, I must needs suffer death, which I know I have well deserved. But yet I beseech you grant me one petition for my soul's health." The lord, at the instance of the people that stood about, so it did not concern his life, was content to grant it him.

Then the fellow said: "I desire you, my lord, that after I am hanged, to come three mornings fresh and fasting, and kiss me on the bare arse." Whereunto the lord answered: "The devil kiss thine arse"—and so let him go.

84. *Of him that had his goose stole*

A man that had a goose stole from him went and complained to the curate and desired him to do so much as help that he had his goose again. The curate said he would. So on Sunday, the curate—as though he would curse—went up into the pulpit and bad everybody sit down. So when they were set he said: "Why sit ye not down?"

"We be set already," quod they.

"Nay (quod the curate), he that did steal the goose sitteth not."

"Yes, that I do," quod he.

"Sayest thou that?" quod the curate. "I charge thee, on pain of cursing, to bring the goose home again."

85. *Of the beggar that said he was kin to King Philip of Macedon*

There came a beggar to King Philip of Macedon on a time and prayed the king to give him somewhat, and farther he said he was his kinsman. And when the king asked him which way, he answered and said how they came both of Adam. Then the king commanded to give him an alms.

When the beggar saw it was but a small piece of money, he said that was not a seemly gift for a king. The king answered: "If I should give every man so much that is my kinsman like as thou art, I should leave nothing for myself."

86. *Of Dante's answer to the jester*

Dante the poet dwelled a while with Can, the Prince de la Scala, with whom also dwelled another Florentine that had neither learning nor prudence, and was a man meet for nothing but to scoff and jest. But yet with his merry toys, he so moved the said Can that he did greatly enrich him. And, because Dante despised his foolishness, this scoffer said to him: "How cometh it, Dante, that thou art held so wise and so well learned and yet art poor and needy? I am an unlearned man and am an ignorant fool, and yet I am far richer than thou art."

To whom Dante answered: "If I may find a lord like and conformable to my manners, as thou hast found to thine, he will likewise make me rich."

87. *Of him that had sore eyes*

One that had sore eyes was warned of the physician that he should in any wise forbear drinking or else lose his eyes, to whom he said: "It is more pleasure for me to lose mine eyes with drinking than to keep them for worms to eat them out."

By this tale ye may perceive that it availeth not to warn some for their own profit.

88. *Of the old woman that had sore eyes*

There was an old woman the which bargained with a surgeon to heal her sore eyes, and when he had made her eyes heal and that she saw better, she covenanted that he should be paid his money and not before. So he laid a medicine to her eyes that should not be taken away the space of five days, in which time she might not look up.[1]

Every day when he came to dress her, he bare away somewhat of her household stuff, table cloths, candlesticks, and dishes. He left nothing that he could carry clean. So when her eyes were hole,[2] she looked up and saw that her household stuff was carried away.

She said to the surgeon that came and required his money for his labor: "Sir, my promise was to pay you when ye made me see better than I did before."

"That is truth," quod he.

"Marry," quod she, "but I see worse now than I did. Before ye laid medicines to mine eyes, I saw much fair stuff in mine house and now I see nothing at all."

89. *Of him that had the custody of a ward*

A certain man that had the custody of a ward and his goods [1] and in short space had spent all away, was by the governor of the city commanded to bring in his books of *Introitus et exitus*, that is to say, of entrance and laying out, and to give account of the orphan's goods. So when he came, he showed first his mouth and said, "Here it went in." And after he showed up his arse and said, "Here it went out, and other books of *Introitus et exitus* I have none."

[1] *look up:* open her eyes
[2] *hole:* healed
[1] *goods:* property

90. *Of the excellent painter that had foul children*

There was a painter in Rome that was an excellent cunning [1] man, and because he had foul [2] children, one said to him: "By my faith, I marvel that you paint so goodly and get so foul children."

"Yea," quod the painter, "I make my children in the dark and I paint those figures by daylight."

91. *Of the scoffer that made a man a soothsayer*

There was a merry scoffing fellow on a time the which took on him to teach a man to be a soothsayer. When they were agreed what he should have for his labor, the scoffer said to the man: "Hold! Eat this round pellet and I warrant thou shalt be a soothsayer."

The man took and put it in his mouth and began to champ thereon, but it savored so ill that he spit it out forthwith and said: "Fi! This pellet that thou givest me to eat savoreth all of a turd."

"Thou sayest truth (quod the scoffer), now thou art a soothsayer [1] and therefore pay me my money."

[1] *cunning:* skillful
[2] *foul:* ugly
[1] The pun here is on truth = sooth.

92. *Of the merchant of Florence called Charles*

A merchant of Florence called Charles came from Avignon to Rome, and as he sat at supper with a great company, one asked him how the Florentines at Avignon fared. He said they were merry and glad—"For they that dwell there a year (quod he), be as men that were frantic and out of their minds."

Then another that sat at supper with them asked this Charles how long he had dwelled there. He answered: "Six months."

"Charles (quod he that asked him the question), thou hast a great wit, for it, that others be about twelve months, thou hast fulfilled in half a year."

93. *Of the Cheshire man called Evlyn*

There dwelled a man in Cheshire called Evlyn which used to go to the town many times, and there he would sit drinking till twelve of the clock at night and then go home. So on a time he carried a little boy, his son, on his shoulder with him. And when the child fell asleep about nine of the clock, the alewife brought him to bed with her children.

At midnight Evlyn went home, and thought no more of his child. As soon as he came home, his wife asked for her child. When she spoke of the child, he looked on his shoulder, and when he saw he was not there, he said he wist nat where he was.

"Out upon thee, whoreson (quod she), thou hast let my child fall into the water" (for he passed over the water of Dee at a bridge).

"Thou liest, whore (quod he), for if he had fallen into the water I should have heard him plump."

94. *Of him that desired to be set upon the pillory*

There were three loitering fellows fell in company on a time, the which went so long together till all their money was spent. When their money was gone, one of them said: "What shall we do now?"

"By my faith (quod another), if I might come where press [1] of people were, I could get money enough for us."

"And I (quod the third), can assemble people together lightly." [2]

So when they came into a little town where a new pillory was set up, he that said he could lightly assemble people together, went to the bailey [3] of the town which was a butcher and desired him that he would give him leave to have the maidenhead of the pillory.

Which request at the first abashed the bailey, for he wist not what he meant thereby. Wherefore he took counsel of his neighbors what was best to do, and they bade him set up the knave and spare not.

So when he was on the pillory he looked about and saw his two fellows busy in the holes of the butchers' aprons, where they used to put their money. Then he said: "There now, go to apace." The people gaped up still [4] and laughed. And when he saw that his fellows had sped their matters and were going away, he said to the people: "Now turn the pillory once about and then I will come down." So they, laughing heartily, did.

When the fellow was come down from the pillory, the bailey said to him: "By my faith, thou art a good fellow, and because thou hast made us so good sport, hold, I will give thee a groat to

[1] *press:* a crowd
[2] *lightly:* easily
[3] *bailey:* chief magistrate
[4] *gaped up still:* i.e., remained looking up at him

drink—" and so put his hand in the hole of his apron. But there he found never a penny.

"Cockes arms! (quod the bailey), my purse is picked and my money is gone."

"Sir (quod the fellow), I trust ye will bear me record that I have it not."

"No, by the mass," quod he, "thou were on the pillory the while."

"Then, no force," [5] quod the fellow, and went his way.

95. *Of the widow's daughter that was sent to the abbot with a couple of capons*

There was an abbot that had a widow to his tenant, which widow on a time sent her daughter with a couple of capons to the abbot. And when the maiden came with her present, she found the abbot sitting at dinner, to whom she said: "Much good do it thee, my lord!"

"Ha! welcome, maiden," quod he.

"My lord (quod she), my mother hath sent thee here a couple of capons."

"God a mercy, maiden," quod he. And so he made her to be set down at his own table to eat some meat.

Among other meats, the abbot had then a green goose with sorrel sauce whereof he did eat. So one that sat at the abbot's table gave the rump of the goose to the maid to pick thereon.

She took the rump in her hand and because she saw the abbot and others wet their meat in the sorrel sauce, she said: "My lord, I pray thee give me leave to wet mine arse in thy green sauce."

[5] *no force:* no matter

96. *Of the two men that drank a pint of white wine together*

There came two homely men of the country into a tavern on a time to drink a pint of wine. So they sat still and wist not what wine to call for. At last, hearing every man call for white wine as clear as water of the rock, they bad the drawer bring them a pint of white wine as clear as water of the rock.

The drawer, seeing and perceiving by their words that they were but blunt fellows, he brought them a pint of clear water. The one of them filled the cup and drank to his fellow and said: "Hold, neighbor, by mass, chadde [1] as liefe drink water, save only for the name of wine."

97. *Of the doctor that went with the fowler to catch birds*

There was a doctor [1] on a time which desired a fowler, that went to catch birds with an owl, that he might go with him. The birder was content, and dressed him with bows and set him by his owl and bad him say nothing.

When he saw the birds alight apace, he said: "There be many birds alighted. Draw thy nets—" wherewith the birds flew away. The birder was very angry and blamed him greatly for his speaking. Then he promised to hold his peace.

When the birder was in again and many birds were alighted, master doctor said in Latin: "Aves permultae adsunt—" wherewith the birds flew away. The birder came out right angry and sore displeased and said that by his babbling he had twice lost

[1] *chadde:* ich had (dialect) = I had
[1] *doctor:* professor, scholar

his prey. "Why, thinkest thou, fool (quod the doctor), that the birds do understand Latin?"

This doctor thought that the understanding and not the noise had feared away the birds.

98. *Of him that undertook to teach an ass to read*

There was a certain tyrant, the which to pillage one of his subjects of his goods, commanded him to teach an ass to spell and read. He said it was impossible except he might have space enough thereto. And when the tyrant bad him ask what time he would, he desired ten years respite.

But yet because he undertook a thing impossible, everybody laughed him to scorn. He turned toward his friends and said: "I am nothing afraid, for in that space either I, the ass, or else my lord may die."

By which tale appeareth that it is wholesome to take leisure enough about a thing that is hard to do, specially when a man cannot choose to take it on hand.[1]

99. *Of the friar that confessed the woman*

As a fair young woman of the town of Amilie confessed her to a friar, he began to burn so in concupiscence of the flesh that he enticed her to consent to his will. And they agreed that she should feign herself sick and send for him to shrive her.

Within three days after, she feigned herself sick and lay down in her bed and sent for the same friar to shrive her. When the friar was come and everybody voided [1] out of the chamber, he

[1] *specially . . . hand:* especially when he has no choice
[1] *voided:* emptied

went to bed to the woman and there lay a long space with her.

Her husband, suspecting so long a confession, came into the chamber—whose sudden coming so sore abashed the friar that he went his way and left his breech behind him lying on the bed.

When her husband saw the breech, he said aloud: "This was not a friar but an advouterer." [2] And for great abomination of the deed he called all his household to see it.

And forthwith he went and complained to the warden of that convent and threatened to slay him that had done the deed. The warden, to appease his anger, said that such publishing was to the shame of him and his household. The man said the breech was so openly found that he could not hide it.

The warden to remedy the matter said it was Saint Francis' breech, an holy relic that his brother carried thither for the woman's health, and that he and his convent would come and fetch it home with procession. With those words the man was content.

Anon the warden and his friars, with the cross before them and arrayed in holy vestments, went to the house and took up the breech, and two of them on a cloth of silk bore it solemnly on high between their hands. And everybody that met them kneeled down and kissed it.

So with great ceremony and song they brought it home to their convent. But after, when this was known, ambassadors of the same city went and complained thereof before the Holy See Apostolic.

100. *How a chaplain of Louven deceived an usurer*

In the town of Louven was a chaplain called Antony of whose merry sayings and doings is much talking. As he met on a day one or two of his acquaintance, he desired them home with him

[2] *advouterer:* adulterer

to dinner. But meat had he none, nor money. There was no remedy but to make a shift.

Forth he goeth and into an usurer's kitchen, with whom he was familiar, and privily under his gown he carried out the pot with meat that was sod [1] for the usurer's dinner.

When he came home, he put out the meat and made the pot to be scoured bright and sent a boy with the same pot to the usurer to borrow two groats thereon, and bad the boy take of bill [2] of his hand that such a brass pot he delivered him. The boy did as he was bid. And with the money that he had of the usurer, he bought wine for their dinner.

When the usurer should go to dinner, the pot and meat was gone. Wherefore he alto [3] chid his maid. She said there came nobody all the day but Sir Antony. They asked him and he said he had none. At length, they said in earnest he and no man else had the pot.

"By my faith (quod he), I borrowed such a pot upon a time but I sent it home again—" and so called witness to them and said: "Lo, how perilous it is to deal with men nowadays without writing. They would lay theft to my charge if I had no writing of the usurer's hand—" and so he showed out the writing. And when they understood the deceit, there was good laughing.

101. *Of the same chaplain and one that spited him*

The same Antony dined on a time with a sort [1] of merry fellows among whom there was one that greatly spited him in his scoffs and merry jests. And as they sat laughing and sporting, one

---

[1] *sod:* boiled
[2] *bill:* receipt
[3] *alto:* thoroughly
[1] *sort:* pack

asked which was the most reverent part of man's body. One said the eye, the other the nose, but Antony—because he knew his annoyer would name the clean contrary—said the mouth was the most reverent part.

"Nay," quod his annoyer. "The part that we sit on is the most reverent." And because they marveled why, he made this reason: That he was most honorable among the common people that was first set, and the part that he named was first set. Which saying contented them and they laughed merrily. He was not a little proud of his saying and that he had overcome Antony. This passed forth.

Four or five days after, they were both bid to dinner in another place. When Antony came in, he found his annoyer that sat talking with another while the dinner was making ready. Antony turned his back to him and let a great fart against his face.

His annoyer, greatly disdaining, said: "Walk, knave, with a mischief! Where hast thou been nurtured?"

"Why and disdainest thou?" quod Antony. "If I had saluted thee with my mouth, thou wouldst have saluted me again. And now I greet thee with that part of my body that, by thy own saying, is most honorable, thou callest me knave." Thus he got again his praise that he had lost before.

102. *Of the old man that put himself in his son's hands*

There was a certain old man which let his son to marry and to bring his wife and his children to dwell with him and to take all the house into his own hand and guiding. So a certain time, the old man was set and kept the upper end of the table; afterwards they set him lower, about the midst of the table; thirdly, they set him at the nether end of the table; fourthly, he was set among the servants; fifthly, they made him a couch behind the hall door and cast on him an old sackcloth. Not long after, the old man died.

When he was dead, the young man's son came to him and said: "Father, I pray you give me this old sackcloth that was wont to cover my grandfather."

"What wouldst thou do with it?" said his father.

"Forsooth," said the child, "it shall serve to cover you when ye be old, like as it did my grandfather." At which words of the child this man ought to have been ashamed and sorry. For it is written: "Son, reverence and help thy father in his old age, and make him not thoughtful and heavy in his life, and though he dote [1] forgive it him. He that honoreth his father shall live the longer and shall rejoice in his own children." [2]

103. *Of him that had a fly painted on his shield*

A young man that on a time went a-warfare caused a fly to be painted in his shield, even of the very greatness of a fly. Wherefore some laughed at him and said: "Ye do well, because ye will not be known."

"Yes," quod he, "I do it because I will be known and spoken of. For I will approach so near our enemies that they shall well discern what arms I bear."

Thus it, that was laid to him for a blame of cowardice, was by his sharp wit turned to a show of manliness. And the noble and valiant Archidamus said: "Shot of crossbows, slings, and such like engines of war are no proof of manhood—but when they come and fight hand-to-hand, appeareth who be men and who be not."

[1] *dote:* act foolishly, become senile
[2] *"Son . . . children":* Barbazon, ed. "La Honce Partie" (Hazlitt).

104. *Of th'Emperor Augustus and the old men*

As the noble Emperor Augustus on a time came into a bain,[1] he beheld an old man that had done good service in the wars frot [2] himself against a marble pillar for lack of one to help to wash him. The Emperor, moved with pity, gave an annuity to find [3] him and a servant to wait upon him.

When this was known, a great sort [4] of old men drew them together and stood where the Emperor should pass forth by, every one of them rubbing his own back with a marble stone. The Emperor demanded [5] why they did so.

"Because, noble Emperor," said they, "we be not able to keep servants to do it."

"Why," quod the Emperor, "one of you may claw and frot another's back well enough."

105. *Phocion's oration to the Athenians*

Phocion on a day treating a long oration to the people of Athens pleased them very well; and when he saw that they altogether allowed his words, he turned to his friends and said: "Have I unwarily spoken any hurt?" [1] So much he persuaded himself that nothing could please them that was well and truly spoken.

[1] *bain:* public bath
[2] *frot:* rubbed
[3] *find:* support
[4] *sort:* pack
[5] *demanded:* asked
[1] *"Have I . . . hurt?":* i.e., "What did I say wrong?"

106. *Of Demosthenes and Phocion*

Demosthenes said to Phocion: "If the Athenians fall once in a madness they will slay thee." To whom he answered: "Ye, surely, if they wax mad they will slay me—but if they wax once wise, they will slay thee." For Demosthenes spoke much to the people's pleasure and spoke things rather delightable than wholesome.

107. *Of Phocion that refused Alexander's gift*

What time Alexander, King of Macedon, sent an hundred bezants [1] of gold for a gift to Phocion, he asked them that brought the money how it came that Alexander sent it to him alone, seeing there were many other men in Athens besides him. They answered: "Because he judgeth you alone to be an honest and a good man."

"Therefore," quod he, "let him suffer me to be taken to be such a one still."

Who would not wonder at the clean and uncorrupt courage of this Phocion? He was but a poor man and yet the greatness of the gift could nothing move him. Besides also he showed that they the which, while they minister the commonwealth, abstain not from taking of gifts, neither be nor ought not to be taken for good men.

[1] *bezants:* gold coins

108. *Of Denise the tyrant and his son*

What time Denise the tyrant understood that his son, that should reign after him, had committed advoutry [1] with a worshipful man's wife, angrily he said to him: "Did I, thy father, ever such a deed?"

The young man answered: "No. Ye had not a king to your father."

"Nor thou," said Denise, "art not like to have a son a king except thou leave committing of such wicked deeds."

109. *Of Pomponius the Roman that was brought before Mithridates*

Pomponius, a nobleman of Rome, sore hurt and wounded was taken and brought before Mithridates which asked him this question: "If I cure and heal thy wounds, wilt thou then be my friend?"

He answered him again thus: "If thou wilt be a friend to the Romans, thou shalt then have me thy friend."

This was a noble stomach that preferred the wealth of his country before his own health.

110. *Of Titus and the jester*

Suetonius showeth that Titus the father [1] provoked a scoffer that stood jesting with everybody, that he should likewise say

[1] *advoutry:* adultery
[1] *father:* the elder

somewhat to him. "I will," said the scoffer, "after ye have done your easement." He jested at the Emperor's countenance—he looked always as one that strained himself. On such a visaged man writeth Martial:

> Utere lactucis, ac mollibus utere maluis.
> Nam faciem durum Phebe cacantis habes.²

111. *Of Scipio Nasica and Ennius the poet*

When Scipio Nasica came on a time to speak with Ennius the Poet he asked his maid at the door if he were within, and she said he was not at home. But Nasica perceived that her master bad her say so and that he was within. But for that time, dissembling the matter, he went his way.

Within a few days after, Ennius came to Nasica and knocking at the door asked if he were within. Nasica himself spake out aloud and said he was not at home. Then said Ennius: "What, man, think you that I know not your voice?"

Whereunto Nasica answered and said: "What a dishonest man be you? When I sought you, I believed your maid that said ye were not at home, and ye will not believe me mine own self."

112. *Of Fabius Minutius and his son*

Fabius Minutius was of his son exhorted on a time to get and conquer a place that was meet for them and to their great advantage—the which thing, he said, they might do with the loss of a few men. "Will ye be one of those few?" said Fabius to his son. Thereby showing that it is a point of a good captain to

---

² *Utere . . . habes:* i.e., "You should take lettuces and purgative herbs, Phoebus, For you look like one straining at stool" (Martial, *Epigrams,* III, 89).

care for the least of his soldiers and to save them as near as he could.

The Emperor Antonius Pius loved much this sentence of Scipio, which he would oft say: "I had lever [1] save one citizen than slay a thousand enemies."

113. *Of Aurelian that was displeased because the city Tyna was closed against him*

What time the Emperor Aurelian came to the city Tyna, he found it closed against him, wherefore all angrily he said: "I will not leave a dog alive in this town—" which words rejoiced much his men of war because of the great prey and booty that they thought to win there.

One of the citizens called Heradamon, for fear lest he should be slain among the others, betrayed the city. When Aurelian had taken the city, the first thing he did, he slew Heradamon the traitor to his country. And to his soldiers that came to him and desired that they might according to his promise over-run and spoil the city, he answered: "Go to, I said I would not leave a dog alive. Spare not, kill all the dogs in the town."

By this means the gentle prince rewarded the traitor according to his deserving and disappointed the covetousness of his soldiers.

Imprinted at London in Flete Strete in the house of Thomas Berthelet nere to the Cundite, at the sygne of Lucrece.

Cum privilegio

[1] *lever:* rather

Merry Tales . . . Made by Master Skelton (1567)

Only one copy remains of this book reputed to have been extremely popular in its day and to have established the reputation of John Skelton well into the nineteenth century and beyond. Printed by Thomas Colwell thirty-eight years after Skelton's death (and a year before publication of Skelton's collected works), the jestbook simply strings together jests that have Skelton as a common denominator.

An earlier biographical sketch of Skelton had been published in at least three different editions of John Bale's literary history (1548). The jestbook incorporates such factual matter as Skelton's laureateship (an academic rather than national title) and his rectorship at Diss, dating from 1504. For the most part, however, it seems based on living popular legend.

After Alexander Dyce published it in his Poetical Works of Skelton *(1843) and gave it proper comment, the jestbook lost prestige as biography. W. C. Hazlitt printed it in his* Shakespeare's Jestbooks, 2nd series, 1864. *The unique copy, in the Huntington Library (STC 22618), is the basis of the present text, showing very few variants from Dyce's or Hazlitt's editions.*

Merie Tales

Newly Imprinted & made by Master Skelton Poet Laureat.

¶ Imprinted at London in Fleetstreat beneath the Conduit at the signe of S. John Euangelist, by Thomas Colwell.

CONTENTS

1. *How Skelton came late home to Oxford from Abington*

Skelton was an Englishman born as Scogan was, and he was educated and brought up in Oxford, and there was he made a poet laureate. And on a time he had been at Abington to make merry, where that he had eat salt meats, and he did come late home to Oxford. And he did lie in an inn named ye Tabere, which is now the Angel, and he did drink, and went to bed.

About midnight he was so thirsty or dry that he was constrained to call to the tapster for drink. And the tapster heard him not. Then he cried to his host and his hostess, and to the hosteler, for drink—and no man would hear him. "Alack," said Skelton, "I shall perish for lack of drink! What remedy?" at the last, he did cry out and said: "Fire! Fire! Fire!"

Then Skelton heard every man bustled himself upward, and some of them were naked, and some were half asleep and amazed, and Skelton did cry "Fire! Fire!" still, that every man knew not whether to resort. Skelton did go to bed—and the host and hostess and the tapster with the hosteler did run to Skelton's chamber with candles lighted in their hands, saying: "Where? Where? Where is the fire?"

"Here, here, here," said Skelton, and pointed his finger to his mouth, saying: "Fetch me some drink to quench the fire and the heat and the dryness in my mouth." And so they did.

Wherefore it is good for every man to help his ownself in time of need with some policy or craft—so be it there be no deceit nor falsehood used.

2. *How Skelton dressed the Kendalman in the sweat time*

On a time, Skelton rode from Oxford to London with a Kendalman,[1] and at Uxbridge they 'bated.[2] The Kendalman laid his cap upon the board [3] in the hall, and he went to serve his horse. Skelton took the Kendalman's cap and did put betwixt the lining and the outer side a dish of butter. And when the Kendalman had dressed his horse, he did come into dinner and did put on his cap (that time the sweating sickness was in all England).

At the last, when the butter had taken heat of the Kendalman's head, it did begin to run over his face and about his cheeks. Skelton said: "Sir, you sweat sore. Beware that you have not the sweating sickness." The Kendalman said: "By the misse, Ise wrang! I bus goe till bed." [4]

Skelton said: "I am skilled in physic—and especially in the sweating sickness, that I will warrant any man." "In gewd faith," saith the Kendalman, "do see, and Ise bay for you scot to London." [5]

Then said Skelton: "Get you a kerchief and I will bring you abed." The which was done. Skelton caused the cap to be sod [6] in hot lye and dried it. In the morning, Skelton and the Kendalman did ride merrily to London.

[1] *Kendalman:* a man from Kendal, a northern man
[2] *'bated:* abated, rested
[3] *board:* table
[4] *"By the misse . . . bed":* "By the mass, I'm sick. I'd best go to bed."
[5] *"In gewd faith . . . London":* "In good faith . . . do so and I'll pay for you scot free to London."
[6] *sod:* boiled

3. *How Skelton told the man that Christ was very busy in the woods with them that made faggots*

When Skelton did come to London there were many men at the table at dinner. Amongst all others, there was one said to Skelton: "Be you of Oxford or of Cambridge a scholar?" Skelton said: "I am of Oxford."

"Sir," said the man, "I will put you a question: You do know well that after Christ did rise from death to life, it was 40 days after ere He did ascend into heaven. And He was but certain times with His disciples. And when that He did appear to them, He did never tarry long amongst them but suddenly vanished from them. I would fain know (saith the man to Skelton), where Christ was all these 40 days."

"Where He was," saith Skelton, "God knoweth. He was very busy in the woods among His laborers that did make faggots to burn heretics and such as thou art, the which dost ask such diffuse questions. But now I will tell thee more: When He was not with His mother and His disciples, He was in Paradise—to comfort the holy patriarchs' and prophets' souls, the which before He had set out of hell. And at the day of His ascension, He took them all up with Him into Heaven."

4. *How the Welshman did desire Skelton to aid him in his suit to the king for a patent to sell drink*

Skelton, when he was in London, went to the king's court where there did come to him a Welshman, saying: "Sir, it is so, that many doth come up of my country to the king's court. And some doth get of the king by patent a castle, and some a park, and some a forest, and some one fee and some another, and they do live like honest [1] men. And I should live as honestly as the best if I might have a patent for good drink. Wherefore, I do pray you to write a few words for me in a little bill [2] to give the same to the king's hands, and I will give you well for your labor."

"I am contented," said Skelton.

"Sit down then," said the Welshman, "and write."

"What shall I write?" said Skelton.

The Welshman said: "Write 'drink.' Now," said the Welshman, "write 'more drink.' "

"What now?" said Skelton.

"Write now 'a great deal of drink.' Now," said the Welshman, "put to all this 'drink' 'a little crumb of bread,' and 'a great deal of drink' to it, and read once again."

Skelton did read: "Drink, more drink, and a great deal of drink, and a little crumb of bread, and a great deal of drink to it."

Then the Welshman said: "Put out the 'little crumb of bread' and set in 'all drink' and no 'bread.' And if I might have this signed of the king," said the Welshman, "I care for no more as long as I do live."

"Well then," said Skelton, "when you have this signed of the king, then will I labor for a patent to have bread—that you with your drink and I with the bread may fare well, and seek our living with bag and staff."

5. *Of Swanborn the knave that was buried under Saint Peter's wall in Oxford*

There was dwelling in Oxford a stark knave whose name was Swanborn. And he was such a notable knave that if any scholar

[1] *honest:* prosperous
[2] *bill:* petition

had fallen out th'one with th'other, the one would call th'other "Swanborn"—the which they did take for a worser word than "knave."

His wife would divers times in the week comb his head with a three-footed stool. Then he would run out of the doors weeping; and if any man had asked him what he did ail, otherwhile [1] he would say he had the megrim [2] in his head, or else there was a great smoke within the house.

And if the doors were shut, his wife would beat him under the bed or into the bench hole, and then he would look out at the cat hole. Then would his wife say: "Lookest thou out, whoreson?"

"Yea," would he say. "Thou shalt never let [3] me of my manly looks." Then with her distaff she would pour in at him.

I knew him when that he was a boy in Oxford. He was a little old fellow and would lie as fast as a horse would trot. At last he died and was buried under the wall of S[t]. Peter's church. Then Skelton was desired to make an epitaph upon the church wall, and did write with a coal, saying: "Belsabub his soul save, Qui iacet hic hec a knave: Jam sci mortuus est, Et iacet hic hec a beast: Sepultus est among the weeds: God forgive him his misdeeds!" [4]

6. *How Skelton was complained on to the Bishop of Norwich*

Skelton did keep a musket [1] at Dis, upon the which he was complained on to the Bishop of Norwich. The Bishop sent for

---

[1] *otherwhile:* sometimes
[2] *megrim:* migraine headache
[3] *let:* stop
[4] *"Belsabub . . . misdeeds":* *very* freely translates: Belsabub his soul save, He who lies here lied, the knave; Now he's dead, he's lying still; He always lied and always will, Buried here among the weeds; God forgive him his misdeeds.
[1] *musket:* mistress

Skelton. Skelton did take two capons to give them for a present to the Bishop.

And as soon as he had saluted the Bishop, he said: "My lord, here I have brought you a couple of capons." The Bishop was blind and said: "Who be you?" "I am Skelton," said Skelton. The Bishop said: "A, whore head! I will none of thy capons. Thou keepest unhappy rule in thy house, for the which thou shalt be punished."

"What!" said Skelton, "Is the wind at that door? (and said), God be with you, my lord!" And Skelton with his capons went his way.

The Bishop sent after Skelton to come again. Skelton said: "What! shall I come again to speak with a madman?"

At last he returned to the Bishop which said to him: "I would (said the Bishop), that you should not live such a sclaunderous life, that all your parish should not wonder and complain on you as they do. I pray you amend, and hereafter live honestly, that I hear no more such words of you. And if you will tarry dinner, you shall be welcome. And I thank you (said the Bishop), for your capons."

Skelton said: "My lord, my capons have proper names: The one is named Alpha, the other is named Omega. My lord (said Skelton), this capon is named Alpha—this is the first capon that I did ever give to you. And this capon is named Omega—and this is the last capon that ever I will give you. And so, fare you well," said Skelton.

7. *How Skelton, when he came from the Bishop, made a sermon*

Skelton, the next Sunday after, went into the pulpit to preach and said: "Vos estis, vos estis—that is to say, 'You be, you be.' And what be you? (said Skelton) I say that you be a sort [1] of

[1] *sort:* pack

knaves—yea, and a man might say worse than knaves. And why? I shall show you.

"You have complained of me to the bishop that I do keep a fair wench in my house. I do tell you, if you had any fair wives it were somewhat to help me at need—I am a man as you be. You have foul wives and I have a fair wench, of the which I have begotten a fair boy, as I do think and as you all shall see.

"Thou, wife (said Skelton), that hast my child, be not afraid. Bring me hither my child to me—" the which was done. And he, showing his child naked to all the parish, said: "How say you, neighbors all? Is not this child as fair as is the best of all yours? It hath nose, eyes, hands, and feet, as well as any of yours. It is not like a pig nor a calf nor like no foul nor no monstrous beast.

"If I had (said Skelton), brought forth this child without arms or legs, or that it were deformed, being a monstrous thing, I would never have blamed you to have complained to the bishop of me. But to complain without a cause—I say, as I said before in my antetheme, 'vos estis,' you be, and have been and will and shall be knaves, to complain of me without a cause reasonable.

"For you be presumptuous and do exalt yourselves, and therefore you shall be made low—as I shall show you a familiar example of a parish priest, the which did make a sermon in Rome. And he did take that for his antetheme (the which of late days is named a 'theme') and said: 'Qui se exaltat humilabitui, et qui se humiliat exaltabitur—that is to say, he that doth exalt himself or doth extoll himself shall be made meek, and he that doth humble himself or is meek shall be exalted, extolled, or elevated, or sublimated, or such like.

" 'And that I will show you by this my cap. This cap was first my hood when that I was a student in Jucalico, and then it was so proud that it would not be contented but it would slip and fall from my shoulders. I perceiving this, that he was proud, what then did I? Shortly to conclude, I did make of him a pair of breeches to my hose, to bring him low.

" 'And when that I did see, know, or perceive that he was in that case, and almost worn clean out, what did I then to extoll him up again? You all may see that this my cap was made of it that was my breeches.'

"Therefore," said Skelton, "vos estis—therefore you be, as I did say before: If that you exalt yourself and cannot be contented that I have my wench still, some of you shall wear horns. And therefore vos estis—and so, farewell."

It is merry in the hall when beards wag all.

8. *How the friar asked leave of Skelton to preach at Dis, which Skelton would not grant*

There was a friar the which did come to Skelton to have license to preach at Dis. "What, would you preach there?" said Skelton. "Do not you think that I am sufficient to preach there in mine own cure?"

"Sir," said the friar, "I am the limitor [1] of Norwich, and once a year one of our place doth use to preach with you, to take the devotion of the people. And if I may have your good will, so be it—or else I will come and preach against your will, by the authority of the Bishop of Rome. For I have his bulls to preach in every place, and therefore I will be there on Sunday next coming." "Come not there, friar, I do counsel thee," said Skelton.

The Sunday next following, Skelton laid watch for the coming of the friar. And as soon as Skelton had knowledge of the friar, he went into the pulpit to preach. At last the friar did come into the church with the Bishop of Rome's bull in his hand. Skelton then said to all his parish: "See, see, see—" and pointed to the friar.

All the parish gazed on the friar. Then said Skelton: "Masters, here is as wonderful a thing as ever was seen. You all do know

[1] *limitor:* a friar licensed to beg within a given, limited territory

that it is a thing daily seen, a bull doth beget a calf. But here, contrary to all nature, a calf hath gotten a bull. For this friar, being a calf, hath gotten a bull of the Bishop of Rome."

The friar, being ashamed, would never after that time presume to preach at Dis.

9. *How Skelton handled the friar that would needs lie with him in his inn*

As Skelton rid into the country there was a friar that happened in at an alehouse whereas Skelton was lodged, and there the friar did desire to have lodging. The alewife said: "Sir, I have but one bed whereas Master Skelton doth lie."

"Sir," said the friar, "I pray you that I may lie with you." Skelton said: "Master friar, I do use to have no man to lie with me." "Sir," said the friar, "I have lain with as good men as you, and for my money I do look to have lodging as well as you." "Well," said Skelton, "I do see then that you will lie with me." "Yea, sir," said the friar.

Skelton did fill all the cups in the house and whittled [1] the friar that, at the last, the friar was in mine eames peason.[2] Then said Skelton: "Master friar, get you to bed and I will come to bed within a while."

The friar went and did lie upright and snorted like a sow. Skelton went to the chamber and did see that the friar did lie so, said to the wife: "Give me a washing betle." [3] Skelton then cast down the clothes and the friar did lie stark naked. Then Skelton did shite upon the friar's navel and belly, and then he did take the washing betle and did strike an hard stroke upon the navel and belly of the friar, and did put out the candle and went out of the chamber.

[1] *whittled:* plied with drink
[2] *mine eames peason:* at peace with the world
[3] *betle:* stick

The friar felt his belly and smelt a foul savor had thought he had been gored, and cried out and said: "Help! help! help! I am killed!" They of the house with Skelton went into the chamber and asked what the friar did ail. The friar said: "I am killed. One hath thrust me in the belly." "Fo," said Skelton, "thou drunken soul, thou dost lie. Thou hast beshitten thyself. Fo (said Skelton), let us go out of the chamber, for the knave doth stink."

The friar was shamed and cried for water. "Out with the whoreson," said Skelton, "and wrap the sheets together and put the friar in the hog stye or in the barn." The friar said: "Give me some water into the barn—" and there the friar did wash himself and did lie there all the night long. The chamber and the bed was dressed, and the sheets shifted, and then Skelton went to bed.

10. *How the Cardinal desired Skelton to make an epitaph upon his grave*

Thomas Wolsey, Cardinal and Archbishop of York, had made a regal tomb to lie in after he was dead, and he desired Master Skelton to make for his tomb an epitaph (which is a memorial to show the life, with the acts, of a noble man). Skelton said: "If it do like your grace, I can not make an epitaph unless that I do see your tomb."

The Cardinal said: "I do pray you to meet with me tomorrow at the West Monastery and there shall you see my tomb a-making."

The 'pointment kept and Skelton—seeing the sumptuous cost, more pertaining for an emperor or a maximus king than for such a man as he was (although cardinals will compare with kings)—"Well," said Skelton, "if it shall like your grace to creep into this tomb while you be alive, I can make an epitaph. For

I am sure that when that you be dead, you shall never have it."
The which was verified of truth.

11. *How the hosteler did bite Skelton's mare under the tail, for biting him by the arm*

Skelton used much to ride on a mare. And on a time he happened into an inn where there was a foolish hosteler. Skelton said: "Hosteler, hast thou any mare's bread?"

"No, sir," said the hosteler, "I have good horse bread, but I have no mare's bread."

Skelton said: "I must have mare's bread."

"Sir," said the hosteler, "there is no mare's bread to get in all the town."

"Well," said Skelton, "for this once, serve my mare with horse bread."

In the meantime, Skelton commanded the hosteler to saddle his mare and the hosteler did gird the mare hard. And the hosteler was in his jerkin, and his shirt sleeves were above his elbows, and in the girding of the mare hard, the mare bit the hosteler by the arm, and bit him sore.

The hosteler was angry and did bite the mare under the tail, saying: "Ah, whore! Is it good biting by the bare arm?"

Skelton said then: "Why, fellow, hast thou hurt my mare?"

"Yea," said the hosteler, "ka me, ka thee [1]—if she do hurt me, I will displease her."

---

[1] *ka me, ka thee:* i.e., tit for tat

12. *How the cobbler told Master Skelton it is good sleeping in a
whole skin*

In the Parish of Dis where as Skelton was Parson, there dwelled
a cobbler, being half a souter,[1] which was a tall man and a great
sloven, otherwise named a slouch. The King's Majesty having
wars beyond the sea, Skelton said to this aforesaid doughty man:
"Neighbor, you be a tall man, and in the King's wars you must
bear a standard."

"A standard?" said the cobbler. "What a thing is that?"

Skelton said: "It is a great banner, such a one as thou dost
use to bear in Rogation week. And a lord's or a knight's or a
gentleman's arms shall be upon it, and the soldiers, that be
under the aforesaid persons, fighting under the banner!"

"Fighting?" said the cobbler. "I can no skill in fighting."

"No," said Skelton, "thou shalt not fight—but hold up and
advance the banner."

"By my fay," said the cobbler, "I can no skill in the matter."

"Well," said Skelton, "there is no remedy but thou shalt forth
to do the King's service in his wars. For in all this country there
is not a more likelier man to do such a feat as thou art."

"Sir," said the cobbler, "I will give you a fat capon, that I
may be at home."

"No," said Skelton, "I will not have none of thy capons—for
thou shalt do the King service in his wars."

"Why," said the cobbler, "what should I do? Will you have me
to go in the King's wars and to be killed for my labor? Then I
shall be well at ease, for I shall have my 'mends [2] in mine own
hands."

"What, knave!" said Skelton, "art thou a coward, having so
great bones?"

[1] *souter:* shoemaker
[2] *'mends:* amendments, atonements

"No," said the cobbler, "I am not afraid. It is good to sleep in a whole skin."

"Why," said Skelton, "thou shalt be harnessed [3] to keep away the strokes from thy skin."

"By my fay," said the cobbler, "if I must needs forth, I will see how Ich shall be ordered." [4]

Skelton did harness the doughty squirrel and did put an helmet on his head. And when the helmet was on the cobbler's head, the cobbler said: "What shall those holes serve for?"

Skelton said: "Holes to look out to see thy enemies."

"Yea," said the cobbler, "then am I in worser case than ever I was. For then one may come and thrust a nail into one of the holes and prick out mine eye. Therefore (said the cobbler to Master Skelton), I will not go to war. My wife shall go in my stead. For she can fight and play the devil with her distaff, and with stool, staff, cup, or candlestick. For, by my fay, Ich am sick, I chill go home to bed. I think I shall die."

13. *How Master Skelton's miller deceived him many times by playing the thief, and how he was pardoned by Master Skelton, after the stealing away of a priest out of his bed at midnight*

When Master Skelton did dwell in the country, he was agreed with a miller to have his corn ground toll free. And many times when his maidens should bake, they wanted of their meal and complained to their mistress that they could not make their stint of bread. Mistress Skelton, being very angry, told her husband of it.

Then Master Skelton sent for his miller and asked him how it chanced that he deceived him of his corn. "I!" said John Miller,

---

[3] *harnessed:* i.e., in armor
[4] *"I will . . . ordered":* I want to see how I shall be outfitted

"nay, surely I never deceived you. If that you can prove that by me, do with me as you list."

"Surely," said Skelton, "if I do find thee false anymore, thou shalt be hanged up by the neck." So Skelton appointed one of his servants to stand at the mill while the corn was a-grinding.

John Miller, being a notable thief, would fain have deceived him as he had done before, but being afraid of Skelton's servant, caused his wife to put one of her children into the mill dam and to cry—"Help, help, my child is drowned!"

With that, John Miller and all went out of the mill. And Skelton's servant, being diligent to help the child, thought not of the meal—and the while, the miller's boy was ready with a sack and stole away the corn.

So, when they had taken up the child and all was safe, they came in again; and so the servant, having his grist, went home mistrusting nothing. And when the maids came to bake again, as they did before, so they lacked of their meal again.

Master Skelton called for his man, and asked him how it chanced that he was deceived, and he said that he could not tell— "For I did your commandment."

And then Master Skelton sent for the miller and said: "Thou hast not used me well, for I want of my meal."

"Why, what would you have me do?" said the miller. "You have set your own man to watch me."

"Well, then," said Skelton, "if thou dost not tell me which way thou hast played the thief with me, thou shalt be hanged."

"I pray you be good master unto me, and I will tell you the truth. Your servant would not from my mill, and when I saw none other remedy, I caused my wife to put one of my children into the water, and to cry that it was drowned. And whiles we were helping of the child out, one of my boys did steal your corn."

"Yea," said Skelton, "if thou have such pretty fetches,[1] you can do more than this. And therefore if thou dost not one thing that I shall tell thee, I will follow the law on thee."

[1] *fetches:* tricks

"What is that?" said the miller.

"If that thou dost not steal my cup off the table when I am set at meat, thou shalt not escape my hands."

"O, good master," said John Miller, "I pray you forgive me, and let me not do this. I am not able to do it."

"Thou shalt never be forgiven," said Skelton, "without thou dooest it."

When the miller saw no remedy, he went and charged one of his boys in an evening (when that Skelton was at supper) to set fire in one of his hog styes, far from any house, fordoing [2] any harm. And it chanced that one of Skelton's servants came out and spied the fire, and he cried: "Help! help! for all that my master hath is like to be burnt!"

His master, hearing this, rose from his supper with all the company, and went to quench the fire. And the while, John Miller came in and stole away his cup, and went his way.

The fire being quickly slaked, Skelton came in with his friends and reasoned with his friends which way they thought the fire should come. And every man made answer as they thought good. And as they were reasoning, Skelton called for a cup of beer— and in no wise, his cup which he used to drink in would not be found.

Skelton was very angry that his cup was missing, and asked which way it should be gone, and no man could tell him of it. At last he bethought him of the miller and said: "Surely he, that thief, hath done this deed, and he is worthy to be hanged." And he sent for the miller.

So the miller told him all how he had done. "Truly," said Skelton, "thou art a notable knave. And without thou canst do me one other feat, thou shalt die."

"O, good master," said the miller, "you promised to pardon me, and will you now break your promise?"

"Aye," said Skelton, "without thou canst steal the sheets off my bed when my wife and I am asleep, thou shalt be hanged— that all such knaves shall take example by thee."

[2] *fordoing:* preventing

"Alas!" said the miller, "which way shall I do this thing? It is impossible for me to get them while you be there."

"Well," said Skelton, "without thou do it, thou knowest the danger." [3]

The miller went his way, being very heavy, and studied which way he might do this deed. He having a little boy which knew all the corners of Skelton's house and where he lay, upon a night when they were all busy, the boy crept in under his bed with a pot of yeast. And when Skelton and his wife were fast asleep, he all to [4] 'nointed the sheets with yeast as far as he could reach.

At last Skelton awaked and felt the sheets all wet, waked his wife, and said: "What! hast thou beshitten the bed?"

And she said: "Nay, it is you that have done it, I think—for I am sure it is not I." And so there fell a great strife between Skelton and his wife, thinking that the bed had been beshitten—and calling for the maid to give them a clean pair of sheets.

And so they arose, and the maid took the foul sheets and threw them underneath the bed, thinking the next morning to have fetched them away. The next time the maids should go to washing, they looked all about and could not find the sheets—for Jack, the miller's boy, had stolen them away.

Then the miller was sent for again, to know where the sheets were become. And the miller told Master Skelton all how he devised to steal the sheets. "How say ye," said Skelton to his friends, "is not this a notable thief? Is he not worthy to be hanged that can do these deeds?"

"O, good master," quoth the miller, "now forgive me according to your promise. For I have done all that you have commanded me, and I trust now you will pardon me."

"Nay," quoth Skelton, "thou shalt do yet one other feat, and that shall be this: Thou shalt steal master parson out of his bed at midnight, that he shall not know where he is become."

The miller made great moan and lamented, saying: "I can not tell in the world how I shall do, for I am never able to do

[3] *danger:* penalty
[4] *all to:* thoroughly

this feat." "Well," said Skelton, "thou shalt do it or else thou shalt find no favor at my hands. And therefore go thy way."

The miller, being sorry, devised with himself which way he might bring this thing to pass. And two or three nights after, he gathered a number of snails and 'greed with the sexton of the church to have the key of the church door, and went into the church between the hours of eleven and twelve in the night, and took the snails, and lighted a sort [5] of little wax candles, and set upon every snail one. And the snails crept about the church with the same candles upon their backs.

And then he went into the vestry and put a cope [6] upon his back and stood very solemnly at the high altar with a book in his hand, and afterward tolled the bell that the priest, lying in the churchyard, might hear him. The priest, hearing the bell toll, started out of his sleep and looked out of his window, and saw such a light in the church, was very much amazed, and thought surely that the church had been on fire—and went for to see what wonder it should be.

And when he came there, he found the church door open and went up into the choir, and seeing the miller standing in his vestments, and a book in his hand, praying devoutly—and all the lights in the church—thought surely with himself it was some angel come down from heaven, or some other great miracle—blessed himself, and said: "In the name of the Father, the Son and the Holy Ghost, what art thou that standest here in this holy place?"

"O," said the miller, "I am Saint Peter which kept the keys of heaven gate, and thou knowest that none can enter into heaven except I let him in. And I am sent out from heaven for thee."

"For me!" quoth the priest. "Good Saint Peter, worship may thou be! I am glad to hear that news."

"Because thou hast done good deeds," said the miller, "and served God, He hath sent for thee afore doomsday come, that thou shalt not know the troubles of the world."

[5] *sort:* pack
[6] *cope:* priest's vestment

"O, blessed be God!" said the priest. "I am very well contented for to go. Yet if it would please God to let me go home and distribute such things as I have to the poor, I would be very glad."

"No," said the miller. "If thou dost delight more in thy goods than in the joys of heaven, thou art not for God. Therefore prepare thyself and go into this bag which I have brought for thee."

The miller having a great quarter sack, the poor priest went into it, thinking verily he had gone to heaven (yet was very sorry to part from his goods), asked Saint Peter how long it would be ere he came there. The miller said he should be there quickly —and in he got the priest and tied up the sack, and put out the lights and laid every thing in their place, and took the priest on his back and locked the church doors, and to go.

And when he came to go over the church stile, the priest was very heavy, and the miller cast him over the stile so that the priest cried—"Oh! O, good Saint Peter (said the priest), whither go I now?"

"O," said the miller, "these be the pangs that ye must abide before you come to heaven."

"Oh," quoth the priest, "I would I were there once!"

Up he got the priest again, and carried him till he came to the top of a high hill, a little from his house, and cast him down the hill, that his head had many shrewd raps, that his neck was almost burst. "Oh, good Saint Peter," said the priest, "where am I now?"

"You are almost now at heaven—" and carried him with much ado till he came to his own house, and then the miller threw him over the threshold. "O, good Saint Peter," said the priest, "where am I now? This is the sorest pang that ever I 'bided."

"O," said that miller, "give God thanks that thou hast had patience to abide all this pain, for now thou art going up into heaven—" and tied a rope about the sack and drew him up to the top of the chimney, and there let him hang.

"Oh, good Saint Peter, tell me now where I am," said the priest.

"Marry," said he, "thou art now in the top of John Miller's chimney."

"A vengeance on thee, knave!" said the priest. "Hast thou made me believe all this while that I was going up into heaven? Well, now I am here, and ever I come down again, I will make thee to repent it."

But John Miller was glad that he had brought him there.

And in the morning, the sexton rang all in to service, and when the people were come to church, the priest was lacking. The parish asked the sexton where the priest was and the sexton said: "I can not tell." Then the parish sent to Master Skelton and told how their priest was lacking to say them service.

Master Skelton marveled at that, and bethought him of the crafty doing of the miller, sent for John Miller. And when the miller was come, Skelton said: "Canst thou tell where the parish priest is?" The miller up and told him altogether how he had done. Master Skelton, considering the matter, said to the miller: "Why, thou unreverent knave, hast thou handled the poor priest on this fashion, and put on the holy ornaments upon a knave's back! Thou shalt be hanged, and [7] it cost me all the good I have!"

John Miller fell upon his knees and desired Master Skelton to pardon him: "For I did nothing (said the miller), but that you said you would forgive me."

"Nay, not so," said Skelton. "But if thou canst steal my gelding out of my stable, my two men watching him, I will pardon thee. And if they take thee, they shall strike off thy head—" for Skelton thought it better that such a false knave should lose his head than to live.

Then John Miller was very sad, and bethought him how to bring it to pass. Then he remembered that there was a man left hanging upon the gallows the day before, and went privily in the night and took him down and cut off his head and put it upon a pole, and brake a hole into the stable, and put in a candle lighted, thrusting in the head a little and a little.

[7] *and:* if

The men watching the stable, seeing that, got themselves near to the hole (thinking that it was his head), and one of them with his sword cut it off. Then they for gladness presented it unto their master, leaving the stable door open. Then John Miller went in and stole away the gelding.

Master Skelton, looking upon the head, saw it was the thief's head that was left hanging upon the gallows, said: "Alas, how oft hath this false knave deceived us! Go quickly to the stable again, for I think my gelding is gone."

His men, going back again, found it even so. Then they came again and told their master his horse was gone. "Ah, I thought so, you doltish knaves!" said Skelton. "But if I had sent wise men about it, it had not been so."

Then Skelton sent for the miller and asked him if he could tell where his horse was. "Safe enough, master," said the miller, for he told Skelton all the matter how he had done.

Well Skelton considering his tale, said that he was worthy to be hanged, "For thou dost excel all the thieves that ever I knew or heard of, but for my promise's sake I forgive thee—upon condition thou wilt become an honest man and leave all thy craft and false dealing." And thus John Miller 'scaped unpunished.

14. *How Skelton was in prison at the commandment of the Cardinal*

On a time Skelton did meet with certain friends of his at Charing Cross after that he was in prison at my Lord Cardinal's commandment, and his friend said: "I am glad you be abroad among your friends, for you have been long pent in." Skelton said: "By the mass, I am glad I am out indeed, for I have been pent in like a roach or fish, at Westminster in prison."

The Cardinal, hearing of those words, sent for him again. Skelton, kneeling of his knees before him, after long communication, desired the Cardinal to grant him a boon. "Thou shalt have none," said the Cardinal.

The assistants desired that he might have it granted, for they thought it should be some merry pastime that he will show "your Grace." "Say on, thou whore head," said the Cardinal to Skelton.

"I pray your grace to let me lie down and wallow, for I can kneel no longer."

15. *How the vintner's wife put water into Skelton's wine*

Skelton did love well a cup of good wine. And on a day, he did make merry in a tavern in London. And the morrow after, he sent to the same place again for a quart of the same wine he drunk of before. The which was clean changed and brewed again.

Skelton, perceiving this, went to the tavern and did sit down in a chair and did sigh very sore, and made great lamentation. The wife of the house, perceiving this, said to Master Skelton: "How is it with you, Master Skelton?"

He answered and said "I did never so evil." And then he did reach another great sigh, saying: "I am afraid that I shall never be saved nor come to heaven."

"Why," said the wife, "should you despair so much in God's mercy?"

"Nay," said he, "it is past all remedy."

Then said the wife: "I do pray you break your mind unto me."

"O," said Skelton, "I would gladly show you the cause of my dolor if that I wist that you would keep my counsel."

"Sir," said she, "I have been made of counsel of greater matters than you can show me."

"Nay, nay," said Skelton. "My matter passeth all other matters, for I think I shall sink to hell for my great offenses. For I sent this day to you for wine to say mass withal. And we have a strong law that every priest is bound to put into his chalice, when he doth sing or say mass, some wine and water—the which doth signify the water and blood that did run out of Christ's side when Longeous the blind knight did thrust a spear to Christ's heart—and this day I did put no water into my wine, when that I did put wine into my chalice."

"Then," said the vintner's wife, "be merry, Master Skelton—and keep my counsel—for, by my faith, I did put into the vessel of wine that I did send you of today ten gallons of water. And therefore take no thought, Master Skelton, for I warrant you."

Then said Skelton: "Dame, I do beshrew [1] thee for thy labor, for I thought so much before."

For through such uses and brewing of wine may men be deceived, and be hurt by drinking of such evil wine. For all wines must be strong and fair and well colored. It must have a redolent savor. It must be cold and sprinkling in the piece [2] or in the glass.

Thus endeth the merry Tales of Master Skelton, very pleasant for the recreation of the mind.

[1] *beshrew:* curse
[2] *piece:* cask

Selections from the Mirrour
of Mirth (1583)

The Mirrour of Mirth *is represented here by a dozen jests, sufficient to show what had happened to jestbooks over the one hundred years since Caxton's "Alfonce" and "Poge." The first edition of 1583 contained thirty-nine jests, all translated from the popular French work of Bonaventure Des Periers, who had died in 1544. The edition of 1592 dropped nine of the jests and added a new one.*

The translation is attributed to Thomas Deloney, who later combined dramatic technique and jestbook style to produce novels as popular in his day as in our own.

The basis for the present text is the edition of 1583 in the Library of Trinity College, Cambridge. A copy of the 1592 edition is in the Folger Library. The 1583 text has been reproduced in facsimile with introduction and notes by J. Woodrow Hassell, Jr. (Columbia, S.C.: Univ. of So. Carolina Press, 1959).

THE
Mirrour of Mirth,
and pleasant Conceits:

CONTAINING,

Many proper and pleasaunt inuentions, for the recreation and delight of many, and to the hurt and
hinderance of none.

Framed in French by that Worshipfull and learned Gentleman
Bonaduenture de Pe.iers, Groom to the right excellent
and vertuous Princesse, the Queene of Nauara:
And Englished by R. D.

At London,
¶ Printed by Roger
Warde : dwelling a litle aboue Holburne
Conduit, at the Signe of the Talbot.
1583.

CONTENTS

12. Of a certain student in the law and of the 'pothecary that
taught him physic

To the courteous and gentle Readers

It was the custom of a certain Philosopher (right gentle and
courteous readers) when he perceived the people to wax weary
by his long and tedious orations, and to drop out of doors ere
he had done, to take his harp in hand, which he so finely fingered
that the sweet and pleasant sound thereof procured the people
to come running in faster than before they went forth—whose
dulled spirits being revived with that pleasant melody and their
minds (before cloyed with over-many circumstances of gravity)
being by this means marvelously delighted—did the better and
with greater ease continue the time of his conclusion; whose
excellent policy in this point hath attained so great commenda-
tion that it is set forth for an example to all posterities.

If, then, you find yourselves overladen, either by the means
of worldly cares or with the intolerable burden of over-great
studies, (if the deeds of this Philosopher were to be followed)
I would wish you no greater or better pleasure than he showed
to his people—considering that mirth and melody cutteth off
care, unburdeneth the mind of sorrow, healeth the grieved heart,
and filleth both soul and body with inestimable comfort. And
therefore many mighty and excellent Princes, whose heads are
troubled with divers and sundry enormities, do for this cause
entertain and accept of such persons whose pleasant nature and
disposition may move them to delight.

Sith, then, moderate pleasure is not only convenient but also
profitable and necessary for us, I have presumed here upon your
courtesy for the recreation of your minds, to send unto your
sight this simple and rude work—the grace and beauty whereof,
being stripped from his country guise [1] and now newly wrapped

---

[1] *country guise:* i.e., original language (French)

in this strange attire, is not only blemished by means of the translator's unskillfulness but, as it were, spoiled both of favor and fashion.

Yet if it please you to pardon his imperfection and to accept his good will, he shall not only be encouraged to mend his amiss but also hereafter present you with such as may better countervail [2] your courtesy and save his own credit. Thus, loath to be over-tedious in so mean a matter, I commend you to the protection of the celestial powers and this to your friendly consideration.

Yours in all humility,
T. D.

1. *Of a chorister that sang the counter-tenor in the Church of St. Hilary's at Poitiers, that compared the Canons to their pottages*

In the Church of St. Hilary's at Poitiers, sometimes there was a singing man that sang the counter-tenor who, for that he was a very good fellow and would drink hard (as commonly such men will do), was well beloved amongst the Canons and they called him oftentimes to dinner and to supper. And because of the familiar acquaintance that he had with them, it seemed to him that there was none of them all but that sought and desired his furtherance. By reason whereof he would say first to one and then to another: "Sir, you know how long time it is since I first served in this Church. It is now high time that I might hereafter be provided for. I pray you speak for me when you are together in your Chapel Court. I require no great thing. Although you, my masters, have great livings, I would be content with one of the least."

[2] *countervail:* compensate

His request was well taken and allowed of them all—being several which gave him a good answer, saying that it was reason he should be remembered and: "Although the Chapel Court will not consider of thee, rather than thou shouldest want, we will give thee part of ours." This said they to him when they were alone. Well, at all their going in and coming out of the Chapel Court he gave attendance, desiring them to remember him. And they did answer him with one voice, saying: "Stay a while and thou shalt not be forgotten, but shalt have the first place that is vacant."

But when it came to the pinch there was always some excuse: either that the benefice was too great and therefore one of the Masters had it; or that it was too little, and therefore he should have a better; or that they were constrained to give it to one of their brethern's kinsmen—but without fail he should have the next that did fall. And with these words they kept off this singing man, so that the time went away. And he served still without any reward.

And in the meanwhile, he gave always some present (according to his slender ability) to them whom he knew might give their voices in the Chapel Court, as: the first new fruits he could buy; sometimes chickens; sometimes pigeons, rabbits, partridges, and such like, according to the season—which the poor singing man bought either at the market or at the poulterer's, making them believe that they cost him nothing. And they took always that which was given them.

In the end, this chorister—perceiving himself never the nearer nor one whit the better, but that he lost his time, his money, and his pains—determined to make no longer suit, but studied to show them what opinion he had of them. And to bring this to pass, he found the means to gather five or six crowns together. And during the time that he was providing them (for it required time), he began to make more account of "my masters" the Canons than before, and to use himself more soberly.

And when he espied time convenient, he came to the chiefest amongst them and prayed them one after another to dine with him the next Sunday following at his house—saying unto them that, in nine or ten years that he had been in their service, he could do no less than to bestow one dinner on them; and he would entertain them—though not so well as they were worthy, yet according to his power in the best manner that he might or could devise.

They promised him one after another to come together. But they were not so negligent but that every one of them made their provision at home against the day appointed, fearing to have a slender dinner of this singing man's provision—giving better credit to his words than to his kitchen.

At the hour and time set down, each of them sent their own ordinary provision [1] to his house and he said unto them: "My friends, my masters and yours dooth me great wrong. Are they afraid they shall not be well used? They need not send their dinner hither, for I have provided meat for them, I thank God." But he took all that came and put all together in a great pot that he had provided on purpose in a corner of the kitchen.

At the last came the Canons to dinner and sat down in order, according to their dignities. This singing man at the first set before them their pottage [2] that he had put together in a great pot—but God knoweth in what order. For one had sent a capon in stewed broth, another saffron broth, another chickens in white broth, another powdered beef and turnips, another a leg of mutton in herb pottage. Some sent their meat sodden [3] and some roasted.

When the Canons saw this kind of service, they had no stomaches to eat, but tarried each man to see when their own provision would come in—not thinking that it was on the table before them. The chorister, or singing man, went to and fro very busy, as one that was careful to see them well served—beholding always their countenances that sat at the table.

The first service being somewhat too long, they could forbear

---

[1] *ordinary provision:* ? steward
[2] *pottage:* stew
[3] *sodden:* boiled

no longer but said unto him: "I pray thee take away these pottages and give us those that we sent hither."

"These are yours," said he.

"Ours?" said they. "That they are not."

"Yes, truly," quoth he, "they are—" saying to one—"Here is your turnips"; to another—"Here is your stewed broth"; to another—"Here is your herb pottage"; to another—"Here is your white broth"; and to another—"These are your saffron pottages." Then they began each man to know his own pottage, and to behold one another.

"Now, truly," said they, "we were never thus used. But is this the order to feast the Canons? Now the Devil take all, I thought this fool would mock us."

Then spake another, saying: "I had the best pottage that was eat of this seven years."

"And I," said another, "had well provided for my dinner."

"And my heart gave me," said the fourth, "that it had been better to have dined at home."

When the singing man had given ear a while unto their talk, he said: "My masters, if all your pottages were so good as ye fain they were, how can it be possible that they should become naught in so short a time? I have kept them by the fire close covered. What could I have done better to them?"

"Yea, marry," said they. "But where didst thou learn to put them thus together? Thou mightest well know that they would not be good, being thus mixed."

"Well, then," said he, "I perceive that which is good by itself alone is naught, being mixed with other things. Now, truly," said he, "I must needs believe you, if it be but by yourselves,[4] my Masters. For when ye be each one alone by yourselves there is nothing better than ye are. You promise then mountains. But when you are together in your Chapel Court, then are ye like to your pottages."

Then they understood well what he meant. "Ha, well," said they. "We perceive now to what end this thy doing was. Thou

___

[4] *by yourselves:* by analogy to yourselves

hast good cause to be considered. But in the meantime, shall we not dine?"

"Yes, that you shall," said he, "better than you are worthy." Then he brought them other meat that he had prepared and set it before them, wherewith they were pleased.

When they had well dined, they went away, and concluded from that time forth that he should be provided for—the which was done. And thus his invention and device of pottages did prevail more than all his requests and importunate suits before time.

2. *Of three sisters newly married that did each of them make a good answer to their husbands the first night of their wedding*

In the country of Anjou there was in times past a gentleman that was rich and of a good stock, but he was somewhat subject to his pleasure. This gentleman had three daughters that were fair and well nurtured and of such age and years that the youngest might well enough resist the violence of a man. It happened so, that they were without a mother. And because their father was yet of lusty years, he used still his old customs—which were to keep a good house and to entertain and receive merry and pleasant company, where the order was to play, to dance, to revel, and to make good cheer.

And for that he was negligent and not careful in the ordering of his house and overseeing of his household, his daughters had opportunity, leisure, and liberty enough to talk and laugh with young gentlemen, whose talk (I warrant you) was not how to make cheap corn, nor concerning the governance of the public wealth—as the sequel shows. Also their father on his part played the lover as well as others, which made the young gentlewomen the more bolder to love and to be beloved; for as the old cocks crow, the young ones learn. And they, having gentle hearts, knowing that they were gentlewomen of a good house, thought it a thing very ungrateful and full of reproach to be beloved and not to love again.

These reasons therefore considered—being all three of them played, entertained, loved, and followed every day and hour—at length, they suffered themselves to be taken and snared in love —taking such compassion on their paramours that they spared not to pleasure them in whatsoever they did demand. At which play and sport they sped so well that the marks and signs began to appear.

For the eldest daughter (being somewhat more forward than the rest) was greatly abashed because there was no way to keep it secret. For in a house where the mother is missing, there is small regard of the daughter's doings; or at the least if there happen a mischance, they know ways and remedies to prevent it. But the maiden, knowing no way to hide this from her father, determined to make him privy to her secret practices.

Which when he understood, he was at the first very sorry and greatly displeased. But he despaired not, for that he was of that stamp of men that take not things to the heart. And to say the truth, what need a man torment and vex himself for a thing when it is done; it is but rather to make it worse.

Well, he sent his daughter into the country three or four miles off, to an aunt that she had, under color of sickness (because that by the counsel of the physicians, the change of the air was very good for her), tarrying there until she was delivered with child. But as it is commonly seen, one misfortune falleth upon another's neck: for, as his eldest daughter had in a manner dispatched her business and emptied her belly, the second sister was also sped.

The father perceiving this said: "I see that my daughters would not that the world should be left desolate." And upon this event (doubting belike the worst), he came to his youngest daughter, who was not yet with child but she had done her good will in the matter to her power: "Well, daughter," said he, "how doest thou? Hast not thou followed thy elder sisters' steps?" The young damsel began to change color and to blush, which the father took for open confession. "Very well," said he, "God send us good luck and keep us from evil."

Yet nevertheless, he thought it high time to provide for his affairs, and therefore he determined to marry his three daughters. But here was the mischief. He knew not to whom. For to offer them to his neighbors it was in vain because their doings in his house was known, or at the least suspected. On the other side, to marry them to those that had abused his daughters was a thing that could not well be done, for it may be each of them had more than one. And if peradventure there was but one man that had done the deed, ye know few men will put their trust in one that will so willingly lay her legs open before she knows who shall be her husband.

And for these considerations, the father thought it more expedient and necessary to seek his sons-in-law further from home. And as those men which of nature are pleasant and merry and love to frequent company, are happy and fortunate in their doings, even so this gentleman failed not of his purpose—to find out that which he sought for, which was in the country of Brittaine, where he was well known as well for the name of his house as for the lands and goods ¹ he had in that country, not far from the town of Nantes. By means whereof he had good occasion to make his journey thither. To conclude, when he was in the said country—as well by friends that he made as through himself— he proffered the marriage of his three daughters. To which the Brittains gave some ear, so that there was choice enough.

But amongst all the rest there was one gentleman of Brittaine who was rich and of a good stock, the which had three sons of good years and well made like men, good dancers, clean legged, well footed, and excellent at all games—whose like was not to be had in all the whole country—whereof this gentleman was very glad. And because the prolonging of the time was not best, he concluded the match with the father of these young men: that his three sons should marry his three daughters, and that

¹ *goods:* property

one bridal should serve for all; that is, they should all three be married on one day.

And to bring this to pass, the three brethern prepared themselves with all speed to depart into Anjou with the gentleman father of the three daughters. Now you must note that, although they were Brittains, there was not one of the three but knew fashions; for they had played youthful pranks with the Brittainish maids, which are of a good inclination that way, as the talk goeth. But to our matter—

When they were come to the gentleman's house, they beheld the countenances of the three gentlewomen, every one his, and found them all fresh, fair, and pleasant, and also wise and well spoken. Well, the marriage was concluded and all things prepared. But the night before the wedding should be, the father called his three daughters aside into a chamber and said unto them these words:

"Ye know what fault you have all three committed, and what pain you have put me unto. If I had been of the nature of these rigorous, cruel and hard-hearted fathers, I had cast you off and you should never have enjoyed any of my goods. But for my part, you see, I had rather redress things that are amiss than to put you to shame, and myself in perpetual trouble through your follies. I have here brought for each of you a husband. Therefore prepare yourselves to make much of them and cherish them, and pluck up good hearts. You shall have no harm. If they happen to perceive or spy anything by any of you, to your own peril be it. Nevertheless, you have as yet done them no offense.

"And therefore henceforth take heed to yourselves and govern yourselves so that there may be found no fault in your doings. And I promise you for my part that I will both forget and forgive all faults past. And besides all this, I assure you, she that can give unto her husband the best answer to please him the first night, being in bed together, should have for her part two hundred crowns more than the others. Now, therefore, go your ways and remember my words." After these wholesome admonitions he went to bed and his daughters also, being nothing oblivious in this matter.

The bridal day was the next morrow. They went to the church and were married early in the morning. There was great cheer, with dancing and leaping about the house—which being past, the beds were made wherein the brides were bravely laid, unto whom their husbands shortly after came.

What time, the eldest sporting with his new bedfellow, and feeling her belly very lank, merely put forth these speeches: "I doubt, my beloved, the birds be fled and gone."

Unto whom she presently replied: "Keep you then in the nest."

The second sister's husband, handling her, feeling her belly hard and round, began thus: "How now, wife. The barn is already full."

"Beat then at the gate," quoth she.

The third sister's husband, in sporting himself in like sort and finding his wife skillful in the game, presently spoke in this manner: "I perceive the way was beaten before."

The damsel answered: "You may the better find the path."

The night being past and the day come, they came all three before their father and declared unto him what had chanced, and what was their answers. Now would I know to which of the three he ought to give the two hundred crowns. If therefore your skill be so good, declare the truth of this difficult matter.

3. *Of a certain man in Pickardy that withdrew his wife from her disordinate love, through the admonition that he gave her in the presence of her parents*

There was in times past a king of France whose name we do not well know, and although we did, yet should it be secret because of this matter whereof we mean to speak. Nevertheless, it is said that he was a good king and worthy of the crown. He would bend his ear to hear the talk as well of the poor as of the rich, for thereby he understood the truth of things, which cannot be so well when one goeth by hearsay— But to the purpose—

This good king would walk through the countries of his kingdom, and many times would go into the cities and towns in a disguised garment to understand the truth and order of things. Upon a day, he thought to visit the country of Pickardy in his royal person, notwithstanding using many times his accustomed privateness.

Being at Soissons, he sent for the chiefest of the town and caused them to sit down with him at his table—in token of great courtesy, requesting them very gently to rehearse and tell some stories, either merry tales or such as were grave and sad. Amongst others, there was one that began to declare to the king this story following:

And it like your grace (said he), it came to pass not long since in one of the towns of Pickardy that a certain justice, who liveth yet, buried his wife after they had lived together a good season. And because he liked so well the first, he had a desire to marry the second time and took to wife a maiden fresh and fair, come of a good kindred. Yet, notwithstanding, she was not equal to him either in goods or in qualities.

For he was of good years and half spent, and she in the flower of her youth, wanton and full of pleasure—so that he was not able to satisfy her youth according to her desire. For when she began to have a little taste of the joys and pleasures of this world, she felt quickly that her husband did but set her a-longing. And although he gave her good entertainment, as well in her apparel, in fair words, and showing to her a merry countenance, nevertheless, all this served but to set fire in the tow,[1] so that at the last it flamed out in such sort that she determined with herself to borrow of some other that which her husband wanted to perform.

At the last she found out a new lover with whom she used

---

[1] *set fire in the tow:* i.e., kindle the candle of her lust

her pleasure for a time. But not content with him, she got another and then another—so that in short time she had such a company that they hindered one another coming in unto her, both at lawful and unlawful hours, to take their pleasure on her. By which means she had laid aside the remembrance of her honor, giving herself wholly to her lust and pleasure.

In the meantime, her husband knew nothing—or, at the least if he did, he armed himself with patience, being content to bear the penance of his own folly; because that his years being more than half spent, he had so unadvisedly taken to wife a maid of so young and tender years.

Well, this train continued so long till it was commonly talked on in the town and in every man's mouth; wherewith his friends were grieved so sore that one of them could not refrain but came and told him thereof—declaring unto him the rumor and noise that was spread abroad, so that if he did not provide a remedy he would give occasion unto all the world to think that he was content withal. And in the end, all his friends would despise and forsake his company, and he should be abhorred of all honest men.

When he understood the talk of his friend, he made a sign of great displeasure and sorrow, as one that knew nothing thereof, and promised to see a remedy therein with as much speed as was possible. But when he was alone by himself, he thought it was a thing out of his power to remedy, but that the shame would continue and remain still. And he thought his wife should of herself in respect of him and of her honor call back her folly and beware—otherwise, all the strong walls, bolts, and locks would not hold her in nor stay her disordinate affection.

Furthermore, he reasoned with himself that he, being a man sober and wise, ought not to set his care towards the bridling of a vain and evil given woman—the which thing kept him from searching out the truth of the matter too rashly. Notwithstanding, for that he would not seem as one not careful of his domestical affairs (the which was esteemed of all men most dishonest and wicked), he bethought him on a remedy which he thought above all others was most expedient and necessary.

The remedy was this: He determined to buy a house which joined to his backside and of two he purposed to make one, saying that he would have a going in and out at his backside as well as at the street side. Which device was speedily finished and a door was made in the secretest place that might be, unto which he caused to be made half a dozen of keys. And he forgot not to make a gallery very proper for the goers and comers.

These things being thus prepared, he appointed a day to have all his wife's principal and chief parents [2] and kindred to dinner, and not one of his own kindred at that time. He gave them good entertainment, and made them great cheer. After dinner was done, before any of them did rise from the table, he began to speak unto them these words following, in the presence of his wife:

"My masters and gentlewomen all that are here present, you know how long it is since I married your kinswoman that sitteth here by me. I have had now time and leisure to consider that it was not to me she ought to have been married, because the match between her and me was not equal. But when a thing is done that may not be undone, we must be content to tarry the end."

Then, turning himself towards his wife, he said unto her: "Wife, I have not long since suffered rebukes through your naughty and evil government, the which hath grieved me at the heart. It hath been showed me that there commeth hither young men at all hours of the day to keep you company. Truly, it is a thing greatly to your dishonor and mine, which if I had perceived before now I would have provided a remedy for. But yet it is better late than never.

"I pray you speak unto those that frequent your company, that hereafter they may come to you in more secret manner— which they may the better do because of a door on the back-

[2] *parents:* close relatives

side which I caused to be made for them, of which door here are half a dozen keys for you to give to each of your lovers one. And if there be not keys enough I will cause more to be made, for the smith is at your commandment.

"And bid them so to part the time of their meeting as may be most profitable both for them and you. For if you will not abstain from sin and evil doing, at the least do it so secretly that the world have no occasion to speak of the same, to your shame and mine."

When the young wife had heard the talk that her husband had made unto her in the presence of her parents and friends, she began to be ashamed of her doings, and remembered with herself the wrong and injury that she had done to her husband —to the dishonor of him, herself, and her kindred. So that then she had such remorse of conscience that from that time forward, she shut the gate against all her lovers and forsook all her disordinate affections and unlawful pleasures, and afterwards lived with her husband like an honest and virtuous wife—in all honor and contentation ³ of them both.

When the King had heard this story he was desirous to know who was the party, saying: "Now, by the faith of a gentleman, he is one of the patientest men in my kingdom. He would sure do some virtuous act, seeing he is imbued with such patience." And at the very same time the King made him his general attorney in Pickardy.

As for me, if I knew the name of this honest man, I would give him immortal praise. But time hath done great wrong to hide his name, that deserved well to be placed in the Chronicles —yea! to have been canonized. For he was a very martyr in this world, and I believe he is happy in the world to come.

³ *contentation:* contentment

4. *Of a Doctor of degree that was so sore hurt with an oxe that he could not tell in which leg it was*

There was upon a time a certain Doctor riding through the streets towards the Schools, who met in the way by chance a company of oxen that a butcher's boy did drive—one of which oxen came so near to M. Doctor that he touched his gown as he passed upon his mule. Wherewithal, he being sore afraid cried out aloud: "Help, my masters, help! This oxe hath killed me! I am dead!"

At this cry the people came running together, thinking by his cry that he was grievously hurt. One kept him upon the one side, another on the other side, upon his mule.

And amongst his great cries, he called his servant who was named Cornelius: "Come hither (said he), go thy ways to the Schools and tell them that I am dead. An oxe hath killed me and that I cannot come to make my lecture."

The students were sore troubled to hear these news, and so were the other Doctors. Whereupon they appointed some to go see him—which found him laid along upon a bed, and the Surgeon by him that had his rolling bands, his oil, his ointments, his whites of eggs, and all his implements necessary in such a chance.

M. Doctor complained on his right leg so sore that he could not endure to have his hose pulled off, but that it must needs be ripped. When the surgeon had seen his bare leg, he found no skin broken nor bruised, nor no appearance of hurt, although that M. Doctor cried still: "I am dead, my friend!"

And when the Surgeon did touch it with his hand, he cried the louder: "Thou killest me! Thou killest me!"

"And where is it that it grieveth you most?" said the Surgeon.

"Dost thou not see," said he, "how an oxe hath killed me—and askest thou me where my pain lyeth?"

Then the Surgeon asked him: "Is it here, Sir?"

"No," quoth he.

"Nor here?"

"No, neither." To be short, it could not be found.

"O, good God," said the Doctor, "what a pain is this! that these folks cannot find where my pain lyeth. Is it not swollen?" (said he to the barber [1]).

"No, sir," said he.

"It must needs be," then said the Doctor, "that it is in the other leg. For I know well enough that the oxe did strike me on one of my legs."

There was no remedy but that the other hose must be pulled off and the leg searched. But there was as much harm as in the first leg. "Good lord," quoth the Doctor, "this Surgeon hath no skill. Go fetch me another."

When he was come and could find nothing, the Doctor began to wonder, saying: "This is a strange matter, that such a great oxe should strike me and do me no harm." Then calling his man, he said: "Come hither, Cornelius. When the oxe did hurt me, in which leg was it? Was it not in this, next the wall?"

"Ita,[2] Domine," said his servant.

Then quoth he: "It must needs be in this leg, and so I said at the first. But they thought I mocked them."

The Surgeon perceiving that M. Doctor had no harm, but only was afraid, for to content his mind he gave it a little ointment and bound his leg with a cloth—saying unto him that the dressing would serve at that time. "And afterward," said he, "Master Doctor, when you can tell me in which leg it is, another salve shall be laid unto it."

[1] *barber:* the Surgeon
[2] *Ita:* yes

5. *A comparison of soothsayers and tellers of fortune to the good wife that carried a pail of milk to the market*

The common talk of soothsayers and tellers of fortune is to promise great riches, saying they know the secrets of nature, which the wisest men never knew. Their doings is like smoke in the sun, so that their soothsaying may rather be termed false saying, and we cannot compare it better than to a good wife that sometime carried a pail of milk to the market—thinking to sell it as pleased her, making her reckoning thus:

First, she would sell her milk for 2 pence, and with this 2 pence buy 12 eggs which she would set to brood under a hen, and she would have 12 chickens. These chickens being grown up, she would carve them and by that means they should be capons. These capons would be worth (being young) 5 pence apiece—that is, just a crown, with the which she would buy 2 pigs, a sow and a boar; and they growing great would bring forth 12 others, the which she would sell (after she had kept them a while) for 5 groats apiece; that is, just 20 shillings.

Then she would buy a mare that would bring forth a fair foal, the which would grow up and be so gentle and fair he would play skip, leap, and fling and cry "Wc he he he" after every beast that should pass by. And for the joy she conceived of her supposed colt, in her jollity counterfeiting to show his lustiness, her pail of milk fell down off her head and was all spilt. There lay her eggs, her chickens, her capons, her pigs, her mare, her colt, and all upon the ground. Even so these soothsayers—after that they have furnished, burnished, blotted and spotted, louted and flouted, putrefied and corrupted, promised and not performed, their best box being broken, they may go count with this good wife.

6. *Of King Solomon that made the philosophical stone and the cause why these soothsayers cannot prevail in their doings*

The cause why soothsayers, witches and wizards cannot bring all their matters to pass as they would, all the world doth not know. But Marie the Prophetess showeth the cause why in a book that she hath made of the great excellency and knowledge of the art—exhorting the philosophers and giving them courage not to despair, and she sayeth that the philosophers' stone is so worthy and so precious that amongst other her wonderful virtues and excellencies, she hath power to command spirits. And whosoever hath it, he may bind, loose, warrant, torment, martyr, help out of prison, go through bolts and locks—to be short, he may juggle, play with both hands, and do what he list, if he know how to use his fortune.

It is so (sayeth she), that Solomon had the perfection of this stone and knew by divine inspiration the great and wonderful property of the same, which was to constrain the devils, as we have said. And therefore so soon as he had made it, he concluded to make all the spirits come and appear before him. But, first, he caused to be made a cauldron of brass of a wonderful and huge greatness, for it was nothing less than all the whole circuit of the Forest of Sherborn but that it wanted half a foot or thereabouts—it is all a matter—we will not strive for a tittle. Marry, ye must note that it must be somewhat rounder, and it was needful to be so great, for to serve that turn that he minded.

And after the same manner he caused to be made a cover, so close and just as was possible. And also in like manner he caused a hole to be made and cast in the ground, large and deep enough for to bury his cauldron.

When he had prepared all these things, he made to come before him by virtue of the stone all the spirits that were dispersed in this world, little and great, beginning with the emperors of the four corners of the earth. Then he made the kings to come, dukes, earls, barons, lords, knights, esquires, captains, heads of bands, petty captains, soldiers afoot and on horseback, to great numbers.

When they were all come, Solomon commanded them by the virtue aforesaid that they should all go into that said pan that was buried in the ground. The spirits could not gainsay, but were fain to go in—but ye may well think that it was with great grief. So soon as they were all in, Solomon caused the cover to be set on and glued fast with the glue of Sapience; [1] and therein leaving the devils, caused it also to be covered with earth until the hole was filled up with whom his mind and purpose was that the world should be no more infected, and that men might afterward live in peace and tranquillity, and that all virtue and godliness might reign upon the earth.

And it came to pass presently after that, that men began to be merry and glad, content, lively, gallant, frolick, gentle, amiable, and pleasant. O, how all things went forward! The earth brought forth all manner of fruit without man's labor. The wolves did not devour the cattle. The lions, tigers, and wild boars were as tame as other beasts. To be short, all the earth seemed a Paradise whilst these runnigate [2] devils were enclosed in this deep dungeon.

But what happened after a long time? As kingdoms chance to change, the towns and cities decay and new are builded. So, there was a king who had a great desire to build a city. And Fortune would that it came into his head to raise it in the proper place where as these devils were enclosed. This king set people on work for to make this city, the which he would have mighty, strong, and invincible, and therefore it required terrible and deep foundations to make the walls.

Hereupon, the pioneers digged so low that one amongst the rest discovered the cauldron wherein these spirits were—who,

[1] *Sapience:* wisdom
[2] *runnigate:* renegade

after that he had stricken upon it and that his companions did perceive it, thought they should have been made rich forever and that there was hidden some inestimable riches. But it was not in their power to break it open of a sudden. For, besides that greatness, it was out of measure thick. And therefore it was necessary that the king should know thereof, who, when he had seen it, thought even as the pioneers did. For who would ever have thought that devils were therein, when it was thought that there was none in the world—for in long time before there was no talk of them.

This king did well remember that the kings his predecessors had infinite riches, so as he could not judge but that they had buried and hid therein some great treasure and that it was appointed him of destiny to find it out and to enjoy that wealth, that he might be the richest king in the world. To conclude, he set as many men of work as there was about the cauldron at the first.

And whilst they were battering and beating upon it to get it open, the devils were at their watch, listening and giving ear what it should be, so that they could not tell what to think— whether they should be had out to hanging or that their judgement had been made since they were put there. Now these braziers [3] and batterers had beaten upon it so long that they beat out a great piece of the cover and made a way to go in. But it was no sooner open than the devils, you may be sure, strived to get out by the heaps—making such a noise and cry that the king and all his people was so amazed with fear that they fell down as dead.

And these spirits got them to their feet and away they go, every one to his old corner, but that perhaps some of them were amazed to see the countries and kingdoms altered and changed since their imprisonment. By means whereof they were fain for a time to stray as vagabonds, not knowing of what country they were because they heard not their parish bell. But all the way as they went they did so many mischiefs that it was horrible to

[3] *braziers:* brass workers

declare. For instead of one mischief that they did in times past to vex the world, they invented a thousand: They killed, they overthrew, they cast down, spoiled and overwhelmed all things. All went to shivers, for the devils were loose.

In those days there were many philosophers, for the sooth-sayers and augurers were called philosophers by excellency, be-cause that Solomon had left them by writing the manner and form to make the holy stone—the which they brought to an art and kept schools of philosophy as we do of grammar, in such sort that many attained to the knowledge; considering also that these cursed spirits did not trouble their brain whilst they were enclosed. But so soon as they were at liberty, remembering how Solomon had misused them by virtue of this stone, the first thing they did was to go to the philosophers' forges and to cast them down.

And also they found the means to deface, scrape out, break, and falsify all the books that they could find out, of the said science, so that they left them so obscure and hard that men know not what they seek. And they were minded altogether to abolish and root it out, but that, God would not suffer them. Yet His permission they had to go and come, for to hinder the best learned in their business in such sort that when anyone taketh pains to attain the perfection thereof, and hath in a manner brought it to pass, then commeth the devil. And he breaketh a box which is full of this precious matter, and in less than an hour maketh the poor philosopher lose all the pains that he hath taken in ten or twelve years—so that he is to begin again: not because hogs have rooted it up and spoiled it, but the devils, which are worse.

And this is the cause why so few soothsayers attain to their enterprises. Not for that the science is not so true as it was at first, but because the wicked spirits are enemies of this gift and seek utterly to overthrow it—and because it may be one day that one may have the grace to do as well as Solomon ever did. If by good luck he happen in our days, I pray him by these presents that he forget not to conjure, adjure, excommunicate, root out, destroy, exterminate, confound, and utterly abolish these wicked spirits, enemies to nature and all good things, that thus hinder not only the poor soothsayers but also all men and women. For they put into their heads a thousand wrongs and a thousand fantasies—yea, and they themselves enter into these old witches, making them very devils. And hereof commeth those words that are spoken of a wicked woman: "She hath a devilish head."

7. Of Giles the joiner, how he did revenge himself of a greyhound that came always and beguiled him of his dinner

There was on a time at Poitiers a joiner [1] named Giles that labored to get his living so well as he could—having lost his wife who had left him a daughter of the age of nine or ten years, being content with her service, and had no other boy nor maid. He made provision on the Saturday to serve him all the week after. And in the morning he would get his little pot on the fire that his daughter made to boil, and found himself as well content with his ordinary provision as a richer man would be with his.

Now it is commonly said, it is good to have a neighbor neither too poor nor too rich. For if he be poor, he will always be craving, being not able to help thee at need. And if he be rich, he will keep thee under subjection and thou must be fain to suffer him, and art afraid to borrow of him. This joiner had to his neighbor a gentleman who was somewhat too great a Sir for his poor estate and loved hunting very well. And he did usually keep a great company of hounds in his house, to hunt the hare —the which pastime was to be had not far without the town.

Amongst all his hounds, he had a very fair greyhound that did many shrewd turns in that town. For he would come into every man's house, and the victuals he found he would devour.

[1] *joiner:* cabinetmaker

There was nothing for him neither too hot nor too heavy, were it bread, beef, cheese, or anything else—all was one. And chiefly he did most harm to the poor joiner, for there was but a wall between the gentleman and him. By the means whereof, this greyhound was smelling and seeking about his house at all hours of the day; and look what he found, he carried it quite away.

And also the hound had this subtlety: that with his paw he would cast down the pot that boiled upon the fire and would take up the meat and run his way, so that oftentimes the poor joiner had but a slender and cold dinner. Which thing grieved him sore. For after his labor and pains taken in his work, he was beguiled of his dinner before he could sit down at table. And (which was worst of all) he durst not complain. But he meaned to be revenged, whatever should happen.

Upon a day when he spied the greyhound going to get his prey, he followeth after him with a great square truncheon in his hand, and he found him busy about his pot to get out the meat. He made no more ado but shut the gate and got hold on the greyhound—to whom in short time he gave five or six dry stripes with his square upon the back, and spared him not at all, and then cast away his square truncheon and took up a small hazel wand in his hand (an ell long or thereabout). Wherewithall, he followed the greyhound out of the doors, that cried as though he had been killed (as indeed he was little better), and laid on him in the street, saying: "Ha, whoreson cur, get thee hence with a mischief, and come no more here to eat up my dinner—" making a show as though he had stricken with nothing but that small rod. But it was with a rod so soft as a footstool wherewith he had so blessed the greyhound that the gentleman never eat hare after of his taking.

8. *Of Blondeau the merry cobbler that was never sad or heavy in his lifetime but twice, and how he provided remedy for it* . . .

There was sometimes dwelling in Paris a cobbler named Blondeau that had a little shop in a corner where he mended shoes, getting his living thereby merrily. And above all, he loved good wine, and could tell them that went unto it where the best was, for he would be sure to spy out the best and take his part. All the day long he would sing as he sat at his work and make the neighbors merry. He was never seen all the days of his life heavy and sad but twice.

The one time was after that he had found an old naule [1] in an iron pot in which was a store of old money—some of silver and some of brass—whereof he knew not the value. Then he began to be heavy and sad, and would sing no more. His mind ran all on his pot of trash that he had found. He thought to himself that the money was not current. "I cannot," said he, "get neither bread nor wine for it, and if I show it to the goldsmiths, they will bewray [2] me or have their part of my finding—and yet they will not give me half of that it is worth." Then another time he was afraid that he had not hidden his pot well, and that someone or other came to steal it away. There was almost no hour but he would go from his shop to remove his pot. He was in the greatest trouble and pain that could be.

But at the last he bethought himself, saying: "How the Devil commeth it that I am so troubled with my pot. Every man perceiveth by me that I have something in my head. I would the Devil had it, so I had never seen it." Which said, on a sudden he took the pot with the money and cast it into the river, and there drowned all his care. This being done, he was the merriest man alive and began in his accustomed manner to sing as joy-

[1] *naule:* awl
[2] *bewray:* disclose, betray

fully as ever he did. Neither was his mind any more grieved or molested.

Another time, he was offended with a gentleman that dwelled right over against his shop who had an ape that did a thousand shrewd turns to Blondeau. For he, being in a window, watched the cobbler when he cut out pieces of leather for his shoes and beheld how he did; and so soon as poor Blondeau was gone to dinner or to any other place about his business, the same ape would come down to go into the cobbler's shop and take his cutting knife and cut out the leather as he had seen Blondeau do. And this was his custom and use at all times that Blondeau was gone out, so that the poor man was fain to eat and drink a great while in his shop, and durst not go abroad unless he had locked up his leather. And if he had forgotten at any time to shut it up, then the ape would not forget to cut out pieces, which thing did trouble him very much. And also he durst do no harm to the ape, for fear of his master.

When he was so weary of this displeasure that he could forbear no longer, he thought he would be revenged. And perceiving it was the ape's property to counterfeit him in all things (for if Blondeau had whet his knife, so would this ape do; if he had thrust with his naule, this ape would do so after him; and if that he had pulled out his threads at length, the ape would pull out as he had seen him do), upon a time he did whet his cutting knife and made it as sharp as a razor. And at that time when he espied the ape to look earnestly upon him, he began to put his cutting knife against his throat and to go with it to and fro, as though he would have cut his own throat. And when he had done this twice or thrice, that the ape might learn it, he laid down his knife and shut his shop door and went home to dinner.

This ape by and by commeth down and entereth his shop, thinking to try this new game and pastime that he had never seen before. And he taketh up the paring knife and straightways put it to his throat, going with it to and fro as he had seen Blondeau the cobbler do. But he put it too near his throat and, taking no regard, cut his own throat, whereof he died within an hour after. And thus Blondeau was revenged of the ape, without any danger of his master. And then he framed himself to his old custom again—in singing and making good cheer—and so he continued even unto the end of his life. . . .

9. *Of the feats and memorial acts of a fox that belonged to a bailey of Maine la Inhes, and how he was taken and put to death*

In the town of Maine la Inhes in the low country of Maine, which is situate in the borders of the barren country, there was sometimes a bailey that was a good companion, according to the order of the country, who delighted in many things and had in his house many tame beasts. Among the which he had a fox that he brought up and kept of a young one, whose tail was cut off and wherefore was called the Curtail Fox. This fox was crafty of nature, but yet he degenerated from his kind in being conversant with men, and had so good a wit for a fox that if he could have spoken he would have showed to many men that they were but beasts.

He knew when the bailey of the house did make a feast, seeing the folks in the house busy, especially the cook. He would go to the poulters and bring home conies,[1] capons, pigeons, chickens, and wild fowl according to the season, and would steal them so cunningly that he was never taken doing the deed. And thus he furnished his master's kitchen marvelously well. Nevertheless, he went to and fro so often that he began to be suspected of the poulters and others. For he always found new crafts, stealing still more and more. At the last, they conspired to kill him, which they durst not do openly, for fear of his master that was

[1] *conies:* rabbits

chief lord of the town. But each one determined to trap him in the night.

Now this fox, when he went about to seek his prey, would come in at the cellar window or by a low light, or else watch whilst they had come to the door without a candle, and then did he steal in like a rat. And as he had inventions and ways to come in, so had he in like manner policies to get out with his prey. Many times the poulterers determined his death with a crossbow bent, watching for him. But the fox would prevent them for all their policy and did never come there so long as they watched. But a man could not have his eyes any sooner closed but the fox would be presently provided. If there were any snares or gins [2] laid for him, he knew as well how to escape the danger as if he himself had laid them. So that they could never be so circumspect as to take him, although he never came away empty.

Yet, being many times prevented of his purpose, he was sore displeased because he could not do such service to the cook as he was used to do. And therefore, being of good years, he began to take heed. And also he thought that they made no account of him as they did afore time, because he did them small service in his age. And chiefly for this he began to be mischievous crafty, and to eat and kill up his master's fowl. So that everybody being in bed he would step to the perch and now take a capon, another time a hen, and they did not mistrust him—thinking that it had been the weasel or the polecat. But in the end (as all mischiefs come to light) he went and came so often that a little wench lying in the stable for God's sake, perceived him and bewrayed [3] all.

And from thenceforth the great blame was laid on the fox. For it was reported to Master Bailey that Curtail his fox did eat up and devour his fowls. This fox would be in every corner to listen and hear what was spoken against him, and he used commonly to be under the table when his master was at dinner and supper. But after his master heard of his fashions, he so

[2] *gins:* traps
[3] *bewrayed:* disclosed

hated him that upon a time being at dinner, and the fox being behind the folks, Master Bailey began to say: "What say you to my fox that eateth up all my hens and capons? I will be revenged of him within these three days."

The fox understanding this, knew it was no more good tarrying in the town, and he tarried not until the three days were past, but he banished himself and fled into the fields amongst the wild foxes. You may be sure his farewell was not without making spoil of somewhat. But being now amongst his kind, he had something ado to acquaint himself with them—for during the time that he remained in the town, he had learned to speak good yelpish of the dogs and their manner also, and went with them on hunting and under the color of friendship would deceive the wild foxes and put them into the hands of the dogs. This the foxes remembering, refused both the receiving of him into their company and to put their confidence in him anymore. But he used rhetoric and made partly his excuse and partly asked forgiveness.

And then he made them believe that he knew the means to make them live at ease like kings, because he knew all the poultry in the country, and the hours and times fit to seek their prey. And thus in the end they believed him through his fair words and made him their captain. Wherewithal they found themselves content for a time, for their captain Curtail brought them to such places as they had enough. But the mischief was that they would use themselves too much to the civil life not fit for them. For the people of the country, seeing them thus in bands and companies, set dogs after them and made always some of them to come short home.

But in the meantime Captain Curtail, that crafty fox, saved himself at all times. For he kept the backward, to that end that when the dogs were busy and occupied with the first band, he might have leisure to save himself and escape from the view of them. And also he would never go into the hole but amongst the company of other foxes. And when the hounds were ready to thrust in, he would so bite and fight with his fellows that he would constrain them to go forth, to the end that whilst the dogs were occupied in running after them he might save himself.

But the poor Curtail Fox could not so well shift for himself but in the end he was caught. Forasmuch as the clowns [4] of the country knew well enough that he was the cause of all mischief and shrewd turns that were done thereabout, so that they swore his death and dispatched each of them a messenger to all the gentlemen of the country, requesting their help and desiring them for the profit of the country to lend them their dogs to dispatch the country of that mischievous fox. To the which the gentlemen did willingly agree and gave good answer to the messengers—and also the most part of them had of a long time sought their pastime and could not find anything.

In the end they brought out so many dogs that there were enough both for the Curtail Fox and his fellows, so that he might well bite and drive out the rest, but it would not prevail. For at the last when there was no more left, his turn must needs follow next. He was taken quick and haled out of a corner of his hole, with digging him out, for the dogs could not come at him nor make him to come forth of his hole.

Well, at the last poor Curtail was taken and led alive into the town of Maine whereas his judgement was given and was sacrificed in the open market place for the thefts, robberies, pilferies, crafts, fraud, deceits, injuries, wrongs, conspiracies, treasons, murthers, and other grievous faults and injuries by him committed and done, and was executed before a great multitude standing by to see the execution.

The people came flocking thither in heaps, for he was known well twenty mile compass to be the most ungracious fox that ever the earth bare. Some say, for all that, many honest folks bewailed his death because he had done so many proper feats, and therefore they said it was pity that he should be put to death, being a fox of so good understanding. But in the end they could not have the mastery, although they had laid hands on their weapons to have saved his life—for he was hanged and

[4] *clowns:* farmers

strangled for a notable thief at the castle of Maine. And thus may you see that there is no mischief nor wickedness but is punished at the last.

10. *Of a gentleman that in the night time cried after his hawks and of the carter that whipped his horses*

There is a kind of people that have choleric humors, or melancholy or phlegmatic, it must needs be one of the three (for the sanguine complexion is always good, so they say), whereof the vapor forgeth into the brain that maketh them become fantastical, lunatic, erratic, schismatic, and all the actics that may be spoken—for the which there is found no remedy by any purgation that may be given. Therefore, having a desire to help such afflicted people and to pleasure their wives, friends, parents, and kindred and all those that shall have to do, I will here in few words briefly declare an example that came to pass and happened, how they shall do when they have anybody so taken, chiefly with night dreams—for it is a great pain to rest neither day nor night.

There was a gentleman in the country and land of Province, a man of reasonable good years and rich, which greatly loved hunting and took therein so great delight and pleasure in the daytime that in the night he would rise up in his sleep and begin to cry, to halloo, and "whup" after his hounds, as if he had been abroad in the daytime. Wherewith he was sore displeased and so were his friends, for there could not sleep one body that was in the house for him. And also many times he wakened and dis-eased the neighbors, he would cry out so loud and so long time after his birds. But for other qualities he was reasonable and also he was well known as well for his honesty and gentleness as for this his imperfection which was so troublesome that by reason thereof all the world called him the Falconer.

Upon a day in following his hawks, he was far from home and strayed so far that the night overtook him so that he knew not whither to go. But he turned so long through the mountains and woods that at the last, being very late, he came to a house that was upon the highway alone, whereas the goodman did sometimes lodge foot folks that were belated in the night because there was no other lodging near hand.

When he came thither, the goodman of the house was in bed and his household—whom he caused for to rise, desiring him that he might have lodging for that night because it was both cold and foul weather. The goodman opened the door and let him in, and put his horse in the stable amongst the neat,[1] and showed him a bed on the ground—for there was no chamber above.

There was at that time in the house a carter, new come from the fair at Pesenest, which was laid in another bed hard by, who awaked at the gentleman's coming, wherewith he was angry, for he was weary with travail[2] and was but new fallen asleep. And such people of their nature are not very courteous. At his sudden waking, he said to the gentleman: "Who the devil brought you hither so late?"

This gentleman, being alone and in a place unknown, spake as he could, saying: "My friend, the occasion is in following my hawks. Suffer me, I pray thee, to tarry here until the morning and then I will away."

This carter, being better awaked, and looking earnestly upon the gentleman, began straightway to know him—for he had seen him often times at Aix in Province, and had oftentimes heard tell what a sleeper he was. The gentleman knew not him, but in pulling off his clothes he said: "Friend, I pray thee, be not offended with me for this one night, for I have an impediment which is to cry in the night after my hawks. For I love hawking so, that me think every night I am at the game."

"Oho," said the carter. "It taketh me after the same manner,

[1] *neat:* cattle
[2] *travail:* work

for I think I am always whipping of my horses and driving my cart, and I can by no means leave it."

"Well," said the gentleman, "one night will soon be passed over. We will therefore bear one with another." He goeth to bed but he was very little entered into his first sleep but that he started out of his bed and went crying about the house: "Sa haw—sa haw—sa haw—whup, whup, whup."

At this cry, the carter awaked and taketh his whip that stood by him and yerked [3] the gentleman to and fro about the house, crying: "Ha ree, brown, bayard, dun—go—what brown—hob, hob—why, hy, ho, ree!" He so yerked the poor gentleman, ye need not ask how, who waked with the yerks of the whip and instead of crying after his hawks, he changed his tune and cried out for help, saying: "I am slain!"

But the carter fetched him to and fro still about the house, until at the last the poor gentleman was fain to get him under the table and there couch and speak not a word, tarrying there until the carter had passed his rage over—who, when he perceived that the gentleman had hidden himself, set down his whip, went to bed, and began to snort like one that had been in his dead sleep.

The goodman of the house rose, lighted a candle, and found the gentleman hidden underneath the board [4] in such a little corner as would scant serve a cat to go in—and all his body and legs were so painted with lashes as if it had been the picture of Christ. The which surely was a great miracle, for never after that did he once rise up to cry after his hawks as before he was wont to do in his sleep—whereat his friends and kindred did much marvel that knew his quality. But he told them what had happened. Never one man was more bound to another than was the gentleman to the carter who had healed him of such an infirmity as that was.

[3] *yerked:* whipped
[4] *board:* table

11. *Of a monk that answered altogether by syllables*

A certain monk traveling the country arrived in an inn at supper time. The host willed him to sit down among others that had already begun supper. The monk, to overtake them, began to lay on load [1] with his teeth, and with such an appetite as though he had eat no meat in three or four days before. The old lad had put himself in his doublet, the better to fill his paunch—the which being perceived by one that sat at the table, he began to ask the monk many questions that were not greatly to his mind for he was busy filling of his belly. Because he would not lose much time, he answered the party that spake to him altogether in syllables. And I think he was practiced with this language long before, for he was very expert in it. The questions and the answers were these:

"What garment do you wear?"

"Strong."

"What wine do ye drink?"

"Red."

"What flesh do ye eat?"

"Beef."

"How many monks are ye?"

"Nine."

"How like you this wine?"

"Good."

"You drink no such at home?"

"No."

"What eat ye upon Fridays?"

"Eggs."

"How many have each of you?"

"Two."

And this while, he lost not one mouthful of meat, for his teeth

[1] *lay on load:* get busy

were still going, and yet answered well and readily to all his demands. If he said his matins so short, out of doubt he was a notable pillar of the Church.

12. *Of a certain student in the law and of the 'pothecary that taught him physic*

There was upon a time a certain scholar, that had dwelled at Toulouse a certain time, passing by a little town not far from Cahors in Quercy named Saint Antony's—there for to practice his texts of law. Not that he had greatly therein profited, for he had most studied humane letters wherein he had very good knowledge. But he thought, seeing he began to profess the law, not to stray or wander from the same until he could answer therein as well as another.

So soon as he was come to Saint Antony's (as in such little towns a man is quickly spied and marked), there came a 'pothecary to be acquainted with him, saying—"Sir, you are welcome to the town," and so began to fall in talk with him, who amongst other talk spake certain words as touching physic. When the 'pothecary had heard him speak, he said unto him: "Sir, so far as I can perceive, you are a physician."

"No, that I am not," said he. "But I have read somewhat of physic."

"I know well enough, sir, that you will not declare what you are because you mean not to tarry long in this town. But truly, sir, if you would, you should not find it least for your profit. We have at this present never a physician in these quarters. He that we had is lately dead, and died worth three or four thousand pound. If that you will remain and dwell here (for here is good being), I will lodge you in my house and so you and I shall live well when ye are once known. Sir," said the 'pothecary, "I pray you take the pains to come and dine with me."

The scholar, understanding the 'pothecary's words, that was no fool (for he had traveled into many places to see and know fashions) was content to go with him to dinner and thought this to himself: "I will try the chance and if this man will do as he sayeth, I shall make good shift, for this is a rude country and there is not one body that knoweth me. And therefore we will see what will come to pass."

The 'pothecary brought him to his house to dinner. After dinner, having always this talk in their mouths, they agreed together to be cousins. And for to make our tale short, the 'pothecary made the scholar believe that he was a physician.

And then the scholar said unto him: "First of all, you shall understand that I never had great practice in our art as you do think. But my mind was to have gone to Paris to have studied another year and then to have fallen to the practice at the town from whence I came. But seeing I have found you, and that I know you are a man that can show me pleasure and I in like manner unto you, let us look about to do our business, for I am content at your request to tarry."

"Sir," said the 'pothecary, "take no care. I will teach you all the practice of physic in less than fifteen days. I have of a long time used the company of physicians, both in France and in other places. I know their fashions and their receipts all by heart. Moreover, in this country ye need but set a good countenance on it and go by guess, and you shall be counted the best physician in all the world."

And then the 'pothecary began to teach him how he should write an ounce, half ounce, a quarter of an ounce, a dram, a handfull, a quantity. And another day he taught him the names of drugs that were most common, and to mix, to strain, to 'still, to make compounds and simples and such like things. This continued ten or twelve days, during the which time he kept his chamber, causing the 'pothecary to say that he was not well. The which 'pothecary blazed abroad that this physician was the best learned man that ever came to that town. Whereof they of the town were very glad, and began to entertain him, and to make much of him so soon as he came abroad, they striving who should make him the best cheer. And you would have said that already they longed to be sick, to try this new physician, and to set him a-work to the end he might have a better will and desire to tarry there.

But M. Doctor made himself to be sought for and entered not haunting the company of many folks, but kept a great countenance and set a good face on the matter, and above other things he did not depart from the 'pothecary that had taught him his cunning. In short time, there came urines to him from all parts.

Now, in those places, they must judge by the urines whether the patient be a man or a woman, and in what part their pain and sickness lay, and of what age they were. But this physician could do more than that, for he could tell them who was their father and mother and whether they were married or no, and how many children they had. To conclude, he could tell all even from the old to the new, and all by the help of his M. the 'pothecary. For when he saw anybody brought a water, the 'pothecary would question with them whilst the physician was above, and would ask them from end to end all these former things. And then he caused them stay until he was gone up and declared to M. Doctor all that he had learned of them that brought the urines.

The physician, taking their waters, would hold them up and look on them, putting his hand between the urinal and the light, and would shake it and turn it with all the gestures in such cases required. Then he would say: "It is a woman's water." ("Yea, truly, sir, it is so.") "She had a great pain in her left side under the breast," or "Pain in the head" (as the 'pothecary had given him instructions). "It is not three months since she was delivered of a daughter." The bringer of this urine did begin greatly to marvel at his great knowledge and would go away and declare unto everybody what the physician had said. So that from mouth to mouth the report went that there to the town was come such an odd fellow that there was not his like to be found.

And if by fortune his 'pothecary was not by or at hand, then would he draw the worm out of their nose himself, in saying: "Very sick." To which the bringer of the urine would say "he" or "she—" by the means whereof he would say after a little pausing: "Is not this a man's water?" "Yea, truly, sir, it is a man's water," would the bringer say. "I spied that," by-and-by would the physician say.

But when he came to minister and give physic unto anyone, then would he have always his 'pothecary, who spake one unto another physic Latin—which was in those days fine stuff. And under this Latin the 'pothecary would name him the whole receipt, making a show as though they spake of other things. In the which, I leave you to consider whether it were not a good sight to see a physician write under a 'pothecary.

In effect, whether it was because of the good opinion the people had on him or by any other chance, those that were sick felt themselves well by his ordinances and appointments. They thought not themselves well that came not to this physician, and they were persuaded that it was good being sick whilst he was there. For they thought if he went once his way, they should never recover again the like. And happy was he that could present him with the greatest gifts. So that in six or seven months, he had gotten good store of crowns, and also his 'pothecary by means one of another, and therefore he prepared himself to depart from Saint Antony's, saying that he had received letters from his country by the which he heard news that he must needs depart for a time. But he would not fail to return again shortly.

It was to Paris that he came, where afterwards he fell to study physic. And it may be afterward, for all his further knowledge, he was not so good a physician as when he was 'prentice. I mean his doings came not so prosperously to pass. And many times fortune helpeth more those that are ignorant than those that have knowledge and skill. For a man of knowledge useth too much discretion in his doings. He thinketh of the circumstance and hath a fear and a doubt, which giveth unto men a mistrust in themselves that doth discourage them to deal in many things. And as it is commonly said, better it is to fall into the hands of a lucky physician than to him that is learned and hath good skill.

The physician of Italy knew this well enough who, when he had nothing to do, did write two or three hundred kind of receipts for divers sicknesses and diseases—of the which he took a great number and put them in the pocket of his coat or into his bosom, so that when anybody came unto him with urines he drew out one of the receipts by chance (as the lots are drawn at the Lottery) and gave it to the bringer of the urine, saying unto him or her: "Dio te la daga buona." [1] And if it sped well so it was, and if it sped ill—"Suo damno." [2] For thus goeth the world.

[1] *"Dio . . . buona":* i.e., "May God give thee good luck."
[2] *"Suo damno":* i.e., "Tough luck."

Finis

GLOSSARY

Adew. adieu
Adventure. chance
Advice. estimate
Advouterer, avoutry. adultery
Al(l)to. altogether, thoroughly
Ambagious. long-winded
And. if
Annual. annual appointment
Antetheme. text of sermon
Antler. buck deer
Appaired. grew worse.
Appointed. arranged, made appointment
Assay. try
Astonied. paralyzed, numb
Adventure. occurrence
Avised. advised
Avaled. doffed
Avoid. clear off
A-wreaked. avenged

Baillie(if). chief magistrate
Bain. public bath
Balk. ceiling beam
Barber. surgeon
To bash. become abashed
'Bated. abided
'Bating. stopping place
Beaver. drinking companion, servant(?)
Beshrew. curse
Betle. stick

Bewray. curse, disclose, betray
Bezants. gold coins
Bill. petition, recipe
Board. table
Borrow. pledge
Botels. bales
Bouked. washed
Boult. sift
Braziers. brass workers
Budget. purse, wallet
Bull. a mock
Bush. hair

Can. ken, know
Cap. take off cap
Capax. impressionable
Carrick. galley
Cast. decided
Cause. case
Cautele. trick
Chamlet. expensive cloth
Channel. open sewer
Chapman. customer, retailer
Cheer. countenance
Chepe. bargain
Cherished. took care of
Chincough. whooping cough
Chose you. suit yourself
Clerk. scholar, clerk
Close. secretly
Clouted. cleated
Clowns. farmers

Clubbish. uncouth
Collop. slice
Compass. circle
Conditions. habits, behavior, manners
Conies. rabbits
Conject. conjecture
Consenting. involved in
Contentation. contentment
Continent. at once, immediately
Cope. vestment
Counter. debtor's prison
Countervail(e). compensate
Courage. state of mind, heart
Covenant. bargain
Cover knave. hat
Crack, crake. boast
Cunning. skillful
Cure. pastime
Curious. fastidious

Danger. dependence, penalty
Dangerous. careful
Dele. distribute, little bit
Demanded. asked, petitioned
Denied. refused
Depart. share, separate
Did. ordered, put on
Dirige. funeral service
Disease. discomfort
Dispend. spend
Disport. recreation, relaxation
Do. order to be made or done, put on
Do off. doff, take off
Doctor. scholar, professor
Dole. charity
Dommage. hurt
Dote. act foolishly
Doubt. fear
Dout. put out
Draught. privy
Duty. debt

Effect. office
Enough. cooked enough
Enured with. used to
Esprised. enflamed

Fabulator. fabulist, fable maker, storyteller
Fail. err
Fallacy. trick, deception
Fault of kind. natural fault
Fet. fetch
Fetches. tricks
Find. support
Flesh shambles. slaughter house, meat market
Force. care
Fordoing. preventing
Formi(y)ce. ant
Foul. ugly
Found. support, take care of; confounded
Franklin. freeholder, country gentleman
Friar limito(u)r. friar licensed to beg in limited territory
Friar minor. Franciscan
Frot. rubbed

Gage. pawn
Gins. traps
Glister. enema
Godse(i)p. cousin, godparent, close friend
Good(s). property, money
Goodly. prosperous
Gorget. collar, armor
Gossip. cousin, godparent, close friend
Grise. step
Grutching. grudging
Guerished. flourished

Heedling. headlong
Hey. trap, snare
High. loud
Hight. named
Hold. bet
Hole. hale, heal
Honest(ly). decent, prosperous
Hoved. hovered, heaved
How well. although

Incontinent. at once, immediately, intently
Indicals. indexes
Ita. yes

Janway. Genoese
Jape. trick
Japed. mocked, made jest of

Kendal(l)man. man from Kendal in north country

Laborer. farm worker, rustic
Last. load, shoe pattern
Leasing. fib
Leman. mistress.
Let(t). prevent, stop, interrupt
Lewd. unlearned, stupid
Lever. rather
Libel. list
Light(ly). easy, readily, swiftly
Limito(u)r. friar licensed to beg within limited territory
List. please
Lust. desire
Lye. dregs

Maculed. guilty
Mails. scales
Male. wallet
Matter. case
Medecine. physician
Megrim. migraine headache
Mete. measure
Mickle. much
Midst. middle
Minion. dainty
Misericorde. mercy
Miten. quarter-farthing
Mowe. be able to
Musket. mistress

Naule. awl
Neat. cattle
Neck. back
Ne wot(e). know not
News. novelties
Nice. foolish

Niggin(ship). niggard
No force. no matter, never mind
Nothid. nothing
Nourished. reared

Obligation. contract
Ordinary provision. ?steward
Otherwhile. often, sometimes
Over eve. in the evening
Over night. at night

Pageants. practical jokes
Parbraking. vomiting
Parents. close relatives
Paul's. St. Paul's church or churchyard
P'aventure. per adventure, perchance
Peaked. sneaked
'Peased. appeased
Pick. throw
Pickthank. sycophant
Piece. cask
Pieces. points
Placebo. vespers for the dead
Plaisance. pleasure
'Pointed. appointed, arranged
Poller. confidence man
Polling fellow. confidence man
Portingale. Portugal
Pottage(s). stew
Poundgarnet. pomegranate
Prepensed. planned
Press. crowd
Price. prize
Pricked. stimulated
Privity. conspiracy
Prove. try
Puissance. army, force

Quick. alive, lively
Quit. acquit, repay

Rains. small of the back
Rascal. fawn, young deer
Ravished. dressed in ecclesiastical garments
Rayed. streaked

Reins. kidneys, small of back
Reluced. reflected
Remember. remind, recall
Remercy. thank
Requiring. asking
Rivage. river bank
Rood. wooden cross
Room(s). offices, places
Rowned. whispered
Rude. unlearned
Runnigate. renegade

Sacring. sacrament
Sadly. quietly
Sale. soul
Sapience. wisdom
Scath. damage, pain
Secure. engaged, safe
Sepulture. burial
Servage. servitude
Shift. undershirt
Shottish. good-for-nothing
Shrove. confessed
Siege board. toilet seat
Silly. poor, innocent
Sith(en). since
Sod(den). boiled
Soddenly. soaking wet
Soft(ly). slow
Sonde. channel
Sort. pack
Souter, sutor. shoemaker
Sparred. barred
Sped. taken care of
Sped of. succeeded with
Spittle house. hospital
'Ssayed. assayed, tried
Standing-field. battlefield
Strait. tight
Straught. stretched

Strive. argue
Strouting. bulging
Sure. secret
Surely. securely, safely
Sweven(s). dream

Tolleth. count, measure
Thank. reward
Thaugh. needed
'Tofore. heretofore
Toteth. looked all over
Travail. work
Trencher. dish
Triste. sad
Trow. believe

Unethe, unnethe. hardly, scarcely
Unthrift. ne'er-do-well
Using. visiting

Villein. rustic, peasant
Vitaile. food

Waiter. watchman, guard
Wardropp. dressing room
Waster. club
Watch. sleepless night
Waxed. grew, paled
Ween. imagine
Well avised. determined
Which. who, what, that
White friar. Carmelite friar
Whittled. plied with drink
Will. want, wish
Wis(t). knew
Wode(ness). mad
Wot(e), wottest. know
Wyte. fault

Yerked. whipped
Yet. still